A Vision of Voices

A Vision of Voices

JOHN CROSBY AND THE SANTA FE OPERA

Craig A. Smith

UNIVERSITY OF NEW MEXICO PRESS • ALBUQUERQUE

© 2015 by the UNIVERSITY OF NEW MEXICO PRESS

All rights reserved. Published 2015
Printed in the United States of America

20 19 18 17 16 15   1 2 3 4 5 6

Library of Congress Cataloging-in-Publication Data
Smith, Craig A., 1953–
  A vision of voices : John Crosby and The Santa Fe Opera / Craig A. Smith.
    pages cm
  Includes bibliographical references and index.
  ISBN 978-0-8263-5575-1 (pbk. : alk. paper)
  — ISBN 978-0-8263-5576-8 (electronic)
  1. Crosby, John, 1926–2002. 2. Santa Fe Opera.
  3. Impresarios—United States—Biography. I. Title.
  ML429.C67S54 2015
  782.1092—dc23
  [B]

                          2014024274

Cover illustrations: photograph by Robert Godwin and oil painting by
    Mikael Melbye, courtesy The Santa Fe Opera.
Title page illustration: © Al Hirschfeld, reproduced by arrangement with
    Hirschfeld's exclusive representative, the Margo Feiden Galleries Ltd.,
    New York. wwwalhirschfeld.com
Designed by Lisa Tremaine
Composed in Stempel Garamond, cut in Germany in 1924 and based on the
    Garmonds of the late fifteenth century. An elegant Humanist-Garalde, Stempel
    Garamond is highly readable, one of many reasons it is still used today.

To the memory of John O'Hea Crosby
and his enduring accomplishments

Special thanks to Nancy Zeckendorf—colleague, friend, and associate of John Crosby—and the additional underwriters whose support made this book possible: June and Thomas Catron, Edgar Foster Daniels, Bruce B. Donnell, Maryon Davies Lewis, Patricia A. McFate, Greig Porter, Regina Sarfaty Rickless, Mara and Charles W. Robinson, and James R. Seitz Jr.

Contents

Color plates follow page 144

A Note on the Text

Titles of operatic works are given in accordance with The Santa Fe Opera's program book listings. In general, titles are given in the original language except in the case of comic operas with English text and/or dialogue or where custom dictates otherwise. For example, Mozart's *Così fan tutte* is rendered in Italian, but *Le nozze di Figaro* is known as *The Marriage of Figaro*. Similarly, Offenbach's *Orfée aux Enfers* is *Orpheus in the Underworld*, and his *Les contes d'Hoffman* is *The Tales of Hoffman*.

John Crosby was a man of letters not only through his own education and his honorary degrees, but in his correspondence. Sample missives have been placed throughout this book to illustrate his peculiar combination of business acumen, sensitivity, humor, temper, intransigence, and patience, and to buttress the conclusions and opinions stated.

All extracts from John Crosby's letters are presented unaltered as they appear in The Santa Fe Opera files. Such extracts have not been given a confirming note, as the date that accompanies them indicates placement in the records. Material drawn from Crosby's transcribed oral history and autobiographical sketch has been punctuated according to standard style.

Preface

From the heart of Santa Fe, the Plaza, take San Francisco Street west to Guadalupe Street. Turn right and go north, past shops and homes and the venerable Rosario Cemetery, to where Guadalupe merges with U.S. Highway 84/285. From there, the northbound side of the busy three-lane road gradually winds its way up to the top of a hill. There it passes between high concrete walls and beneath a bridge that marks where the old westerly turnoff to Tano Road used to be. That was decades ago, when the hill was steeper and higher than it is today, and the now far-flung city was quietly compact.

From the crest, as the highway descends quickly down the concrete slope, a huge expanse of northern New Mexico's mesas, mountains, and plains opens out in a visual symphony of color and pattern. Don't marvel too much at it, though, or you may miss the three consecutive road signs on the right alerting you to the upcoming exit to the village of Tesuque.

As you pass the last sign, an imposing structure springs into view on the left in the middle distance. It stands proudly on an eminence, with adobe-colored walls as fluently strong as New Mexico's mountains and a soaring white roof suggesting clouds and lightning come down from the upper air and given shape. It is The Santa Fe Opera—a destination for thousands of opera lovers every year, the main anchor of Santa Fe's thriving arts scene, and a consistent presenter of works that meld orchestral music, dance, theatrical values, and superb singing into a union of high and often heaven-storming quality.

The opera company, its theater, its campus, its outreach, and much of Santa Fe's international arts destination status would not exist without the one man who created the company and then guided its fortunes for forty-five years: John O'Hea Crosby. Variously a polymath and an impresario, an amateur but accomplished engineer and hydrologist, a martinet of an administrator and a welcoming friend, he led a richly concentrated life devoted to the company that was the child of both his brain and heart. It was in some ways a closed life for a multifaceted and often contradictory personality, one into which he admitted few people, either personally or professionally, and of which he himself may not have known what lay behind every door. But it was a life that also radiated genius, insight, and an unending pursuit of excellence.

To Board president: June 6, 1974

Necessity is the mother of invention, and one can have a very intriguing time being resourceful. Sometimes the public may not realize the fun we have this way—making costumes for "Pelleas" from bath mats, etc. We do not mean to jerry-rig our productions or maintenance; but we do want to keep putting our money on what counts. Quality counts, always. Quantity must take a second place, if necessary. Martha Graham could not have stayed in business if it had not been for the leotard.

Given Crosby's unwavering attention to his opera company for so many decades, it is not hard to imagine his spirit perambulating about the grounds during rehearsals and performances—with, as some believe, a ghostly baton in one hand and an ever-present phantom cigarette in the other.[1] The shade would cock an ear to the sound of the fountain in the entry plaza as Crosby remembered his countless memos on, and constant attention to, the precious resource of water. He would wonder if the several wells on the opera grounds had been properly programmed to increase their pumping at intermission, when scores of toilets would need constant flushing in a short period of time. Certainly he would nod with satisfaction at the bar sales and the gift shop transactions adding needed cash to company coffers to supplement ticket sales, grants, and donations. Surely he would count the house; oversee the arrival and departure of hundreds of cars; and in the interim, float backstage to be sure that the production was running smoothly and that the conductor was taking good care of *his* orchestra. With that done, he would make his way through the company's business offices—for even with staff gone for the day, he could sense and judge how operations were going and where morale stood.

If John Crosby's ghost wanders the grounds, his body lies three miles south, just north of the quiet grounds of Rosario, in the venerable Santa Fe National Cemetery. As a veteran of World War II, he had fully earned the dignity of burial there. A simple flat headstone marks his grave at section 26, site 46: *John O Crosby, Cpl US Army, World War II, Jul 12, 1926–Dec 15, 2002*.[2] His parents, Aileen O'Hea Crosby and Laurence Alden Crosby, are buried in the cemetery as well, in death, as in life, not far away from their son.

Despite the honor, it would have been more appropriate had Crosby been laid to rest within the purlieus of his beloved house, even as Richard Wagner lies in the grounds of Haus Wahnfried in Bayreuth, Germany. Reposing where he had lived for so many years, Crosby would be near the sounds of pianos and lawn mowers, office bustle and vocal pyrotechnics, storm and thunder and whistling winds. All around would be the plantings he conceived, the roads he graded himself, the pool he swam in, and the buildings he carefully planned for years, even before many could be built. And overhead in the New Mexico sky he loved, countless stars would look down on the fulfillment of a dream.

From the time he was thirty, Crosby was an exceptionally influential figure in the world of opera. His skills ranged from visionary dreamer to tough-minded businessman, artistic explorer to conservative programmer, competent conductor to lynx-eyed production critic. He also was a marketing genius, whose creation was impeccably branded from the first. The Santa Fe Opera was his life, and through it, he changed Santa Fe, the state of New Mexico, and the operatic world. His devotion to top festival quality, to the works of the great German composer Richard Strauss, to new and sometimes envelope-ripping repertoire, to commissions and revivals, and to stringent financial control and obsessive oversight bore a rich, sometimes prickly, and still-enduring harvest.

The prickliness came from Crosby's own character. He was raised

in comfortable circumstances, the child of a New England father descended from John and Priscilla Alden of the *Mayflower* and an Anglo-Irish mother who mastered both science and music before her marriage. The family was devoutly Roman Catholic, but Crosby was a gay man in a period during which it was indeed the love that dare not whisper, let alone speak, its name—a circumstance that created in him a reticence even beyond that caused by his genetic inheritance and upbringing. Just a cursory look at his behavior might suggest that he suffered from some form of autism spectrum disorder, perhaps Asperger's Syndrome, that led him to be astonishingly brilliant at facts and figures yet more than a lap behind when it came to many basic interpersonal skills. Certainly the idea was common meat for discussion among many staff and board members over time, and there was little doubt among those who worked closely with him that his Great Stone Face silences were as much internally and chemically driven as they were a modality of his negotiating skills.[3]

To an agent (telegram): August 24, 1973

REFUSE TO DO ANYMORE BUSINESS WITH YOUR OFFICE SINCE
I NEVER DO BUSINESS WITH LIARS.

In fact, Crosby was emotionally contradictory. He could take a sudden and total aversion to someone for any or no reason, and he could rip a person's heart out one moment and then treat them with gentlemanly courtesy the next, especially when the situation had to do with a failure to keep the company functioning at its highest possible level. Yet he also had a deep, if well-hidden, core of warm affection for his family, for some few trusted associates and colleagues, and for an even closer circle of intimate friends. When people were in trouble, he could be both affectionate and sympathetic. He subsumed himself in his creation with an almost religious sense of self-abnegation, although he insisted on being regarded as The Santa Fe Opera's avatar even more than he wanted to be seen as a man named John Crosby. The opera was his child, spouse, and lover, and the people associated with it were all deeply influenced by the sturdy aura of his own personality. Yet he was also a man of basically simple tastes, who could be seen of a Sunday morning in a local supermarket, buying picnic supplies for one of his pool parties.[4]

CHAPTER ONE

Setting the Stage

Prologue

The summer evening of July 3, 1957, was a fine one in Santa Fe. The day had been clement after rain the night before, and the Northern New Mexico temperature, which had soared into the mid-90s, was fast dropping into the low 60s, a regular and welcome characteristic of the 7,000-foot mountains-and-mesas climate.[1]

As the hour trended toward 9:00 p.m., a necklace of car lights, made up of strands from Albuquerque, Los Alamos, Española, Tesuque, Santa Fe itself, and points beyond, stretched along the new two-lane, north–south U.S. Highway 84. They came together at a point some seven and a half miles north of the capital city, where from the sky they could have been seen turning onto a rough road rising up a low hill just west of the small village of Tesuque. At the top of the steep dirt incline, the cars clustered together in a small parking lot like a convocation of fireflies, quickly darkening. To the near northwest, a bowl of other light stood, drawing in the hundreds of figures who hurried toward it.

Their destination was a building that would normally be highly unlikely to find at the top of an earth-packed road near a sparsely populated town in a vast state: a small redwood theater, seating just 480 people,[2] tucked into the lee side of a rolling hill. It was an outdoor amphitheater, in concept reminiscent of a Greek theater, where the only roof was the sky and the gods could look easily down on man's attempts to weave love, hate, woe, and wonder into a cathartic experience. A small canopy arched over the stage and orchestra pit, which itself was fronted by a high but shallow reflecting pool. The complex was near a former guest ranch that perched several hundred yards away on the other side of the hill, seeming, with its adobe architecture, to melt into the ground. In contrast, although the theater itself was anchored to the New Mexico earth, its open design linked it to the sky and its stars. One could easily imagine it floating upward and away, fueled by the power of music.

Tonight the entire site teemed with activity, light, and sound. Young men directed arriving cars into patterns of parked vehicles. Box office employees handed out tickets and soothed ruffled customers who had left their precious admittance pasteboards back home on the hall table. Bartenders readied their stock, from soft drinks to stronger waters. Singers vocalized backstage, the sound coming dimly through the night. In the pit, orchestra members tuned their instruments and went over difficult passages. The confused yet creative sounds energized the air, filling it with expectation. Flowing under all was the murmur of eager audience members filing into the house and finding their seats on the long wooden benches—or for a lucky few, in boxes formed with low canvas screens containing patio chairs.

The arrivals were variously attired in everything from formal evening dresses and white tie and tails to jeans, concha belts, and boots; from sack suits and daytime dresses to tuxedos and cocktail frocks. Through the open rear of the stage, the lights of the nuclear city of Los Alamos could be seen twinkling in the distance. A waxing moon rode high above all.

Precisely at 9:00 p.m., the house lights dimmed.[3] Excited conversation faded into silence. A trim man with just nine days to go until his thirty-first birthday entered the pit to applause. His obvious energy was notable, given that he had been working nonstop for months, something of which the packed house was well aware. He bowed, acknowledged the orchestra, and raised his baton. A snare drum rolled, and people rose as one to place hands over hearts and sing the national anthem. Then silence again, a pause—and the baton danced once more, calling forth a wiry melody from the violins, soon tossed back and forth between instrumental choirs. Stage lights rose, figures moved onto the playing area, and Giacomo Puccini's *Madame Butterfly* flowered in front of hundreds of eager eyes and soared into hundreds of listening ears. Something new had come to the venerable world of opera: the first night of the first season of The Santa Fe Opera.

That opening night marked the fulfillment of a dream for the conductor, John O'Hea Crosby. He had not only imagined the entire enterprise but helped pour his theater's concrete slab, plant the blossoms in its flower beds, inspect its plumbing, plot out its finances, and steer it through the lurking shoals that threaten any new artistic entity. Fortunately, he was not alone. He had brought many others along with him on the journey, and they formed a strong cadre of support. In the audience were his parents, Aileen O'Hea Crosby and Laurence Alden Crosby, who had bravely funded their son's undertaking to the tune of $200,000 and would soon provide even more money, as well as contributing their own labor as gardeners and costume supervisors, artist greeters, and even restroom janitors. Also proudly present was Leopold Sachse, former intendant of the Hamburg Staatsoper and a Crosby mentor at Columbia University in New York. He had helped persuade the senior Crosbys that their son's audacious vision was both worthy and workable.[4] Then there were the business people and patrons whom Crosby and his supportive friends in both New York and Santa Fe had persuaded to back the company and sit on its young board, and the mostly twenty-something singers, directors, designers, technical personnel, orchestra members, and office staff who were together bringing Puccini to vibrant life.[5] It was a young company in every way, but more sagely overseen than many other fledgling endeavors, let alone established musical organizations. Even in the heart-stopping excitement of an opening night, plans for the decades ahead were already spinning in the brain of the young conductor-impresario. And with those plans in mind, he had already begun to maneuver his supporters neatly into positions from which they would continue to assist what he knew would be a growing, glowing, grand enterprise.

For there was something about the young John Crosby—a firmness of purpose allied with persuasive charm and endless energy—that drew others to him and his ambitions. He was a pied piper, who took his eager train of followers not inside a rocky cliff to disappear forever but into the theatrical wings and then onstage, making do and

The theater shortly before opening night, 1957, from the air. Note the two spotlights on the roof of the entrance building. The complex has grown tremendously since this image was taken, but the rugged New Mexico terrain remains the same. Photographer unknown. Courtesy The Santa Fe Opera.

finding the way as they went along. He preached a message of messianic intensity that drew like-minded people together, with an awareness of obstacles ahead that was both blithe and confident, nervous and engaged. The feeling was that with Crosby at the helm, the group would flourish as a unified cooperative no matter what challenges loomed. It did, too. As Crosby himself observed fifteen years later, "The Santa Fe Opera began as an experimental commune, in the best sense"—a visionary organization driven by one man whose combination of musical ability, hard-headed worldly knowledge, and personal inspiration was irresistible.[6]

Opening night did not stand alone. In the coming nine weeks, Puccini's lyrically tragic *Madame Butterfly* was joined by six other operas.[7] They were contemporary master Igor Stravinsky's acerbic *The Rake's Progress*; Richard Strauss's comedy *Ariadne auf Naxos*; Giovanni Battista Pergolesi's pert *La Serva Padrona*, playing on a double bill with American composer Marvin David Levy's contemporary comedy *The Tower*; Wolfgang Amadeus Mozart's sardonic *Così fan tutte*; and Gioacchino Rossini's sly *The Barber of Seville*. All were heard in English, with the singers alternating from night to night in now starring, now supporting roles—a big change from most opera houses of the period, in which stars orbited high and secondary artists trod the earth far below. In an amazing accomplishment for a tiny new company, a number of the shows played to capacity audiences, and all shows were enthusiastically received. National as well as local critics were there to evaluate and judge, and they unanimously lauded the achievement, noting the high level of both musical and dramatic verity. The Santa Fe Opera was news from the first.[8]

The success was so solid that one could almost forget the difficulties inherent in such a project, although they dogged the company nonetheless. One big element of adversity came with the theater's design: the weather. Throughout the company's history, the New Mexico atmosphere has not always been as benign as on that opening night. The second night's *Così fan tutte* went well, but when *The Rake's Progress* came around, a wild rainstorm forced a postponement, even as Stravinsky himself sat in the audience and the cast and orchestra huddled backstage.[9] Then, as now, one of The Santa Fe Opera's most obvious and beloved characteristics—its open-to-the-elements environment—could be both tremendously charming and meteorologically confounding.

During this first season, Crosby established the model his company would follow strictly, during his forty-five-year tenure as general director and even after. On the artistic side of the scale were a balanced repertoire, inclusion of new works from the start, dramatically apt singers, cohesive production values, and an exactly plotted and necessarily rigid production schedule. On the administrative side were meticulous cost and personnel controls, a capable if overworked staff, and a financial restraint that sometimes led to Crosby being compared to a modern-day Ebenezer Scrooge: for with Crosby, if a prop or costume component could be saved and recycled rather than thrown out, or borrowed rather than bought, it would be. Although, to be fair, he never was one to stint on either operating funds or capital when good results and solid success could be predicted—and when the money was in hand. His gambling on tastes and fashions in music was always balanced by an artistic and administrative conscience of a high order, or, to put it more bluntly, he always hedged his bets on unusual pieces with a strong supporting cadre of box office favorites.

To the President of the Opera Association of New Mexico:
December 7, 1963

On page 2, paragraph #2 the word "budget" crops up again, and all
I can say is that the written statements prepared by me for the
board must stand as identified—that is, ESTIMATE.

Crosby also exhibited the personality, characteristics, and mysteries
that marked his entire life. From enigma to impresario to entrepreneur,
at thirty-one he possessed the focused personality and directness of
purpose that helped him govern his creation for four decades. When it
came to business, he was consistently attentive, even obsessed. When
it came to art, he was all business. He made sure that creative matters
toed the line as well as administrative ones, from casting and direction
to ticket sales and theater maintenance. Even when difficulties arose,
he looked forward rather than back. That didn't mean he couldn't be
happy at artistic success, even if he seldom showed it, but that he was
always looking ahead, as well as being in the moment, while simultaneously remembering to learn from past triumphs and troubles. In
effect, Crosby surfed the past, present, and future as one.

Personally, in the midst of what really was a dazzling success,
Crosby displayed one overriding personality trait that would never
leave him. He was almost pathologically shy, admitting few people to
his internal circle and even fewer as he aged.[10] That created a conun-
drum for a man intent on working in the friction-filled and personality-
ridden world of opera—how to succeed in such a heart-on-the-sleeve
atmosphere with a cautious and sometimes unwelcoming character at
his core. He also expected everyone to maintain as closely uniform a
commitment to the company as he did—in point of fact, an absolute
one—and few persons could consistently live up to such demands.
As a result, now and later, his temper could flare suddenly at a problem or failure, at times to the point of emotional explosions or physical reactions. Symptomatic of the stress he labored under were the
ever-present cigarettes he chain-smoked like an oral security blanket,
as well as his indulgence in copious amounts of alcohol at parties, after
performances, or even just at the end of the workday. They helped at
times to keep the stopper in the Crosby genie bottle.[11]

Seen from today's perspective, it was nothing short of astounding that anyone would think they could found an opera company in what was considered the wilds of the West, let alone succeed by attracting faithful supporters, creditable performers, and a composer as world famous as Igor Stravinsky. In 1957, Santa Fe was a state capital and a recognized visual and literary arts destination, as well as a refuge for people with tuberculosis and other pulmonary ailments. It had limitless natural beauty, pure air, and serene surroundings. Its population had more than doubled from the 1930s to the 1950s and stood, at that point, just over 30,000. Yet it still was tiny by metropolitan standards and something of a jumping-off place. At twelve hours by air, or more than forty by train, from the East Coast, it was hard to reach and not yet equipped for the flood of visitors that an opera company would need to attract to sustain itself.[12] It was as if someone had suggested starting an international theater group north of the Arctic Circle or a dance company on an island where ships only called every six months.

And yet John Crosby, for all his audaciousness, both guessed and planned accurately. He was the right person in the right place at the right time. His temperament and intelligence, dedication to music, confidence born of privilege, and family support made him the ideal candidate to imagine an unlikely project and bring it to life. In targeting a small town with a rich cultural history and a core of wealthy people who would support high-level arts experiences, he had just the place—one he fortuitously knew and loved from personal experience. The time was definitely ripe as well. The post–World War II economic boom was in full swing, he had family money to back him, and he had plentiful connections with artistic people willing to work hard for modest pay to practice their craft and be part of something of unusual and lasting quality.

Beyond altruism, and even more important, founding The Santa Fe Opera permitted Crosby to live out his artistic dream. He savored the idea of being a creative king and accomplished conductor as well as an administrator, and, in his quietly implacable way, he was determined to achieve the goal. He founded the company to give him an artistically Archimedian place to stand, from which he hoped to move the musical world. That he did so practically, although not always in terms of consistent personal artistic success, was a major triumph and a minor tragedy.[13] Yet the organization that began so audaciously is today one of the most successful in the country and the world, located in one of the most thrillingly beautiful locales possible—and it is one of the top ten destinations for opera lovers around the globe.[14] None of it would be here today, none of the spell could have been cast, none of the foundations laid without the peculiar brilliance and vision of John Crosby. Yet, although his dedication was profound, it also had something of innocence about it—a forthright acceptance yet denial of difficulties in the same way a child can dream of achievement and spiritually achieve it. He had a vision of voices—not only those of singers but also the artistic voices of directors and designers and instrumentalists, the laudatory voices of audience members, and the supportive voices of staff members. And there were the voices of his own confidence and conscience, both pushing and drawing him forward. Listening to them all, balancing them all, he was ready to sail toward future successions on the near horizon.

The Antecedents of an Impresario

For all its glitter, the theatrical world has been considered the haunt of rogues and vagabonds for centuries and the bane of moral folk. That stricture certainly includes the operatic stage, shunned by many despite its insidious attractions. So it seems odd, yet apt in a way, that Crosby's ancestry was firmly New England Puritan (although Roman Catholic) on his father's side and resolutely Irish Roman Catholic on his mother's. The two lines came together in him to produce a highly intelligent and generally reserved personage, something of a sport, who found fulfillment in the arts. But he was also capable of sudden, profane explosions of Irish temper and darts of cold anger as piercing as any colonial divine calling down shame on a sinner— especially when the sin was failure to live up to Crosby's own example and expectations.

The line of Crosby's father, Laurence Alden Crosby, can be traced back to fifteenth-century Stillingfleet in Yorkshire, England. There an ancestral John Crosby was born circa 1440. Two of that John Crosby's sons immigrated to the American colonies between 1635 and 1638 and established flourishing families that quickly spread through what became Maine, Massachusetts, and New Brunswick, Canada.[15]

Frequent names found in an old family Bible and traceable throughout the Crosby line to the present day are James, John, Emily, Caroline, Leland, Alden, Priscilla, and Laurence, often repeated in alternate generations.[16]

The grafting of Mayflower notables John Alden and his wife, Priscilla Mullins Alden, into the Crosby stock came when James Crosby, John Crosby's grandfather, married Emily Alden in the latter part of the nineteenth century.[17] They had three children: Priscilla Standish, Caroline Leland, and Laurence Alden, who was born December 20, 1892, in Bangor, Maine. Laurence was ten when Caroline and James drowned in an April 24, 1902, canoeing accident in Bangor. James managed to get his wife to safety, then returned to try to rescue Caroline; both drowned. After the tragedy, Laurence, Priscilla, and their mother lived in somewhat straitened circumstances; an aunt came to live with them to help out.[18]

Laurence's keen mind and inherent abilities soon showed themselves, rather in the style of a Horatio Alger hero.[19] He began a steady rise to financial and social success. He earned a bachelor of arts degree from Maine's famed Bowdoin College in 1913 and then was awarded a Rhodes Scholarship to Oxford University. At that storied institution, in various years from 1915 through 1919, he showed a love for both the historical and the practical aspects of the legal profession. He successfully took bachelor of arts and bachelor of civil law degrees and later earned a master of arts. In between, he found time to earn another bachelor of civil law degree from Columbia University in New York. He must have loved Oxford dearly. In 1922, he cowrote *Oxford of Today* for Rhodes Scholars who would be attending the school after World War I.

Laurence became a certified member of the New York Bar in 1917, just as he earned his Columbia degree; it was also the year he entered the U.S. Army to serve during World War I for two years. After leaving the army in 1919 as a first lieutenant, he maintained a private law practice for some years, then in 1927 joined the secretive, powerful, and highly successful New York law firm of Sullivan & Cromwell, a political and monetary power behind many modern thrones, from governments and companies to individuals and families.

As Laurence Crosby was attending universities and beginning to establish himself in life, John Crosby's mother, Aileen Mary O'Hea,

Around 1927, toddler John Crosby smiles at the birdie while sitting with a favorite doll on an ornate plush sofa. His white smock foreshadows the white tie and tails he would don for conducting decades later. It also prefigures the comfortably informal shirts he so often wore around the company's campus. Photographer unknown. Courtesy the Crosby family.

was living in London. She had been born there on October 23, 1885,[20] seven years before her future husband. Her father was of Irish descent, with a family tree that, like Laurence Crosby's, extended back to the 1400s.[21] It would seem that O'Hea père was of independent means. The family lived in late Victorian and Edwardian comfort, traveling often and moving in refined Roman Catholic social circles, of which London had several.[22] Aileen was one of ten children, a fact not surprising in view of the era and the family's Roman Catholicism. Some of her siblings later established themselves in Mexico and Australia; others devoted themselves to the religious life. Three of her sisters became Carmelite nuns, and two brothers became priests.

Besides acquiring the usual social accomplishments expected of an upper-middle-class young lady of good birth, Aileen took her music beyond modest drawing-room attainments. She studied violin assiduously as a girl, eventually playing at a professional level.[23] She also studied chemistry at Cambridge University, with an eye to teaching it later—chemistry in the scientific sense rather than in the alternate English usage of pharmacology. She undertook less academic work as well. The 1911 all-England census showed her living in London's Croydon district and teaching "domestic science," the equivalent of home economics.[24]

Four years later, in July 1915, came a pivotal meeting. Aileen was traveling to Mexico to visit one of her brothers when she met Laurence on the steamship *Arabic*, out of Liverpool to New York, which docked July 24, 1915.[25] They bonded aboard ship, and Laurence began writing to her when she returned to London. Discussing their meeting, John Crosby wrote on November 3, 1994, to one of his O'Hea cousins living in Mexico,

> I never met your father, but he obviously figured importantly in my life. My mother (your Aunt Aileen) made a trip from London to Mexico in 1916 [*sic*] for the purpose of visiting her brother and, I believe, helping him in an illness. During her trans-Atlantic crossing she met the man who became my father, so we owe that meeting to your father.

The hopeful course of true love soon hit choppy waters. Aileen's mother disliked Americans intensely, as another of her daughters had previously been jilted by an American suitor. Laurence's academic record, good family background, and Roman Catholicism did not impress the redoubtable Mrs. O'Hea. When Aileen discovered that her mother had destroyed letters Laurence had sent her, she left home, lived in lodgings in London, and supported herself playing the violin in respectable tearooms. That fact affirms her musicianship. One had to have an extensive repertoire and be able to render it with taste and technique to succeed in such a job. It also demanded long hours and consistent attendance, as well as some theatrical flair.

At the same time, she and Laurence resumed their correspondence and eventually became engaged. It was a long engagement. They did not marry until September 5, 1923,[26] in London, after Aileen had faced down—or worn down—her mother. The marriage divided the O'Hea family into two camps, pro- and contra-Aileen, and it appears that the rift took some time to close.

The new Mr. and Mrs. Crosby were a handsome pair, of moderate stature and intelligent bearing. Both were of vest-pocket height, around five feet six and five inches, respectively. Both were slender, quick on their feet, and equally quick of mind. They dressed conservatively and tastefully, showing a preference for quiet clothing. When not attired formally, Aileen tended to wear simple but well-made Liberty print dresses from the notable London store. These favored her pretty figure and left her violin-playing arms free from the elbow down. Laurence's clothing tended to bow ties and crisply ironed long-sleeved shirts that went with his suits.

Shortly after their wedding, Aileen and Laurence went to Cuba, where Laurence, fluent in Spanish, oversaw business for various clients in the flourishing Cuban sugar industry. The couple only returned to the United States for the birth of their first child, James O'Hea Crosby, on December 5, 1924, in New York, when Aileen was thirty-nine and Laurence was thirty-two. John O'Hea Crosby followed a year and a half later, on July 12, 1926, also in New York, when Aileen was forty-one and Laurence was thirty-four.[27]

The pair's long engagement and devotion despite family opposition, as well as their age difference, were rather unusual for the period. Even though their social class demanded conformity, they were willing to be socially—if not spiritually—unorthodox. In fact, formal religion was important in the home. Both their sons were brought up as practicing Roman Catholics and accompanied their parents to Mass weekly and on Catholic holy days. The brothers maintained a warm relationship all through John Crosby's life, although during their adult years, they were not geographically close.

Soon, other work in the Spanish-speaking Southern Hemisphere called Laurence Crosby. Around 1928, as James Crosby recalled,

My father had (previously) been sent by his New York law firm to South America, to carry out affairs in most of the many countries in the west coast. Upon his return to New York, the law firm in Wall Street asked him to go south again . . . and he said that was too much for his family—and they said right away, "Take them all with you," which he did, for two full years.[28]

The Crosbys based themselves in the cultural and cosmopolitan city of Buenos Aires, with its museums, opera house, and busy political and social life, while Laurence traveled throughout Colombia, Peru, Ecuador, and Chile on business for his firm and its clients. The family lived comfortably and went to the coast of Uruguay during the South

American winters. Laurence also continued to make regular trips to Cuba on business, where he began to lay the groundwork in the sugar industry for his own growing wealth during the later 1940s and throughout the 1950s. Eventually, he owned five sugar mills, supervised four others, and held interests in the railway lines that brought the sugar cane to the processing mills.[29]

To his New York bankers: May 26, 1994

In view of the changes in management of my investment council account . . . I want to reconfirm certain standing instructions . . . which have been in place since their inception.

   With reference to the account of John O. Crosby . . . the following securities should not be sold under any circumstances without my authorization: 8,450 Atlantica Del Golfo Sugar Company. . . .

   The reason for these instructions is that the subject securities represent claims against the government of Cuba approved by the United States Foreign Claims Settlement Commission in substantial amounts. We have no knowledge as to whether these claims will ever be paid, or paid in part, or if the interest accruing on these claims since 1960 might be part of any settlement.

   However, it is likely there will be some negotiation concerning these claims if the United States Government continues to consider the question of re-opening trade with Cuba. In that event there may be some fluctuation in the value of these securities.

Laurence's years in Cuba paid him well. The family assets, seized by Cuba's revolutionary government in 1959, included many thousands of shares of Atlantica del Golfo Sugar Co., 100 shares of Camaguey Sugar Co., and savings worth more than $11,000. The total value of the seized assets was put at $608,101 — some $3.74 million today — by the Foreign Claims Settlement Commission of the United States in August 1960, at 6 percent annual interest.[30] For the rest of his life, Laurence Crosby grumbled about the lost family holdings. He held Fidel Castro personally accountable and was especially livid during the Cuban Missile Crisis, as he saw the chance for a return of his and others' property vanish in a haze of threats and diplomacy.[31]

Growing Up

By the time the Crosby boys were old enough to be cognizant of their surroundings, the family was living in Bronxville, New York, a wealthy and exclusive suburban community north of New York City. Their house, on a large estate, was built in 1916. Laurence bought it in 1926, just before he joined Sullivan & Cromwell and shortly after John's birth. It served as a family base even when Aileen and Laurence moved to Cuba in late 1946—at which time they gave a house in East Chester, New York, to John and James as an investment. The elder Crosbys stayed at the Bronxville estate from time to time on return trips to the United States. They lived there again after fleeing Cuba in 1959 and until Laurence retired in 1961, when the couple moved permanently to Santa Fe.[32]

Sited on nearly two acres, the large house was surrounded by thick stands of fir, oak, and elm, as well as by a sturdy stone wall. An immense willow brooded over a pond in the rear that was formed by a stream meandering through the property. Two stone bridges spanned the ends of the pond, giving the estate its evocative name of Twin Bridges. The house was three stories high on its front side and four stories at the rear, where the basement area opened onto a slope. Built of fieldstone and stuccoed in part, it was more than large enough for the four-member family and a staff of servants, including a groundsman-chauffeur, at least one maid, and a cook who made superb biscuits. It was probably a good thing the family had full-time kitchen help, for Aileen was chancy at the stove. Family lore notes that her idea of preparing any cut of meat was to boil it into submission.[33]

The servants, and other people involved with Laurence's business, were considered part of the family orbit. The groundsman-chauffeur once helped James build a large-scale ship model, which Aileen then helped rig with lines and sails. He also stayed in touch with the family for years after his direct association with the clan ended, sending James Crosby's family Italian cakes at Christmastime. In similar fashion, Laurence Crosby's secretary sent Laurence's granddaughters dresses as presents. In later life, John Crosby occasionally wrote friendly letters to the groundsman, with family gossip and updates on Aileen and Laurence's health and activities.[34]

The Great Depression apparently did not affect the family much, although Laurence remained prudent in his disbursements. When friends asked why he had a swimming pool constructed in the early 1930s, he replied that he had the money then but didn't know whether he would have it the following year.[35] That encapsulated the Crosby family's financial creed, which was to buy quality items built to last for years, if not decades, whether clothing, automobiles, furniture, or fixtures. John Crosby followed that bent throughout his life, buying relatively few things but those of quality. He would invest in an expensive, perfectly cut blazer and wear it regularly for more than a decade. And when he discovered a kind of outfit that suited him to wear at the opera during summers, he accumulated a closet full of them—casual zippered shirts, comfortably relaxed pants, and espadrilles (or, later, running shoes). His color range was rather confined, too: black and white for formal wear, and white or blue for day-to-day opera work. Comfortable simplicity was his general creed. Attire for him was not something to prove himself with but something simply to have as needed.[36]

Bronxville was an ideal place for boys to grow up. Both James and John learned to ride at a nearby stable, which boasted miles of bridle paths winding through the lush landscape; both were good horsemen. They had family pets, including cats and, at various times, two English bulldogs, one named Brownie. One dog was the hero of a family story: when a photographer could not get the lads to smile in a mid-1930s photograph, she finally asked if they had a pet that might relax them. The ensuing image showed a shyly smiling young John and a handsome and confident adolescent James sitting with a bulldog between them.[37] A veterinarian once suggested giving one of the dogs whiskey when it was ill. Aileen poured out some of Laurence's most expensively fragrant Scotch, which infuriated the paterfamilias. For a dog, he felt, a cheaper brand would have been just as good. At that, Laurence could be dictatorial in the family circle. He even removed the comics pages from the newspaper every day so the boys would not see them.[38]

"That house was such a gorgeous house, I've never lived in a house like that [since]," James Crosby recalled. "It had a gorgeous lawn in front, and in one corner of the lawn—this'll give you an idea of how big that lawn was—my parents built a tennis court." On the other side

A rather diffident-looking young John Crosby, left, with his handsome and jaunty older brother James, circa 1937. They pose with a favorite English bulldog. According to family lore, the photographer despaired of getting the boys to smile for the camera until she hit on the happy thought of bringing a beloved pet into the picture. Photograph by Lena G. Towsley. Courtesy the Crosby family.

of the house was the swimming pool. The many rooms, which were high, wide, and handsome, included a glassed-in sunroom at the end of the house on the second floor. The lawns were meticulously maintained, and flowers grew profusely.

Like James, John was imprinted with the beauty and security of Twin Bridges as a family hearth, and he retained his love for, and memories of, the property all his life. On August 15, 1995, he wrote to the owner of Twin Bridges, "In May 1986, I drove by and stopped for a moment to look in from the driveway pillars. Everything looked wonderful—the trees, gardens and house, particularly the window box outside the east windows of the dining room. I remember this house so very warmly and my days as a youngster playing in the gardens and the old pond and brook." Around the same time, he also paid what turned out to be a last visit to the property. He was driven out to spend the greater part of a day touring the house and grounds, noting what had been changed and what had been retained. It was a nostalgic, touching excursion for a man who seemed so hard-boiled in other areas of his life.[39] Childhood memories and innocence may have seemed deeply buried in John Crosby, but they were there, sending out springs of remembrance that permeated his life and some of his most benign actions.

The Crosbys were a cultured family, and the boys grew up in a cosmopolitan atmosphere filled with books, conversation, clan stories, and news of the day. Besides Aileen, who was a violinist, there was another musician in the family: Laurence had played guitar from his youth. As the boys grew up, they also studied music: John took piano and violin lessons, and James learned piano, flute, flamenco and classical guitar, and the Greek bouzouki.[40]

Violin became more than a passing fancy for the young John.[41] He started formal study in 1934 at age eight with a teacher in New York. His introduction to the piano came earlier: he explored the instrument on his own before beginning regular lessons at age six. Laurence supported the boys' musical interests. He even bought his sons a special red, child-sized piano with seventy-eight keys. Made in the 1920s by Kohler and Campbell, it had Japanese scenes painted on the music rack and was a complete instrument designed for smaller hands, not a toy. The beloved piano is still in the family today.[42]

Aileen and Laurence were loving but strict parents. James Crosby remembered them as

> very brilliant, but aware of the reasoning [powers] of young
> children and their tastes. My parents didn't like to discipline us,
> but they didn't spoil us. And they insisted, if they said something,
> we had to do it. But they never had to punish us with a stick or
> anything like that. They encouraged us to explore art and music—
> Johnny and I really grew up living the best way. We realized the
> artistic riches we had access to in New York City.

That was certainly true. The boys and their mother were often driven into town or took the half-hour train ride to Grand Central Station to go to museums, libraries, and art galleries and to attend theatrical and musical performances, often followed by a supper. The parents did not need to drag their sons along, for they went eagerly. John especially liked the operettas of Gilbert and Sullivan when he and James first heard them.

But both Crosby sons considered the most pivotal experience of their youth to be a long canoe trip along the sixty-five miles of Maine's Allagash River in 1939.[43] "We went with my father and with our uncle, the husband of my father's sister," James Crosby said. "Four canoes and four guides, one guide in each canoe—and one tourist! The canoes were pretty heavily loaded. That trip lasted at least eight days." They saw the wilderness that thrived along the river; they paddled through huge, silent lakes; they caught fish for meals; they helped hump the boats and equipment over portages; and they slept under the stars at night. James recalled it as a once-in-a-lifetime experience—a feeling, he said, John shared deeply. It contributed greatly to John's love of nature and the outdoors and his awareness of the beauty of untouched landscapes. It was a stern beauty that later found echoes in the Tesuque Hills, when he foresaw an operatic stage crowned with nothing but moon and stars. In a nice mix of adventure and practicality, the long trip to the Canadian border was made by canoe, but the travelers returned home by car.[44]

Given the Crosby family's residences in Spanish-speaking countries, both James and John began speaking the language as children. It took hold quickly in James, who as an adolescent was completely fluent in Spanish. In his adult life, he became as respected and famous in the field of Spanish literature as John was in music.[45] His special study was the work of the Spanish Golden Age poet and satirist Francisco de Quevedo, about whom he wrote many books and articles. He spent time with his family in Spain in 1952, 1962, and 1967–1968, when his three children spent a year in a Spanish school. Before his retirement, James taught at universities and colleges, including Yale, the University of Illinois, Dartmouth, the State University of New York in Albany, and Florida International University. John himself retained some of his early mastery of Spanish into later life, using Spanish phrases now and then in his letters, and he apparently could converse easily with Spanish-speaking locals during his boyhood and young manhood in New Mexico.

Educating a Polymath

When it came to education, Aileen and Laurence, with their Cambridge and Oxford backgrounds, did not consider the Bronxville public schools acceptable for their sons. They especially did not want the boys to lose the quasi-English accents they had picked up from their mother. (Throughout his life, John retained such English idioms as "whilst," "shalt," and "must needs" in his speech, and many of his letters contain such locutions.) As a result, the boys' very earliest schooling took place at home, with other children gathered from throughout the neighborhood.[46] In addition, Aileen and Laurence shared their love of English poetry and literature with their sons. "John's and my parents were very literate," James recalled, "constantly reading mostly novels and history in English. Needless to say, they often read aloud to me and to John. This is how John and I began to appreciate novels and plays." Reflecting that early exposure, in later years, John read biography and history voraciously and constantly.[47] In a more child-appropriate manner, Aileen also read to her sons the stories of A. A. Milne's Winnie-the-Pooh and personalized the adventures of Mr. Toad in Kenneth Grahame's *The Wind in the Willows* with Crosby family references. Maintaining the tradition with her grandchildren was one of her great pleasures in later life.

After their initial home education experiences, the boys were sent to a preparatory school, Pelham Day School in Pelham, New York. There, John Crosby recalled, the curriculum was standard for the day: French, English, arithmetic, Latin, and history. (Laurence, with his knowledge of legal Latin, was attentive to their studies of the classical language.) John did well in school, and like just about any young lad, enjoyed experimenting with chemistry sets and electrical kits. He also fancied working in clay.[48] Although he did not practice sculpture of any kind in later life, that early plastic skill and the consequent coordination developed between hand and eye came in handy when he worked alongside architects, builders, and renovators on his theaters and homes. His keen eye always was alert for perfection. As an example, in 1998, he was insistent that a Stravinsky memorial bust being placed in the new house be both completely true to its subject and correctly installed—absolutely realistic, angled just so, and firmly placed.

When the Pelham period ended, first James and then John were sent to the Hotchkiss School in Lakeville, Connecticut. Founded in 1891, it was established as a top boys boarding school (today it is coeducational). Hotchkiss was also a feeder school for Yale, which James and John both attended, two years apart; they each maintained deep affection for both institutions into maturity and later life.

Despite its many advantages, childhood for John included bouts of chronic illness. During early adolescence, he experienced serious regular sinusitis that often kept him confined to bed or suffering under medical ministrations for days at a time. In his oral history, he explained how that unfortunate situation would introduce him to New Mexico.[49]

> I don't think I had what is called asthma, although that story has persisted for decades. I had what I understood was a sinus problem, causing an infection in the sinuses, and I think the condition began to manifest itself as a real problem when I was perhaps 12 or 13 years old. And, at that time, we did not have all the wonder drugs and hormone pills and antibiotics and so forth that we're accustomed to today. So that the treatment for that condition was pretty much limited to a system of getting into the cavities and flushing them out with saline solution. And that had to go on fairly consistently, which was a rather taxing experience.

The family doctors finally suggested to Laurence, after John's first year at Hotchkiss, that sending him to a dry climate in the West "might be less expensive and it might be more efficient and better for my health."[50] The Crosbys therefore looked at a number of Western boarding schools between Colorado Springs and Phoenix. They wanted a school of academic repute, in an area possible to reach fairly quickly by then-available transportation, and in the healthiest climate possible. Given Laurence and Aileen's fondness for British culture and customs, they probably looked also for an institution that would project both the benefits and the character-building rigors of an English public school. All those needs came together when a friend recommended the Los Alamos Ranch School, which enjoyed an enviable reputation from its founding to its closure.

As a result of the recommendation, Aileen and the young John went to Santa Fe to meet the director of the school, A. J. Connell. It was the first time any of the family had been so far west. As Crosby recalled in his oral history, they

took an airplane from New York to Chicago to Denver to Santa

Fe, and unfortunately I arrived with a high temperature—I think a strep throat or something, so that I was put to bed at La Fonda Hotel—and then Mr. Connell kindly came down from Los Alamos [and] introduced himself. My meeting with him was very brief. He simply came into my bedroom, I was in bed, and said hello, and that was how it [went].[51]

Mr. Connell came in his Boy Scout uniform, for scouting attire was de rigueur at the school. No record exists of the ensuing private interview between Aileen and Connell, but it was clearly satisfactory enough. John was enrolled in the school in November 1940 for his sophomore high school year.

The Ranch School had been founded in 1917 by businessman Ashley Pond, who had suffered from pulmonary problems as a child. It was built with one aim: "To help boys become strong young men through a life of rigorous outdoor living and classical education"[52]— an American version of an English Eton, Harrow, or Rugby.

Starting small at first, the school quickly grew, attracting students from well-off families across the country, but the scions of privileged America found life in the mountains anything but soft. For most of the school's life, students slept on screened porches even in the coldest weather; exercised daily, in the nude when the weather permitted, and combined classes with a heavy curriculum of outdoor exercise and activities. The overall mantra was based on the Boy Scout creed, of which Connell was a lifetime advocate—especially the need to stay strong, mentally acute, and morally upright. Horseback riding, soccer, skiing, skating, hiking, swimming, fishing, cutting trails in the soft tufa rock of the area, overnight camping trips, and cutting brush and wood were among the students' various duties and experiences. Students wore the Scout uniform, including shorts, year-round except during winter recreation and certain outdoor activities. Living in nature so much, even an initially ill-developed boy had the opportunity to become bronzed, active, and fit, as well as comfortable in a variety of challenging situations.

The education was on a philosophical par with the Spartan outdoor life. Connell tended to recruit young graduates from top-flight Ivy League colleges to be faculty members, and they were encouraged to administer their lessons as they wished so long as good student progress was maintained. Again in keeping with the Scout mantra, the curriculum included community service projects. Regular reports to parents covered those activities as well as academic progress and physical development as tracked by the school nurse. Over a quarter of a century, more than six hundred boys were educated there, until the school was taken over and closed so the World War II–era Manhattan Project, with its production goal of an atomic bomb, could be built there.

Crosby recalled, "My scholastic work was not very good at that time because I had really been in rather a bit of a tailspin with this sinus condition, which always was taking me out of school, making me sick and so forth, so I wasn't a very good student until . . . the medical problems had been solved"[53]—which they soon were at the school. Although he was only there for one academic year, 1940 to 1941, John did well physically. His sinus infections were quickly ameliorated, and he became stronger, more mentally focused, and more confident. His interest in the arts was fostered as well. Music lessons were part of the curriculum, as was literature, read privately and aloud in group meetings. Young faculty member Fermor Church handled the school's annual Gilbert and Sullivan productions, and during that school year, John helped assiduously. He did not go back to New York during the spring recess but helped build the scenery and, after vacation, mount the production. He no doubt remembered his childhood exposure to the Savoy operas as he worked on sets and lighting; his interest would bear more fruit years later, when G&S works were performed in Santa Fe.

The boys were not completely segregated from girls their own age. Dances were scheduled with members of the Brownmoor School for Girls in Santa Fe and with other "suitable" young ladies—although the boys wore their Scout uniforms even at formal dances. During one of those dances, the fourteen-year-old John met an older woman who would play a pivotal role in the success of The Santa Fe Opera: the then twenty-seven-year-old Miranda "Mirandi" Masocco, later Levy. (To avoid confusion, I will refer to her as Mirandi throughout this book.) The pair's first meeting was fleeting but, according to Mirandi later, quite enjoyable[54]—although they had relatively little to say to each other beyond social chat and through a more than ten-year age difference.

There was additional exposure to other parts of Northern New

Mexico for the young student. For Christmas in 1940, John, James, and Aileen stayed at the famed Bishop's Lodge resort, formerly the retreat of Santa Fe's nineteenth-century archbishop Jean-Baptiste Lamy, who built the church that is now the Cathedral Basilica of St. Francis of Assisi in Santa Fe. And after John's school year in Los Alamos, John, James, and their parents stayed for a time at Ghost Ranch near Abiquiú in the north, where artist Georgia O'Keeffe lived. Even then, O'Keeffe was awesome and famous. "We youngsters were cautioned not to ride our horses too near her home so as not to disturb her," Crosby recalled.[55] (Decades later, in the summer of 1976, he and O'Keeffe came together under unusual and charming circumstances, when he suggested to her that some of his land near the opera might be suitable for a museum or center devoted to her work. After considering the matter, the artist wrote him a kindly, vague, and complimentary refusal without ever using the word "no."[56])

Back East and vastly improved in health and academic progress, Crosby made the most of his last two years at Hotchkiss in ways he could not have during his first year. He took part in soccer, orchestra, and band; joined the Woods Committee and the chemistry and physics club; and was cast in his senior year in three theater productions: Christopher Marlowe's *Dr. Faustus*, George S. Kaufman and Moss Hart's *You Can't Take It With You*, and George Bernard Shaw's *The Great Catherine*. His nicknames were J. O., Jase, and Jason.[57] He also regularly took part in social activities, including dances, when girls visited Hotchkiss's male bastion from schools such as Emma Willard. He retained his affection for Hotchkiss all his life and even served as an initial interviewer at one point for boys who might be considered for the school—something of a preadmission vetting process. In a letter of March 16, 1965, he wrote a friend, "I recently had a most alarming experience—interviewing a young man for admission to the Prep class at Hotchkiss. How does one interview a 12-year-old?" And on November 13, 1975, he thanked the president of the student body for the school's naming its annual holiday in his honor. "I remember Holidays at Hotchkiss as some of the most wonderful days of my life. The thought of you and all your schoolmates hiking off over the Connecticut hillsides, surely brilliant with autumn colors, makes me indeed very homesick for Hotchkiss." A rather blurred photo in the 1944 yearbook shows Crosby, glasses pushed well back on his nose, racing across the soccer field, his eye presumably on the scrum around the ball. The image conveys both energy and decision, attributes that would soon be further developed during the young man's military service.[58]

A Musician in the Military

With America joining World War II in 1941, John Crosby's later years at Hotchkiss were filled with the foreknowledge that, because he was now in good health, military service was inevitable. At least a third of his Hotchkiss classmates had not returned for their senior year due to enlistment or the draft, something common all across the country in public, private, and parochial schools alike.[59] Both Crosby brothers did their part. James entered the Navy Special Forces from Yale[60]; John was inducted into the army in late summer 1944 after graduation from Hotchkiss.[61] His physical took place August 21, 1944,[62] followed by the usual intensive basic training. After basic, he was shipped off in early 1945 to France.[63] When they arrived, the troops he was with were sent on boxcars east to staging areas, then driven by truck to the location of their divisions. Even though the conflict in the European theater was nearly over, he saw the ravages of war in both France and

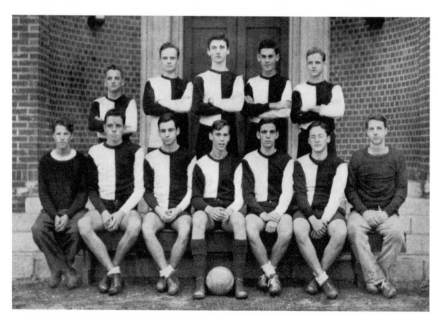

Soccer was one of the teenage John Crosby's favorite sports when he attended the Hotchkiss School. In this 1943 yearbook photograph, he is seen second from right in the first row. He has been caught, unfortunately, with his eyes closed. His slim figure and long legs argue that he was a fast and furious soccer player. Photographer unknown. Courtesy the Hotchkiss School.

John Crosby's 1944 listing in the Hotchkiss school yearbook, the *Mischianza*—Italian for medley or miscellaneous assembly. Note his 1940–1941 "Sabbatical year in the Old West" and his nicknames of J. O., Jase, and Jason. Courtesy the Hotchkiss School.

Germany during his service—and combat at first hand, as he recalled in his oral history. In fact, he was trained as an assistant machine gunner. The team used a Browning water-cooled 30-caliber machine gun. Transportation was by jeep, with a driver, the gunner, the assistant, and ammunition bearers.

> One man carried the tripod and threw it over his shoulders and hit the ground, and he was the gunner. And the assistant gunner placed the machine gun on the tripod and it was ready for the gunner, who was lying there on the ground, to operate. . . . The assistant would place the gun on the tripod, then feed the first belt of ammunition into the gun, and then the ammunition bearers behind him kept bringing him more ammunition as needed.[64]

The young Crosby's combat experience was not long. It ended with the European armistice on V-E Day, May 8, 1945. But he was not reassigned to other battlefield duties. His musical skills and experience had been noted, and the army saw no reason to waste them. After a hiatus of some six to eight weeks after the cessation of hostilities, he was reassigned to a regimental band. He later recalled,

> It was a rather good band, if I may say so, because the regiment I was in had received a number of replacements after the Battle of

the Bulge from units in England, including the units that serviced the Rainbow Club, Piccadilly Circus, London. Some men who'd been with the Glenn Miller Orchestra. So it just so happened in my regiment there were quite a few rather accomplished jazz musicians. And I remember there was even an arranger who worked for Glenn Miller. So that was rather lucky, and we had a pretty fine band as I recall. I think it was about 30 pieces including strings, actually, and I remember I alternated between piano and violin.[65]

Over time, through attrition, the thirty-piece group gradually melted down to a five-piece combo. As bandmates mustered out or were reassigned, Crosby became adept at handling a wide range of instruments. He was doubling not just in brass, but in everything from double bass, accordion, and trombone to violin and piano. His army specialist number was that of a bugler, as there were no specific identification numbers for other different instrumentalists. The thought of the later impresario of The Santa Fe Opera leading swing music, blues ballads, sambas, rumbas, and foxtrots is tantalizing. (One wonders if he ever found people asking him if he were related to two other musical Crosbys, Bing and Bob.) Crosby still felt fairly confident of his instrumental skills decades later. He rather diffidently wrote on March 26, 1966, to conductor Robert Craft that if a professional accordion player could not be found for The Santa Fe Opera's upcoming production of Berg's *Wozzeck*, he would be willing to try and brush up his old squeezebox skills.

Not long after this intensive period of dance-band work, the young musician-soldier was sent to England for rest camp and further study in preparation for his eventual discharge into the civilian population. In October and November 1945 he attended a school set up by Army Operations at Shrivenham, England. There he received certificates of completion for Appreciation of Music 211, Elementary Harmony 109, and History of Music 114.[66] Back with his regiment in late November 1945, he became involved in a USO musical starring Julie Mitchum, Robert Mitchum's sister. He made the orchestral arrangements and conducted the show, leading a Special Service orchestra and also at times throwing in some violin licks. The production went into rehearsal in Munich, opening in the Prince Regent Opera House in early 1946.

It provided Crosby with a "formal conducting debut,"[67] he later recalled humorously, as well as gave him valuable but unwelcome experience in dealing with behind-the-scenes drama. At the time, the Munich Opera company was trying to restart productions by mounting Jacques Offenbach's *The Tales of Hoffman* (in German, *Hoffmanns Erzählungen*), and it deeply resented having to share the theater with an army troupe. The army musicians were not ecstatic, in their turn, at having to alternate stage rehearsals with the German company. Artistic and production skirmishes took place that prefigured many a later headache Crosby would have when running The Santa Fe Opera. He also gained touring experience, shepherding the show around the American Occupation Zone, into and out of theaters that were everything from makeshifts run up quickly by the Army Corps of Engineers to established opera houses redolent of time, luxury, and royal patronage.

In this photo from 1944, James Crosby (left) stands proudly erect in naval uniform; John Crosby (right) is more relaxed in army garb. Photographer unknown. Courtesy the Crosby family.

During his military service,[68] Crosby earned the rank of corporal and a number of medals, including a Company D 37th Tank Battalion, 18th Infantry Special Services, Army of Occupation, European-African medal; the Good Conduct medal; the Eastern Campaign medal; and the World War II Victory medal. He returned to the United States in August 1946 and was processed out of the military at Fort Dix, New Jersey. With a $300 mustering-out gratuity and travel money of $4.75, he went back home to Twin Bridges—and then back to Yale.

Yale and Hindemith

In June 1944, after Hotchkiss and before being drafted, Crosby completed one summer semester at Yale.[69] By enrolling and taking courses, he hoped to hold a place at the school that he could reclaim when he left the service. His major course of study there, as listed on his army papers, was premedical, and he had fourteen credit hours in physics, history, music, English, and zoology.[70]

Crosby did reclaim his place and entered Yale for the 1946–1947 school year. He planned to major in violin performance but soon found the repertoire and technical requirements too onerous. Laurence Crosby was not surprised at his son's inability to master the curriculum and performance demands, but he did not object to John changing his major to music theory and composition (although one might think he would have preferred law or another discipline).[71] Even so, Crosby continued his violin studies with the virtuoso Hugo Kortschak, an Austrian who was dean of music at Yale as well as a former assistant concertmaster of the Chicago Symphony. He also joined the university's orchestra and an amateur theatrical group and was a conductor and orchestrator for undergraduate musical plays. When he conducted the musical comedy *Three Sheets to the Wind* in May 1950, his graduation year, his program biography included the comment that he had played violin in the show *Moonshine* the year before. It also noted, echoing the Crosby family's growing relationship to New Mexico, that he invited the cast "to recuperate with him at his New Mexico Sanatorium" any time.[72]

During his study, John enjoyed his music history classes with the scholarly Beekman Cannon—he recalled him affectionately in a letter of September 28, 1992—and he loved his classes with the legendary German composer Paul Hindemith, famed also as a violist, organist, and music educator. Hindemith had come to the United States in 1940, and he began teaching at Yale in 1941. Among his many students were such later famous composers as Norman dello Joio, Lukas Foss, and Yehudi Wyner, as well as, of course, impresario John Crosby— who was amazed at the inspiration, attention to detail, and abilities the master communicated.

> He was a remarkable teacher, a remarkable man. I mean he was so facile; he had so many interests. He used to give a lecture once a year on the physics of sound, and the lecture would be given up at the physics laboratory at Yale. And the physics faculty would go into the lecture, because they used to say, "He knows more about the physics of sound than we do."[73]

Hindemith believed in personal attention when it came to teaching, and his composition class was never larger than eight students.

JOHN O'HEA CROSBY (Jase). Born July 12, 1926, in New York City, son of Laurence A. and Aileen O'Hea Crosby; brother: James O'H. Crosby, '45W. Prepared at Hotchkiss School. Crosby was in Army, October, 1944—August, 1946 (European theatre); discharged as corporal. Entered Yale with '49M, September, 1946; transferred to '50, February, 1948; majored in theory of music; member, Calhoun (on soccer team); in University Orchestra, 1948–50. Future occupation: teaching, following completion of course at Yale Music School; address, Box 195, Bronxville, N.Y.

The composer had everyone involved in both hands-on and minds-on activities every day. Crosby noted, "Hindemith was a very practical man, a very realistic man, and a very organized person."[74] To give the students a mental and musical workout, he would set difficult tasks. One day they might have to write a piece for a thirty-member military band. Another day, they would find themselves at an imaginary ducal court of the seventeenth or eighteenth century, having to craft a composition for an excellent French horn player, a good cellist, and the duke's daughter, a fair harpsichord player. Or there might be discussions of organ registration or how to write a characteristic and singable melody for voice. Any sort of and size of problem would be tossed to the students, who learned not only to read and interpret scores but to think fast and accurately and get notable and workable material onto music paper quickly and neatly.

Once a problem had been set, Hindemith would specify what form a piece should take—something Mozartean in flavor, for example, with the first movement in sonata-allegro form, the second movement lyrical and expansive, and the third a rousing rondo. Then he would turn his eager journeymen loose. Everyone in the class would take part, with three students at the music stave–ruled blackboards and the others contributing from their desks. Sometimes the seated students would be called up as well to help with executing parts or solving problems, the entire band "supervised by a genius."[75] It was a classic case of teaching individual creativity while stressing the obvious and everlasting need for musicians to work effectively in a group.

Hindemith, a major proponent of sight-singing as a basis for solid musical technique, insisted that his students become fluent in that art as well as in eurhythmics, the practice of incorporating musical

The 1950 Yale University yearbook listing for John Crosby. He looks happy to be graduating and going on to Columbia University for further study. Note that his future occupation is given as teaching—something he certainly did as a mentor for scores of persons who made notable careers in the opera, arts management, and music fields through the years. Courtesy Yale University.

rhythms and stresses into bodily movement. In one challenge, he told them to walk the New Haven flagstones in four-four time while tapping their chest with one finger in three-four time, and tapping an ear with the other hand in six-eight time. That sort of study would prepare students for just about any rhythmic problem in a score, whether they were playing or conducting.[76]

Crosby relished these many creative ingredients that were pouring into his mental crucible. Unhappily, none of his student compositions have survived to show what the eventual founder and conductor of The Santa Fe Opera might have written as a student. It is also unknown whether any of his works ever were publicly performed. But Crosby blossomed in this atmosphere. When the class members were once told to write a fugue for the next day's session, Crosby turned up the next day with three.[77]

Yale was also the setting for an important emotional involvement—Crosby's first known relationship, and a significant one. The fresh-faced and attractive Crosby met classmate Frank Magee Jr. in a seminar, and their mutual attraction was immediate. According to a friend of the time, the pair first got together to study but soon progressed beyond formal dialogue. They quickly became affectionately close companions.[78]

A 1944 graduate of the Phillips Academy in Andover, PA, Magee, like Crosby, had military experience. He was in the U.S. Army Signal Corps in the China Theater from 1944 to 1946.[79] A circa-1950 photograph shows a handsome young man with large, dark eyes, a sensual mouth, thick hair, and a well-cut chin and jaw. According to his résumé of the time, Magee stood 6 feet tall and weighed around 165 pounds. He was well-matched with Crosby, who was of trim build and sharp but shapely features. The pair maintained very close ties for at least a decade, sharing quarters from time to time in New York during the 1950s. Magee also was the opera's business manager from 1958 to 1963,[80] for which Crosby expressed his gratitude in a June 7, 1958, letter to Magee's parents. "Frank has had quite a busy spring in Santa Fe, but I believe he likes the work and finds it stimulating. It certainly has been a great relief to me to have him with us, and he is much appreciated by the other members of the company. . . . I do hope you can come out this summer and hear the performances. New Mexico has some good trout streams too!"

Frank Magee Jr., John Crosby's Yale friend, lover, and companion, circa 1950. Photographer unknown. Courtesy G. L. Davey.

Columbia and New York: Searching for a Dream

After graduation in 1950—with teaching listed as his future occupation in the Yale yearbook[81]—Crosby went on to Columbia University for further study.[82] From 1951 through 1954, he devoted his time to working on conducting skills in a symphonic and operatic repertoire, with Rudolph Thomas, the former conductor of the Hanover State Opera and a leading luminary of the period in New York and international music life. Crosby also took part in the Columbia University Opera Workshop in 1952 and 1953 and worked at times at the Juilliard School from 1952 on as a coach-accompanist. His own performances during this time included six student recitals conducting the Columbia University Orchestra in works by Wolfgang Amadeus Mozart, Ludwig van Beethoven, Franz Schubert, Johannes Brahms, and Richard Wagner. The operatic repertoire he undertook included scenes from Puccini's *La Bohème*, Georges Bizet's *Carmen*, Johann Strauss Jr.'s *Die Fledermaus*, and Wagner's *Die Meistersinger von Nürnberg*, with orchestra and soloists. (All but the Wagner, as major items of the operatic repertoire, would be prominent in Santa Fe Opera seasons later on.) He was conductor and orchestrator for several musicals on the benefit, Junior League, and out-of-town tryout circuit and was even involved in a musical play with the young Elaine Stritch, later a Broadway star. Home alternated between the Bronxville house and shared apartments with friends, including Magee, in New York. He also leased a space as a music studio for study and coachings, where he could practice both piano and violin and work with singers.[83] It is unknown how much of his income came from his work and how much from his well-off parents. During this period, he also met a young man who would later become one of his close professional friends—Edgar Foster Daniels, then a busy actor-singer and later a major supporter of The Santa Fe Opera and, with Crosby, a lover of Richard Strauss's works.[84]

To Luciano Berio: May 1, 1970

Question: re: the arias from standard operas which will be sung in your new work "Opere," we will need orchestral music for such materials selected, and should order that music by early July at the latest to allow for safe delivery and proper practice.

I hope we can avoid use of music protected by copyright, as this
will save royalty fees. In addition to the orchestral music which
we will have on hand for our other performances this summer (*La
Traviata, The Globolinks, Le Rossignol, The Rake's Progress, The
Marriage of Figaro,* and *Anna Bolena*) we also have the orchestra
parts for *The Magic Flute, Così fan tutte, Lucia,* and *Tosca.* . . .

I also have a few personal items which reflect the tastes of
my youth: Parsifal *Good Friday Spell, The Siegfried Idyll, The
Tannhauser Processional,* various medleys of *My Fair Lady* and
the like, endless Strauss (J.) Waltzes and Polkas and the National
Anthem; one or two symphonies of Beethoven, Brahms and Mozart.
Shall we send you our inventory when we get to Santa Fe?

Thanks to his work with Thomas and his own interest in opera, Crosby soon became aware of major changes taking place in the formerly hidebound Metropolitan Opera that would influence the course of operatic endeavor in the entire country. He was among the many eager opera auditors who would spread the new theatrical gospel of the Met's general manager, Rudolf Bing, although few were at such a level as Crosby. In his oral history,[85] he recalled that

A breath of fresh air [was] coming into the production of opera in
the early '50s, when the Metropolitan Opera under the leadership
of Rudolph Bing began to bring in a number of the production
concepts that had developed in Europe in the mid-'30s but had
not moved across to the United States at that time—because of
the Depression and the fact that opera companies were going out
of business, and if they were hanging on, they were hanging on,
you know, by the skin of their teeth. . . . [These new concepts]
were more in line with bringing the performance of opera into the
then-accepted or achieved practices of theatrical performance. In
other words, the costume design, lighting, scenery, and the demands
on the singer to be an actor were being stressed in line with what
the legitimate theater was doing, as opposed to standing in one place
with a painted backdrop behind you and singing your aria.[86]

Like other commentators of the time, Crosby recalled with admiration Bing's productions of Giuseppe Verdi's *Don Carlos, Macbeth,* and

Otello; the Tyrone Guthrie–directed, Fritz Reiner–conducted *Carmen*; and especially the Alfred Lunt–directed, Fritz Steidry–conducted *Così fan tutte* with Eleanor Steber, Blanche Thebom, Patrice Munsel, Richard Tucker, Frank Guarrera, and John Brownlee as superb Mozartean singing actors. Crosby later noted, in a November 30, 1989, letter, "Sir Rudolf really is the great-grandfather of The Santa Fe Opera, which is something I told him on more than one occasion, but which he always tossed off lightly with his elegant wit." (Bing also famously started a small firestorm in fall 1958 when, asked by *Time* what he thought of the new company in New Mexico, he responded, "Where is Santa Fe?" He later genially visited the city and company and even attended the Santa Fe Rodeo, although apparently under slight duress.[87])

To the president of the Santa Fe Rodeo: July 20, 1964

I am most grateful to you for your assistance in securing seats for Mr. Bing at the Rodeo July 10th, and enclosed please find my check in payment of these seats. I am only sorry that I could not persuade Mr. Bing to remain longer at the Rodeo, for we had thought he would enjoy observing the performance, and we had arranged for him to come to the Opera later in the evening.

Crosby took advantage of the many other musical offerings available throughout the metropolis at that time. He noted in his oral history,

New York's wealth of performances attracted young singers and musicians from across the country. One Saturday in 1952, I heard Bruno Walter conduct [Mozart's] *The Magic Flute* at the Metropolitan Opera matinee, took the subway up to Carnegie Hall for Toscanini's concert with the NBC Symphony at 6 p.m., and then went back down to the Met for the evening performance conducted by Fritz Reiner. On three consecutive days at Carnegie Hall, the New York Philharmonic with Walter, the Boston Symphony with Munch, and the Philadelphia Orchestra with Beecham all performed the [Berlioz] *Symphonie Fantastique*. What an experience for young musicians! Such unusual opportunities did not exist elsewhere in the United States.[88]

Also opportune was Crosby's 1955 introduction to Leopold Sachse, a singer, stage director, and the former head of the Hamburg Staatsoper.[89] Sachse at this time worked often at the Metropolitan Opera and had many other directing and producing assignments in New York and elsewhere. He needed an accompanist for a rehearsal of Richard Strauss's *Salome* the day after Easter, April 11. Crosby, alerted by his composer friend Marvin David Levy, filled in. He pleased the stern taskmaster and continued to work for him at Sachse's American Theatre Wing—a major accomplishment, given that Sachse was known to dismiss an accompanist for one wrong note—and eventually confided his hopes for his own opera company to the director. Crosby had begun discussing the possibility of founding a festival theater as early as 1955,[90] when he began feasibility talks with friends in New York and Santa Fe. And once begun, he not only ran with it, he leapt with it, leapfrogging across the advice of naysayers and assembling a theoretical company structure in his head. That foreshadowed his later years at the opera, when he could summon an answer to just about any question, whether it dealt with casts of twenty years ago or ticket income from the last season, from his marvelous and meticulous memory.

Another famed conductor came into Crosby's orbit during this period—the Hungarian-born autocrat Fritz Reiner, during Reiner's final years at the Metropolitan Opera.[91] Crosby attended every performance he could when Reiner was conducting—the master's famous tiny beat influenced his own conducting—and he also met Reiner's wife, who always sat in the front left of the theater near where Crosby took standing room. When he finally told her who he was and that he followed every Reiner performance he could, she laughingly promised to inform her husband of Crosby's hero worship. (Crosby had at least one coaching session with Reiner in later years, although it appears to have been a rather quick lesson in between planes in Chicago. Apparently, Crosby went to visit Reiner at his apartment, where the coaching took place.[92])

The young musician also studied with legendary French conductor Pierre Monteux at his summer school in Maine during the summers of 1955 and 1956. There he even sang Germont père in scenes from Verdi's *La Traviata* in 1956, as most of the singers there at the time were sopranos, and tenors and baritones were in short supply. He wrote a humorous letter to Sachse detailing the challenges of both studying conducting and mastering a major Verdi role in the tight-packed hours of an intense summer music camp.[93] When Monteux died in 1964, Crosby telegraphed his wife, "On behalf of The Santa Fe Opera Company, and particularly those of us who had the honor to know Maître personally may I express our deepest sympathy to you. . . . His memory will always be an inspiration to us."[94]

Another influence in Crosby's musical career and his hopes for founding an opera company came from the great Spanish soprano, Lucrezia Bori, who encouraged him in his aspirations and left the company a bequest of $25,000 on her death.[95]

For Crosby and American opera, times and forces were converging toward an important synthesis. Dramatic verity was beginning to hold a strong place in productions, where previously vocal display had held pride of place. The pendulum was swinging from the era of the star singer to that of a vocal ensemble versed in theatrical skills, with due support from orchestra and stagecraft.

Crosby's interest in this and his growing friendships with singers, theater personnel, and instrumentalists supported his burgeoning dream of his own company and podium. In the next few years, he would draw on his relationships with these mentors and friends as his concept of an international opera festival in Santa Fe crystallized.

CHAPTER TWO

Casting and Rehearsals

To a correspondent: January 9, 1997

Thank you for your letter of January 4th. I am sorry I find it truly impossible to identify the ten greatest operas of all time.

The Crosbys and New Mexico

Crosby's attraction to Santa Fe began with his Los Alamos Ranch School experiences, and his family's interest in the area quickly grew from there as well. In the summer of 1943, John Crosby wrangled at Bishop's Lodge. And after James Crosby completed his Navy service and John Crosby left the army, according to one account, they worked at the lodge during the summers of 1947 and 1948. There, they lived behind Archbishop Lamy's famous chapel in a two-bedroom apartment. They took groups on trail rides in the morning, taught children's riding in the afternoon, and did basic farriery as necessary. Sometimes they took pack trips out overnight, cooking sausages, bacon, and eggs over a campfire.[1] And in 1948, James, John, and their parents purchased a total of forty-seven acres of land on Tano Road, on high ground at Tano Point, some distance south of what became The Santa Fe Opera complex.[2] (That the brothers could afford land as well as their parents argues that the family's prosperity was notable, although the prices would seem ludicrously low now: they paid something like $15 an acre.) It offers wonderful views even today: in the late 1940s, with Santa Fe a small city with a small population, the daylight would show immense expanses of land meeting a far-off horizon, and the night would reveal uncountable stars.

Even undeveloped, it was a family magnet. In the summer of 1949, James Crosby recalled, "Johnny and I spent the whole summer camping out on the land. We lived in tents. When my parents arrived, we went down to the Bishop's Lodge and then we stayed there."[3] Aileen and her sons rode often, and Laurence joined them. The family used to have a short 16 mm film clip showing Laurence, Aileen, and a Bishop's Lodge employee riding hell-for-leather down a steep hill, quite a change from the Bronxville bridle paths.[4] "We used to ride from the Bishop's Lodge . . . up to the beginning of the feet of the mountains," James Crosby said. "Sometimes a group of us would camp up there for a night or two nights or something like that. So Johnny and I got to know the range of those gorgeous mountains just north of Santa Fe."[5] The experience fed something deep in both brothers; it nourished the love of nature that had begun for them with the Allagash River excursion.

In 1950, Crosby designed and the brothers oversaw the construction of a house compound of several buildings on the family land. Both James and John helped local workmen drill a well for the complex,[6] which combined modern convenience and a design-for-living concept with Spanish colonial and even Asian influences. Two separate wings were linked by walkways that joined at a central block that served as a summer kitchen.[7] It was an ideal approach for a family, the climate, and the time. Privacy was available for the different generations, but the family members still had easy access to each other. The compound was a family hub for decades, including those years when James's three children were youngsters and visited their grandparents regularly during the summers. Crosby himself occupied the home for two or three months each summer from 1950 through 1956, at which time he went to live at the newly acquired San Juan Ranch property where the opera was to be built. James and his family stayed at the home each summer from 1950 through 1969. Aileen and Laurence occupied the home from 1961 to 1972, when Aileen died.[8]

What were Aileen and Laurence Crosby like? Answering the question requires presenting several viewpoints, as people show different, detailed sides of their character to those they interact with, depending on the degree of intimacy and the type of situation.

Uniformly, everyone who knew Laurence either in his middle or old age described him as pleasant, kind, and very much a gentleman—although also very much the head of the family. As his sons grew, he appears to have been able to transform the role of supervising father into friend and confidant as well. He favored bow ties with his suits and wore several watches set to different time zones at once.[9] Unlike what one might expect from a wealthy and influential man, he was practical in his approach to things and, at least in Santa Fe, did not use privilege or position as an excuse to demand service. For example, at times a deliveryman at a downtown bookstore would think the weather and road conditions too severe to drop a book off at the Tano Point house. Laurence then would cheerfully put on his coat and drive his Woodie station wagon to the store to get his purchase, undeterred by mud or snow or rain.[10]

Opinions on Aileen Crosby differ. Early company members recalled that Aileen would welcome the singers with hot coffee or tea or chocolate at the ranch after every performance[11] and that she was a supportive presence—even helping clean out the ladies' restroom before performances.[12] Another early colleague of Crosby's recalled her as "more English than the English,"[13] in the negative sense of the comparison. A friend of Crosby's from before the establishment of the company used the words "overbearing" and "domineering."[14] Those qualities apparently came into play when she succeeded in removing Frank Magee from both John's personal orbit and the opera, presumably around Magee's final season with the company, in 1963. The experience was described with significant tact by longtime trusted Crosby colleague and production stage manager Carolyn Lockwood. "She didn't like people that liked John," Lockwood said frankly. "She was very possessive in many ways. I was there when the big blowup came [over Frank Magee], and that was very unpleasant. And she was the cause. So we missed the midnight plane to New York."[15]

Current Santa Fe Opera general director Charles MacKay encountered Aileen later in her life, when he was at the opera in the summer of 1968 as a pit boy and supply French hornist. (He had worked previously with the parking lot crew at the age of fifteen.) He described her as "a very formidable person and certainly not a people person. I just remember her being very, very severe and sort of grumpy. I can remember her coming through the theater when I was just a kid and we all sort of quaked in our boots."[16] Aileen, when not in formal wear for the evening, wore her simple Liberty of London dresses and penny loafers; she also usually wore a hat.[17] Her silhouette could be recognized easily from a distance, alerting workers to look sharp.

Benjamin Saiz, Santa Fe Opera controller, who has worked for decades for the company in a variety of positions, saw a gentler side of Aileen.[18] "When I first met them here [circa 1964–1965], they were very elegant, very simple . . . they weren't snooty people," he said. The Crosbys faithfully attended Mass at Our Lady of Guadalupe church in Santa Fe, he recalled. Just as she helped clean the ladies' restroom when needed, Aileen was hands-on with other domestic tasks. At the end of each season, when the ranch house was still the residence for many company members, she would go to the ranch with her maids and help bundle the curtains and bedspreads for dry cleaning. The bed linen would be washed, and eventually everything would be tucked away in a locked storage room, ready for the following year. During the off-season, Laurence and Aileen regularly drove over from Tano Point to check that the opera buildings' gates were locked and the fences—in those early days, just barbed wire on four-foot-high fence posts—were intact. During this period, there was a real chance that wandering cattle from the neighboring pueblo lands would come onto the campus if the fences were not maintained, and thus the elder Crosbys became fence and range riders.

As to be expected, the Crosby grandchildren saw the warmest side of their grandmother. Besides writing the children special letters and stories, every summer she wrapped the toys they had played with the previous summer and put them on their beds as presents that were both familiar and a surprise.[19] When the adults enjoyed coffee, she would make the grandchildren their own version of the beverage with water and brown sugar. And Aileen welcomed her daughter-in-law, James' wife, into the family with open arms.[20] Laurence was equally affectionate, if somewhat more distant with the girls than with Larry. That would have been the norm for a man of his age, class, and training during that period, to notice a boy more than girls.

Aileen suffered from failing health in the mid-1960s, with fairly regular hospital stays. According to John Crosby, his mother began moving toward invalidism immediately after she and Laurence had to flee Cuba, and she declined steadily.[21] She suffered a debilitating stroke around 1968, after which she had to live in a local nursing home until her death. Laurence visited her twice daily during this period, and Crosby kept in regular touch with her condition while he was in New York in the off-season.[22] When in town, he visited her regularly. After Laurence suffered a slight stroke on October 14, 1971,[23] he spent time at the same nursing home, and after Aileen's death on January 25, 1972, at the age of eighty-seven,[24] Crosby brought Laurence to the opera to live in a special residence he had built for him. (Today it is the company archive and music library.)

```
To the president of the Opera Association of New Mexico:
March 21, 1972

About one week after my mother died I received the enclosure
from St. Vincent's Hospital. I hope the Opera never goes grabbing
like this so quickly.
```

As he became older and began to suffer from dementia, Laurence sometimes wandered away from his paid companions, causing some embarrassing encounters with innocent visitors. In a November 11, 1974, letter to the counselor of educational and cultural affairs for the German Embassy, Crosby wrote, "I must apologize for the confusion of the elderly gentleman whom you met, and who is my father." He went on to explain that Laurence's regular companion was away on a holiday, and that Laurence had "slipped away" from the substitute caretaker. "You will, I am sure, understand my embarrassment, and I deeply appreciate what the experience must have been to you." As a result, later that month Crosby retained a male nurse from New York to come to Santa Fe and live with Laurence as companion and caretaker.[25]

Still, difficulties continued. Once Laurence strode into the business office and announced he was going home to his natal city of Bangor. When asked how he planned to get back to Maine, Laurence said, with dignity, that he planned to walk down to the highway and hitch a ride. After he left the office, an employee alerted the nurse-companion that the elder Crosby was off on another jaunt and needed to be stopped.[26]

"I should advise you," Crosby wrote to Laurence's doctor on September 11, 1975,

> that he tends to become quite disturbed and confused in the late afternoons. Although he is cheerful in the mornings and enjoys lunching downtown, by 5:00 p.m. he can become convinced that the Theater has been robbed, that we must move downtown, that he should go to Maine, etc., etc. His thoughts become very disjointed, and he is inclined to become quite cross. . . . In order to calm him and relax him so that he can prepare for bed, we have to reassure him and talk about 'things to do tomorrow' and often let him have about three drinks."

But even with his confusion and the difficulties it could create, Laurence was generally content. Crosby noted that his father was happy living at the ranch, enjoyed puttering in the garden, and would visit companionably and speak Spanish with the grounds-keeping staff. He also enjoyed spending time with his books and papers, living mostly in the past but able to enjoy much of the present. His illness was leavened further by the companionship of a pet dog, a large and friendly malamute for which he cherished much affection.[27]

Laurence Crosby died January 2, 1980, at age 88.[28] He and his wife are buried in the same plot at the Santa Fe National Cemetery: section X, site 492.[29] As befit one obsessed with detail and history, Crosby kept virtually all their papers, including much material relating to his father's political and business connections at his law firm and papers documenting the family's Cuban assets. He also kept years' worth of his father's dry-cleaning bills—and his own. (Much of that ephemera was dispersed or destroyed on or after Crosby's own death, due to space limitations at The Santa Fe Opera.) Other items were treated in practical ways after Laurence's death. Crosby notified James on April 4, 1980, that some of Aileen and Laurence's old clothing, which was no longer usable even for charitable purposes, had been burned, and some in better condition had been given to needy families in Chimayó. Crosby kept Laurence's army uniforms, academic caps and gowns, and college blazer in case James or his children might eventually want them. He also kept a few items of Aileen's clothing, which he sent as mementos to his two nieces with a charming letter to each.[30]

Crosby's relationship with James and his family was a combination of companionably fraternal and warmly, if nondemonstrably, avuncular. James married in the summer of 1950,[31] and he and his wife Elizabeth Jane Wyszynski—"Betty" or "B. J." in the family—had three children: Elizabeth Anne (Lisa) was born in 1954, Laurence

From left, Aileen Crosby, Laurence Crosby, and John Crosby at James Crosby's wedding reception in July 1950. Photographer unknown. Courtesy the Crosby family.

Alden (Larry) in 1956, and Caroline Leland (Caroline) in 1960. Betty and James originally met at Bishop's Lodge in Santa Fe, when Betty was waitressing and the family was staying there in summer 1949. James and Betty divorced when Lisa was a senior in high school, but the relationship remained cordial; James would celebrate Christmas with the family, for example. When Laurence became less lucid, Crosby took over his role as financial adviser to James, regularly made gifts to James for his retirement account, sent presents to his nieces and nephew, and helped generously with one niece's graduate school expenses.[32]

With his nieces and nephew, their uncle was kind, if distant. During the years James and his family came to Santa Fe, "I think I can remember two or three occasions when John actually came up to the house," the younger Laurence Crosby said.[33] "He was always very busy with the opera, and I didn't really get the feeling he knew that much what to do with kids. . . . I don't think it was his thing; I don't think he was terribly comfortable in that environment." He was friendly enough when they met, if not terribly deep or involved, and he had a notable ability for getting out of family visits he didn't want to make. When he was invited to his nephew's wedding, he sent a letter saying he had elective surgery scheduled then—rather an unusual reason for not attending. The young Laurence worked at the opera on the set crew in the technical department in 1974, after his summer high school year. No one knew he was related to the founder until members of his family came out to visit him. In retrospect, he said, it would have been better to keep the relationship secret. Being John Crosby's nephew carried a certain weight of importance with it, as well as suspicion from others. In 1988, on another trip, he fortuitously met the woman who would become his wife; she worked as the company's then box-office manager.

To his niece, Caroline: September 18, 1984, handwritten

Your grandmother was very fond of a shawl which her youngest sister (your great-aunt Monica) gave her when Aunt Monica lived in India. I am sending the shawl to you and hope you might enjoy having it as a little memento. Affectionately, Uncle John

To his niece, Lisa: September 18, 1984, handwritten

Your grandmother was always very amused when she would wear a little fur cape, which your grandfather gave her when they lived in Havana. Part of the amusement was because it was really too warm to wear a fur cape in Havana, but your grandfather felt very keenly that his wife should have one, particularly because lots of the ladies wore them (in Havana). So Granny finally consented, with the understanding that it be a tiny cape! I am sending the cape to you, and hope you will enjoy having it as a memento. Affectionately, Uncle John.

To Lisa,[34] her uncle John "was famous as all get out" and "a star in the family. . . . The opera itself was enthralling and created for me the love of music I've had all my life. When I was a child, I wanted to be an opera singer, of course." She, too, said her relationship with her uncle struck her as "caring but distanced . . . [he was] always very polite and sweet with us, but we weren't sure we knew him very well." When she was six, Lisa was taken to a dress rehearsal of Mozart's *The Marriage of Figaro*, which thrilled her—even though, she recalled, she had to go home after the first act. From then on, when in Santa Fe during the summer, she was taken to everything not considered inappropriate for children. She had her own ideas on appropriateness, though. "I was bitterly, bitterly angry they wouldn't let me go to *Lulu* when it was first performed," she said.

Caroline[35] likewise remembered the first opera she ever saw: Gian Carlo Menotti's *Help! Help! the Globolinks* in 1969. She recounted vivid memories of coming to the opera and sitting in the Crosby family seats—down right, A 2, 4, 6, and 8 in the orchestra, which remained the founder's own for decades. Everyone would be tremendously excited, sitting in anticipation, waiting for their uncle to appear. "And the minute Uncle John's baton would go up, Larry and I would fall asleep," she confided. As an adult, and a Santa Fe resident, Caroline saw her uncle more frequently than did her brother and sister, although not necessarily frequently—"I would say, maybe three times, four times during the summer," she said. "I would always send him a dozen roses on opening night, a dozen red roses. If I went to the opera when my father came to town, I would see him then." As with everyone, Crosby was not physically demonstrative with Caroline, but "he would not back away when I gave him a hug and a kiss. If he were sitting down and I came and gave him a kiss, he might pat my arm. . . . That, to me, was a way for him to be demonstrative. He was not a warm, fuzzy guy kids would climb over." But he did teach her what was most important in reaching a goal, she said: "Excellence."

The children did get birthday presents from their Uncle John when they were young, but Lisa thinks her mother bought them for John, who would have sent her a check for the purpose.[36] "We always knew he was there in the background; we knew he cared about the family. You knew if anything went wrong, there was Mom and Dad and John. The feeling for family was strong, but there was not a lot of contact. He was such a private person."

Crosby had great affection for his sister-in-law, a feeling that continued after she and James divorced. His admiration went back to their wedding and was based in his love of exactitude. At the ceremony, he noted that the fabric scallops on the bride's and bridesmaids' dresses were all the same height from the floor, no matter how tall the wearer was. They had obviously been constructed with the most flattering and formal and balanced look in mind. When Crosby learned that Betty—an art student at the University of New Mexico before her marriage—had designed and sewn them all, he was so impressed that he went out and bought her a sewing machine as a wedding present.[37]

A Vision in the Hills

When John Crosby began seriously to consider establishing a

professional summer opera festival, he had few American models to draw from. Chautauqua Opera in Chautauqua, New York, had begun in 1929, and Colorado's Central City Opera was founded in 1932. Europe had excellent models for review, including Bayreuth in Germany, which was devoted to Wagner's music dramas; the Salzburg Festival in Austria, which included a major operatic component; and Glyndebourne in England, a gem of an intimate opera house. By studying their successes and challenges, as well as those of instrumental festivals such as the Chicago Symphony Orchestra's Ravinia, the Boston Symphony Orchestra's Tanglewood, and the Los Angeles Philharmonic's Hollywood Bowl, Crosby gained useful material for his own endeavor.

In his posthumous autobiographical memoir, his comments look back at his obvious intentions to found his opera company in line with examples of proven success.

> The summertime festivals of music usually came into being by the action of one or two individuals or a noteworthy composer. . . . These festivals were located by choice in the countryside, thereby removing both performer and patrons from the distractions of major metropolitan centers. The festivals are enhanced by the beauty of nature and climate. Performing artists and patrons make a pilgrimage to the festival seeking the inspiration of music in the best of circumstances. Festivals make a firm commitment to give special attention to musical and production standards. Programming will often focus on the works of a particular composer or group of composers.[38]

The company's Tesuque hillside location seems inevitable today, but Crosby at first considered sites in more populous parts of the country, including Connecticut and Maine.[39] The eastern options offered a ready-made and large audience base, as well as shorter travel distances for personnel, patrons, and production materials. But although they were "much more accessible" than the capital of New Mexico, he said later, none were "so perfect as Santa Fe and none could offer the glorious summer sunsets which inspired one to dream of music."[40] Besides, he added drily, the East Coast was a place "where they have a great deal of rain, lots of mosquitoes, and lots of airplanes overhead."[41] Alas, while the first Santa Fe Opera season avoided the planes and the insects, it did suffer from plenty of rain after years of drought.

There was an additional factor that doubtless played into his planning. As a debutant conductor, Crosby saw Santa Fe as offering him a workable location that would probably not be swarmed over by too many pen-wielding critics. He would have a chance to practice and learn his craft while actually performing—in many ways, an ideal situation for a man who intended to go from a few workshop performances to running his own company and conducting two or even three productions each season. Learning on the job is a traditional route to achievement in any field, but there is always the possibility of failure. Crosby planned his route so as to reduce that chance while he gained skill. He already had audacious courage in plenty and what he felt was adequate practical experience to begin his career. As it was, of course, the opening was well-covered nationally, although in several cases by regional stringers rather than by New York critics.

From the beginning, Crosby intended that his music festival would be the beneficiary of Santa Fe's pre-opera arts tradition. Many notable poets, painters, and writers had come to Santa Fe and Taos in the early 1900s and on into the century, including artists Georgia O'Keeffe, Randall Davey, John Sloane, and Gustave Baumann; poet and Chinese-language translator Witter Bynner; and authors D. H. Lawrence, Paul Horgan, Willa Cather, and Oliver La Farge, among many others. Later on, Crosby recalled, "Bynner became a good friend, Baumann championed the festival, and Horgan served as chairman of its board of directors for 10 years."[42] International classical musicians with homes in the Santa Fe area were violist William Primrose and duo-pianists Vitya Vronsky and Victor Babin. Martha Graham had lived and danced there. Other dancers who had visited and performed were Agnes de Mille and Louis Horst. In addition, the area's well of creativity went deep into the indigenous traditions of the Pueblo artists and artisans and the folk traditions of Spanish *santeros* (carvers of saint figures) and other practitioners of Spanish colonial crafts. The rich mixture of arts—visual, literary, Native, Spanish, musical, and performance—yielded an "ideal mixture of beauty and seclusion,"[43] Crosby said. "[Santa Fe's] tradition and hospitality to the visual and literary arts and preservation of the cultures of past centuries convinced me it was well-poised to become the home of The Santa Fe Opera."[44]

Memo to potential project funders: December 21, 1994

Re: Honoring Indians and/or Mexican entity/individual . . .
   Suggestions:
1. Plan: Identify communities, as opposed to individuals, to be honored and thereby avoid the inadvertent exclusion of an individual or part of an entity. More specifically, honor the artists of the communities.
2. Select communities established before the 20th Century so there can be no question about excluding "Anglo" artists, and limit the communities to those within the general geographic area of The Santa Fe Opera, i.e. Northern New Mexico.
3. Rationale: The work of the artists of the pre-20th century Northern New Mexico communities (pueblos and Spanish villages) has had a permanent impact upon the nature of life in this land. Those artists made this land the place for the Opera to be.
4. Note: When the Opera was established in 1957 "Anglo" artists, who began to come to Northern New Mexico at the beginning of the 20th Century, had made a major impact on life in this land, but they came to a great degree because of the accomplishments of the artists who preceded them by one to three to eight centuries (all the way back to the cliff dwellers).
5. Personal Comment: When I began to think about the idea of an opera festival at Santa Fe—about 1953—I was very much convinced that Santa Fe was the right place because the museums were attracting the kind of tourists who appreciated art, and the residents had cherished and preserved the art. Santa Fe was then obviously a city hospitable to the arts. The germ of all this goes back to the very groups you so generously have decided to honor.
6. Number of Names: There are eight northern pueblos and I suppose about a similar number of pre-19th century Spanish villages, including "El Ciudad Royale de la Santa Fe de San Francisco."
7. Ergo, those honored are "The artists of the cliffs, pueblos and villages of Northern New Mexico A.D. 1000-1900."

Other reasons were more practical. Personnel costs are a significant part of any artistic endeavor. By choosing Santa Fe, an out-of-the-way place that projected an exotic and alluring air, Crosby felt he could attract young singers who would be eager to perform, even if they didn't earn top dollar. The same was true of instrumentalists, designers, directors, and technicians. All would come for modest fees to be able to practice their crafts and gain experience while working at a high festival-quality level. The savings, he was sure, could offset the increased costs of transportation from the East to New Mexico.

Crosby also knew that performers and theater people had few summer opportunities, so he had a ready personnel market in which to trade.[45] Most orchestras at the time did not have summer seasons or festivals, and the ones that did already had contracts with their regular players. There were few opportunities to break into the business. Any singers employed at festivals as soloists or in recital would have established careers; journeyman performers were glad enough to find a spot in a Broadway chorus or even to find work warbling on an Atlantic City boardwalk or in an out-of-town revue. As Crosby said, "Surely the fates would smile kindly on The Santa Fe Opera with a wealth of fine young talent available, the opportunity to introduce exciting works heretofore neglected in our country, and in such a beautiful location." Of course, fate generally fights on the side of money and influence—and fortunately for John Crosby, both were available to him through his parents and other supporters, such as Sachse. It was a given that with his innate financial skill, monies would be well looked after and carefully, almost parsimoniously, husbanded.

Meeting Mirandi—and Convincing Santa Fe

Even with a receptive atmosphere and family support, Crosby still faced obstacles—some cultural, others logistical—to creating an opera company in northern New Mexico. Part of the challenge was the locale itself.[46] Although it was able to boast a mix of rural and somewhat mildly cosmopolitan charm in the 1940s and 1950s, Santa Fe was primitive by urban standards. There were no traffic lights (which some would have thought a blessing). The central plaza still had iron horse troughs around the perimeter for watering horses, donkeys, and mules. Burro trains still brought firewood into town to be sold in Burro Alley. The city was isolated by hours from the East Coast, if somewhat less from the West, and the New Mexico terrain made access difficult even to closer locations. Getting to Albuquerque, sixty miles south, or Taos, seventy miles north, could become a difficult quest due to summer storms that produced flash floods or winter weather that could blanket the roads with snow and quickly make them impassable. Finally, of the town's 35,000 residents, few were familiar with the actual experience or even the concept of live opera.

One who was, was Mirandi Masocco. As noted, Crosby had met her before at the Los Alamos Ranch School dances when he was fourteen and she twenty-seven. They had re-encountered each other in 1948. Now, in the 1950s, this extremely well-connected woman with an operatic story of her own became a close Crosby friend and one of the company's most helpful and influential supporters.

Born in 1914 in Venice, Italy,[47] Mirandi was two and a half years old when she and her three sisters became Santa Fe residents. They were traveling to San Francisco to meet their father when their mother died suddenly on the train between Lamy, the stop for Santa Fe, and Albuquerque. Their papers were lost, and they were brought back to Santa Fe, where they became wards of the state and were committed at one point to the care of the Sisters of Loretto at the Catholic sisterhood's academy.

As the sisters grew up, they integrated fully into the Santa Fe community. Mirandi became a favorite of Witter Bynner and his partner, Robert Hunt, whom she met in the shop of noted silversmith Frank Patania, her sister Aurora's husband. From Bynner, Mirandi learned French, history, and geography, and she improved her English; she learned Spanish from the pair's cook. From Hunt, she learned to appreciate opera. Bynner and Hunt also introduced her to the many international celebrities they entertained. One dinner party she attended included J. B. Priestly, Aldous Huxley, and Maria and Christopher Isherwood.

In 1954, then, Mirandi stepped into the operatic planning limelight with timely help for Crosby, who needed to convince influential Santa Feans that an opera project was feasible. He was only twenty-seven, and, in his own words, "I hesitated to embarrass myself before these

[Santa Fe] elders presenting an idea that would likely be misunderstood and was certainly at risk of being deemed the misguided fancy of a confused young man."[48]

However, the initial meetings about The Santa Fe Opera concept took place at Crosby's New York lodging at 129 West 55th Street during 1954 and 1955. In the draft of his memoir, he recalled that

[I began] earnest discussions about the project with young friends both at Santa Fe and New York. Those friends at Santa Fe, whilst seemingly interested, needed assurances that professional singers and musicians would be willing to join the project. My efforts were devoted chiefly to exploring and developing the interest of fellow musicians in New York in the concept of the festival. These included instrumentalists with whom I had performed in orchestras either as a violinist or a conductor, and singers performing in music conservatory opera productions where I worked as a piano accompanist.[49] Pursuing all these contacts with young singers and musicians throughout 1955, it was evident by the end of that year that a performing company could be assembled.[50]

Then his beloved Columbia University mentor, Sachse, parlayed his affection for and interest in Crosby into bold support of his aims.

He was most encouraging and over time gave me much wise counsel about artistic objectives, which he considered very important for the festival in the light of the then-current needs of opera and performers in the United States. Unbeknownst to me, he contacted my parents a year later to express his support for the project and his opinion that I would be qualified to put it together. That contact proved to be most helpful: an endorsement by a distinguished authority in the field.[51]

Other endorsements followed, including from violist Primrose, who told the young impresario, "If you do not do [the opera] someone else will—and soon."[52] Crosby's planning, leavened by Mirandi's introductions, begin to fructify in 1956, but problems remained with the community's naysayers and saboteurs in musical, social, and professional circles. One local impresario who had thought about starting a festival not long before said, "Come into town if you wish, but I will do everything possible to break your knees."[53]

To the American Guild of Musical Artists: February 25, 1971

In regard to the appellation "Covent Garden West" of which you advise me, I find this perhaps more relevant than those who use it may realize. After all, it was AGMA's own distinguished member, the late Leopold Sachse of happy memory, who persuaded my mother, born in London, England, that it might be a good idea to build a little theatre for opera on a hillside north of Santa Fe with room for about 450 patrons!

Over time, and as the magic of Crosby's vision began to seem more attainable, such hostility waned. But there were still different ideas about what shape the project should take and who it should involve.[54] One early supporter wanted to include all the town's music and theater groups in the opera project. Another patron refused to support Crosby if plans included a certain local conductor she disliked. The business community was skeptical because of the recent experience of a summer theater that had come to town, lurched through two seasons, then spectacularly failed, leaving unpaid bills and much bad feeling in its wake. Businessmen understandably wanted assurance that the company could carry its own weight and be more than a one-season wonder. Even in nonoperatic Santa Fe, it was clear that opera was a seemingly bottomless maw when it came to needing money.

Despite the negativity, which peaked in 1956, Mirandi, a fervent believer in Crosby's operatic vision, continued to press the plan. She introduced Crosby to many people of notable wealth and influence who would play major roles in the opera's continued success and solvency through the years. They included arts patrons whose names are revered in company annals: Perrine and Marshall McCune, originally from Pittsburgh; Margaret Weyerhaeuser Driscoll; Alice Howland and Eleanor Brownwell, East Coast natives and devoted friends and companions; and Amelia White and her sister, Martha, whose luxurious compound on Garcia Street now houses the School for Advanced Research. Mirandi also introduced Crosby to a man who became one of his closest friends, as well as his and the opera's attorney for decades: Thomas B. Catron III, member of a notable and influential New Mexico political and legal dynasty.[55]

In May 1956, Mirandi also provided the link that established the opera's location. She was good friends with the owner of the San Juan Ranch, John Levert, originally from New Orleans, and Levert was finding Santa Fe's high altitude detrimental to his health. She took Crosby out to see the adobe-rich ranch, and he at once fell in love with it and its comfortable, resort-like setting. Adobe architecture is no clue as to what the inside of a building may look like, but Levert and his partner, Hendrik ter Weele, had created a lovely and even luxurious ambience. The ranch had seen many distinguished artistic and musical guests, including conductors Fritz Reiner, Efrem Kurtz, Herbert von Karajan, and Joseph Rosenstock, as well as the husband and wife duo conductor Andre Kostelanetz and soprano Lily Pons. The land itself had fulfilled many functions—it had been a pinto bean farm, a fox and mink farm, and a pig farm—before its transformation into a desirable tourist destination.[56]

Crosby was ecstatic at the possibilities. The property had plenty of room for up to twenty-four people to live on the grounds, and the ridged landscape seemed perfect for both acoustic and scenic purposes. Levert and ter Weele were sympathetic to Crosby. Not only were they interested in the idea of a musical venture on the grounds, but they felt that a new highway just east of the ranch—although perfect for bringing in an audience—had spoiled the tranquility they personally valued. They soon agreed on a three-year lease for the property and acreage. Crosby felt his own funds could handle the ranch purchase but not the building of a theater,[57] and it was now that his parents' support became operative. In September 1956, the contract with Levert and ter Weele was signed, and Aileen and Laurence Crosby agreed to stake the venture to the tune of $200,000 initially.[58]

The contract with the ranch owners granted Crosby a number of options.[59] For the most basic, he could lease the ranch and its seventy-six acres of land for $1,000 for the summer months of June, July, and August 1957 and build a theater on the site. He could exercise another lease option before the end of December 1957 to purchase the ranch and most of its furnishings for $80,000, minus $3,000 for a swimming pool he would install. The first lease option was quickly exercised, and Crosby Development Company, a New Mexico corporation with Crosby as the sole stockholder, became the lessee. The corporation served as the legal vehicle for the theater complex's financing and construction. The young impresario put $30,000 down and agreed to pay the balance of $47,000 over ten years, plus interest at an unstated amount.

Still, before exercising the first lease option, Crosby considered using the facilities for a more intimate theatrical venture than a full-sized opera theater. The main patio could hold 150, and with an erected stage platform, he could stage chamber opera. The bedrooms at the ranch could serve as dressing rooms. The main lounge would be ideal for chamber music. Primrose counseled against this, saying it would dilute the company's reputation and weaken attempts to stage full-fledged opera later. Crosby heeded the advice, which meshed with his own desires and intentions.[60]

In mid-October 1956, the Santa Fe segment of Crosby's operatic planning committee held a well-attended reception at Bishop's Lodge.[61] Crosby spoke convincingly of his planning and vision. Sachse attended to speak encouragingly and movingly about the idea. As Crosby noted in his memoir, "It was a milestone on the path of the development of the Festival."[62] He was soon able to assure Sachse in a letter of December 20, 1956: "My friends here are determined to see everything through in the best possible way, and they are as anxious as you that the project be one of artistic distinction and always a unique venture with a happy family of artists participating."

Things began to accelerate. In November 1956, Crosby negotiated a contract with the American Guild of Musical Artists (AGMA), the collective bargaining organization for those working in the opera, choral, and dance fields. On December 10, 1956, the parties inked a three-year agreement covering compensation and work provisions. AGMA accepted the concept of Crosby's brainchild—influenced by Sachse—of an apprentice program for singers, which the founder defined as young people "who had not, prior to their apprenticeship, performed more than six opera roles professionally." The apprentices would receive limited AGMA membership; the principal artists, covered under a different contract format, would be full AGMA members. This permitted Crosby to provide training for young singers while saving him a good deal of money. A professional AGMA chorus would have added significantly to the costs of the first season, perhaps even making it impossible.[63]

Artistic compensation was not overly generous, though, on any level.[64] It was $100 weekly for leading singers during performance weeks and $50 for each rehearsal week. Leading singers could pay $50 a week for a room with private bath and double occupancy at the ranch, including three meals per day, or they could seek lodgings in town. The apprentices lived at the old Montezuma Hotel in downtown Santa Fe. The apprentice weekly stipend was $28, minus $8 for a shared room at the Montezuma. A generous buffet lunch was served each day at the opera for $1—Crosby wanted his personnel in shape to live up to his expectations—and most people took full advantage of the benefit. Travel coverage for all personnel was predicated on an average of $237.09, which covered lower berth train transport between the artist's city of origin and Santa Fe.

In December 1956, Crosby reached another milestone in his plans: a preliminary understanding with the American Federation of Musicians (AFM) for the orchestra members, who would come from opera companies, orchestras, and chamber ensembles around the country. The pact was ratified in January 1957. Compensation was $15 per performance and included one hour of rehearsal time, without compensation, for each opera; additional time was paid at $2 per hour. The schedule guaranteed thirty-two musicians a total of $61 per week, and members could share rooms at the Montezuma, like the apprentices, for $8 a week. The visiting musicians, along with a few from the area, would join the Albuquerque local of the musician's union for a token fee.

Crosby finally revealed plans for a first season of nine weeks, with twenty-eight performances of seven operas. The loosely defined association of interested locals who had been working with him voted to incorporate as a nonprofit corporation, and Catron filed the articles of incorporation with the State Corporation Commission on December 26, 1956.[65] Thus was born The Santa Fe Opera Association, a name soon changed to the Opera Association of New Mexico. It would continue to operate as Crosby's retaining employer until the association merged with the opera proper in 1992. Formally, it retained Crosby as an independent contractor but was the employer of everyone else involved in and working for the company.

From the beginning, Crosby maintained a New York office for the company—an absolute necessity for any organization involved in the performing arts world.[66] He seems to have had a real fondness for locations in the Fifties and Sixties on the East Side. From October 1955 to November 1959, he had a studio at 129 West 56th Street, which he used for Santa Fe Opera business when in the city. He then moved into an apartment at 39 East 67th Street, which served both for a New York office and for living quarters until January 1963. At that point, he took rooms in the Wyndham Hotel at 42 West 58th Street for the company's New York office; when he needed a place to stay, he either rented a room for himself at the Wyndham or stayed with friends. Shortly thereafter, the opera company offices moved to the townhouse of supporter and Crosby friend Robert L. B. Tobin at 711 Park Avenue. In November 1965, Crosby rented an apartment at 141 East 63rd Street, which was used for both professional purposes and living quarters for many years. In December 1971, he purchased a brownstone house built around 1870, fourteen feet wide and five stories high, at 48 East 63rd Street. For decades, it was both the opera's East Coast headquarters and Crosby's own New York home. At first, the company paid little or no rent for the portion of the house dedicated to professional purposes, but by 1986, regular rent was being paid. A letter of October 16 that year to a staff member notes that the executive/finance committee of the board had agreed to raise the rent from $34,000 per year to $59,000, "in order to meet all costs which I have been bearing as owner of the property rented to the Opera." The company utilized the first two floors; Crosby, the third and fourth; and the fifth floor was available as guest quarters or living space for any full-time, live-in assistant Crosby might retain. The brownstone was sold to The Santa Fe Opera in 1999 and continues to be the company's New York office.[67]

Discussion, Details, and the First House

Crosby had already begun moving to build the theater by October 1956. The architects he decided to retain were John W. McHugh and

Van Dorn Hooker of Santa Fe and Farmington, New Mexico, with McHugh handling the actual design. The initial concept included a fully roofed structure with open sides, but this approach was soon dropped. Crosby wrote to Sachse in an undated letter from October 1956,

> I am meeting with the architect at the theatre site this evening after dark. We have a difficulty to cope with. The approaching audience will see the roof of the theatre as they walk to it from their automobiles. The architect and I are very worried about the unsightly appearance of a roof [as one looks down on it]. Under the circumstances, I feel that the ideal design of the theatre should be the classic amphitheater—completely open to the sky.

Not everyone was as pleased with the concept as were Crosby, McHugh, and Sachse. Members of the Santa Fe committee were not certain of the feasibility of the plan, Crosby recalled. But he was determined to convince the doubters, for his own reputation's sake as well as for the sake of public relations. "I do not wish to be faced with a situation in Santa Fe where local people think I am a crazy young man squandering his money," he wrote Sachse on October 14, 1956— by that point, probably a case of wishful thinking. A topographical sketch of the site had been made on October 21, 1956, he informed Sachse in a letter of that date.

McHugh did suggest that some protection from Santa Fe's vaunted evening coolness and "occasional rain" might be considered, including side and overhead arches of steel, over which canvas sheets could be drawn. Other suggestions were charcoal braziers at the sides of the theater to take the chill off the air.[68] Neither was undertaken, due to the probable expense and difficulty of achievement. Besides, Crosby—based on a two-year study of precipitation observation he had made at the family's Tano Point property—expected nature to help out with his endeavors. "Out of 12 performances in July we stand a chance of one shower," Crosby predicted. "Out of 12 performances in August we stand a chance of 2 or 3 showers."[69] In fact, the two study summers of 1955 and 1956 were unusually dry, and 1957 was so wet that Crosby, according to local lore, became beloved of all the area

A close-up of the first theater's stage and orchestra pit, 1957. The playing area was even more exposed to the elements than in the next two houses. The soaring line of the roof reflected acoustician Jack Purcell's dedication to creating the perfect sonic environment for opera. Photographer unknown. Courtesy The Santa Fe Opera.

ranchers and farmers for lifting the drought hoodoo. During the opening season, ten performances were rained out, but ten rain-check performances were added to compensate. Crosby not only wanted to deliver the number of performances he had promised; he could not bear the thought of having to refund monies on a show that had to be canceled. Additional performances solved both challenges, with orchestra, singers, and choristers performing for reduced fees.

Given that the theater would be open to the sky and winds, establishing the best acoustics possible under the circumstances was vital. A Santa Fe friend of Crosby's, Benjamin Sanders, introduced him to Jack Purcell, a young and highly talented acoustical engineer with the firm of Bolt, Beranek, and Newman in Massachusetts. Fascinated by Crosby's concept, Purcell agreed to take the job for a token honorarium, with the proviso that the architect would respect his specifications and work closely with him. McHugh gladly agreed.[70]

There are several stories of how Purcell and Crosby settled on the theater's particular location. All versions agree that a gun was fired multiple times to ascertain the best acoustical "bowl" for sound; but the stories disagree about whether the pair rode horses, drove a jeep, or walked, and who fired the rifle—or was it a pistol, or even a yacht cannon?—to produce echoes. No matter. As the theater was built, the tests proved accurate. The acoustics were excellent, and in those far-off days of low traffic density and dark night skies, contributed to an unbelievable musico-theatrical experience. (Purcell continued his Santa Fe

Opera association for more than four decades, engineering the acoustics of the 1968 theater and the 1998 theater as well as Stieren Orchestra Hall.[71])

McHugh completed preliminary drawings by December 20, 1956. His fee was $3,000. Crosby later recollected that the theater planning and construction, all told, came to $115,000.[72] As much attention was paid to comfort and sightlines as to acoustics. All seats were within the 100 degree angle of the theater's centerline, "which means all seat locations are excellent," Crosby wrote in a letter of January 6, 1957, to Sachse. He added that the eye level in the first row was two inches above the stage floor, which yielded an ideal visual pitch as the seats rose up the amphitheater slope. McHugh's original plans called for the rear of the stage to be closed by sliding doors. These could be opened at appropriate moments in productions, revealing New Mexico's night sky and landscape, with the distant Jemez Mountains and the lights of Los Alamos as scenic elements. Of course, the opening also was needed for the movement of set pieces, because the house was conceived without fly space above, due to concerns about wind danger during storms. "The angle of roof, sound baffles, angle of stage walls, etc., is consistent with his recommendations," Crosby assured Sachse of McHugh's interpretation of Purcell's conclusions.[73]

Even as construction moved ahead, the road had some bumps. On March 25, 1957, McHugh wrote to Crosby, "Get a cigarette before you read this, for it will probably be a somewhat confusing letter, all about bills and contributions." The letter had to do with how much of their fee McHugh and Hooker would donate to the endeavor; construction issues, including the cost of installing a heating plant (or not), and what this would do to the architect's fee and donation; and consultant fees linked to the heating system. Crosby's reply of March 28 demonstrated his complete command of finances and his understanding of their implications, despite McHugh's misgivings. It is a friendly but firm letter and reads in part,

> With regard to the heating: I hear such conflicting reports that
> it is impossible to make any decision through the mails. You are
> no doubt in receipt of my telegram of the 27th. Please set aside
> as much time as possible, as . . . I can only remain in Santa Fe for

April 6 through April 9th. What is more important to me at the moment is the status of construction and schedule of amounts due to Modern Construction Co. April 1st, May 1st, and June 1st. I have made repeated requests concerning this, and have heard nothing. . . . In short, it looks as if there may be many requests for payments in the next few days—and payments in amounts which I have no knowledge of. I must operate this undertaking on a rigid schedule, as I have explained to you before.

That was presumably a reference to the cash disbursement arrangements he had made with Laurence, who, despite his generosity, kept a weather eye on the project and his son both.

Raising the house took just eleven months, including excavating the site, pouring the supporting concrete slabs and house floor, raising the stage roof, and putting the seating and minimal backstage and front-of-house amenities in place. That was a notable accomplishment, even given the complex's small size and the tightly restricted backstage area. When completed, the intimate and inviting structure offered a charming and functional mix of steel, concrete, and oiled redwood. The theater had a swooping though small roof that extended over the orchestra pit and the reflecting pool: Crosby knew that sound can carry over water and wanted every help available for the players and singers, as the entire seating area was open to the skies above and on the sides. He also wanted to keep the audience away from the orchestra during intermissions, and a pool would help with that. The sides of the stage were handsome redwood panels that could open and close for entrances and exits, like the sliding panels at the rear. Seen from the back of the house, the theater gave the impression of calm dignity, and its reddish glow against the New Mexico sky provided a stellar visual experience. The combination of landscape, theater, and sound made it famous overnight; *Time* magazine very soon called it "one of the handsomest operatic settings in the Western Hemisphere."[74]

But backstage amenities were few, with just two dressing rooms, one each for the male and female contingents of singers, and a costume shop about twelve feet square. With no stage elevator, sets had to be wrestled up two flights of stairs. The pit was small and, consequently, so was the orchestra. The first season program lists just nine violins,

John Crosby, by Fabian Bachrach, circa 1950. The young Crosby chose to be photographed holding his glasses rather than wearing them, which lends a certain vulnerability to his expression. But one also can discern strength in the direct gaze of his eyes and the firmness of his mouth. From The Santa Fe Opera files. Courtesy Fabian Bachrach.

four violas, three cellos, one contrabassist, one harpist, one timpanist-percussionist, paired woodwinds, and an English horn, three French horns, two trumpets, and one trombone—a total of thirty-two instruments. *Madame Butterfly* was therefore heard in a greatly reduced version unless uncredited local musicians were added to the band. Eight apprentice singers were chosen to be choristers—two each of soprano, alto, tenor, and bass—and three local female singers filled out the chorus in *The Rake's Progress.*[75] Given the small space, the tendency for winds to sweep through at night, and the rigors of budgeting, the emphasis for the first half dozen seasons, recalled distinguished designer Henry Heymann, was on detailed and opulent costuming, intelligent use of stage properties, carefully planned lighting, and minimal sets, rather than on ornate or heavy scenery. Adopting this approach was something of a given in the next ten years, not only because of the limitations of the house but because the set construction budget sometimes ran out before the sets for all the shows were built. At that point, it was a case of virtue being mined from necessity.

Besides, Crosby rather liked simplicity for itself. In his memoir, he remembered that

> The first theater was situated exactly as is the present structure and indeed there is a fountain and a reflecting pool. The charming and tastefully designed simple structure would fit within the present stage [1998] and first few rows of seats. A governing principle for the design was simplicity. The theater itself was not to detract the eye from the stage. Only 480 persons could be accommodated, mostly on plain wooden benches. For support there were two dressing rooms for the performers and the barest amenities for the audience. Flowers in the garden at the entrance and the plash of the fountain were to ease the mind and set one's mood for the coming performance. Public spaces were not to be cluttered with posters and other paraphernalia.[76]

Before the first season opened, Laurence wrote to his banker on June 23, 1957, from Havana, "Johnny's venture seems near to fruition, and looks so like success, that he and I are beginning to think he should exercise the option he holds to buy the ranch land on which the 'opera house' is built—so I shall probably want to mobilize some more cash." The first season's success confirmed their idea, and the second lease option to purchase was exercised by Crosby Development Company, with title passing in December 1957. More than seventy-six acres, plus the ranch buildings, were bought. Additional purchases beyond the ranch, for both acreage and buildings, were $3,162 for

Mon ami! Igor Stravinsky throws his arms out in greeting to John Crosby at the Lamy railroad station circa 1959–1961, while Vera Stravinsky detrains behind him. John is walking forward to meet the maestro. His body language speaks of diffidence and respect. It's clear, even in half profile, that he is smiling with delight. Photographer unknown. Courtesy The Santa Fe Opera.

19.5 acres in 1963 and $13,782 for a bit more than 519 acres in 1964. The total outlay by Crosby Development Company in eight years was $93,944 for 615 acres, plus the cost of the buildings.[77] Fortunately, Laurence Crosby had remained affluent even after losing his Cuban investments, rebuttressing the family fortunes through canny investing and his legal work.

The Stravinsky Connection

On the Sunday morning of January 6, 1957, with construction well underway, Crosby remarked to Mirandi that having a famous artist associated with the first season would help cement the company's position—and that he hoped to perform Stravinsky's *The Rake's Progress* in place of the originally planned one-act pieces, *The Impresario*, by Mozart, and Gian Carlo Menotti's *Amelia Goes to the Ball.* Mirandi knew Stravinsky, one of the best-known and most respected composers in the world at that time. She had first met Vera and Igor Stravinsky and the composer's protégé and preferred conductor, Robert Craft, in 1950.[78] Stravinsky had conducted during the first Aspen Music Festival that year, and Tesuque-based duo-pianists Vronsky and Babin were soloists. Fascinated with D. H. Lawrence, Stravinsky asked the pianists if they knew anyone who could introduce him to Frieda Lawrence, the writer's widow.[79] They asked Mirandi, who met the Stravinskys in Taos on August 4 and took them that day to visit Frieda Lawrence and then to Santo Domingo Pueblo for a feast day dance. Stravinsky was moved and excited, observing the dance through the rising dust with tears pouring down his face, Mirandi recounted. Witter Bynner then hosted a dinner party for the group. The day's activities had even the energetic Mirandi panting along half a lap behind, with the Stravinskys still fresh and ready for more. The Stravinskys thereafter saw their new friend on regular visits to Santa Fe, and she often traveled to join them at concerts the maestro conducted in other cities. Mirandi was even present at the U.S. premiere of *The Rake's Progress* in 1953 at the Metropolitan Opera, which Fritz Reiner conducted. Crosby also was at that performance, though in standing room.[80]

Now, at this point, Crosby posed a pivotally fateful question to Mirandi: "Wouldn't it be wonderful if we had a name?" She considered for a moment, then went to the phone and placed a call to someone she called "Pussycat."[81]

"I told him the whole thing about the opera," Mirandi remembered of her discussion with Stravinsky. "He said, 'The theater is not ready and you want me to come? Well, you bring everything for the weekend, so I can see what you're doing. Then I will tell you if I go or not.' I said, 'Wonderful.' I hung up. John said, 'Who was that?' I said, 'Stravinsky.' I thought he was going to faint. He said, 'How dare you call him Pussycat? How dare you not call him maestro?'"

Mirandi flew to Los Angeles, presented the plans to Stravinsky (from theater construction to repertoire to casting), and spoke persuasively of the potential great success of the new company. Impressed, Stravinsky agreed to attend if matters proceeded on schedule. It was, like Crosby being in the right place at the right time, a perfect conjunction of people and plans. The Santa Fe Opera was moving toward opening—and with a musical giant in the wings.

CHAPTER THREE

Curtain Up!

Opening Night: The Future in Embryo

After all the strains and stresses of planning and preparation, The Santa Fe Opera's first night was an auspicious start to the company's life and labors. It was a beautiful evening, the cast and orchestra came together wholeheartedly, and the crew worked like heroes.[1]

There was robust, if unintentional, humor amid the extreme attention to detail that any operatic undertaking demands. For one example, the chairs in the boxes would hold rainwater, and as it rained many afternoons, they soon were christened bidets.[2] The entire company would help with emptying and drying the seats, as well as wiping water off the long benches that filled most of the house. Crosby joined in that task on opening night. He also cleaned out the reflecting pool in front of the orchestra pit (skimming suicidal moths from the surface),[3] double-checked the box office's readiness, and gave the parking lot a final glance. How he found time to do that and still make it into the orchestra pit for the downbeat speaks to his commitment, energy, youth, and obsession. He had planned the entire musical and dramatic menu, of course, so he knew things were as ready as they could be, and, as was the case throughout his four-plus decades at the company helm, he made sure everyone was doing his or her tasks responsibly. Not that the crew and cast needed urging. They were invested in the project to the fullest capacity. It was a neck-or-nothing evening ahead.

His parents also pitched in. As we have seen, Aileen Crosby helped scour out the ladies' restroom in the afternoon, while Laurence looked over the grounds and flowerbeds to be sure the plants were in good condition. For from the beginning, the senior Crosbys went beyond the call of investment duty, getting right into the practical aspects of managing and keeping up the theater. The white petunias and yellow snapdragons near the theater entrance were Aileen's special pride. She chose them because they would be more visible at night than darker flowers, and they would add another sense, that of perfumed scent, to the overall experience.[4] The pair looked after their investment while supporting their son unstintingly, with shared enjoyment of New Mexico's enchantment an additional bond.

Summer evenings in Santa Fe can be surprisingly chilly after the warmth of the days. Mirandi decided, after consulting with Crosby, that something needed to be done to help those who did not dress warmly enough. She persuaded officials at the National Guard Armory to loan the company hundreds of blankets from their inventory. That was a good idea on the face of it, but virtually every blanket left the premises that night with departing patrons. The armory fortunately never pressed the case of the missing coverings.[5] Audience members from then on had to come with their own coats, blankets, or ponchos—or else be one of the lucky ones who got a complimentary blue wool blanket to use on cold evenings, the gift of a sympathetic patron (returnable after the show, of course).[6]

The opera's opening night and its first season prefigured the many seasons and repertoire choices to follow under Crosby's control, although more operas were mounted that first summer and in the immediately ensuing years than is typical today. In 1957, seven works, including the two one-acts, were performed, for a total of twenty-eight performances.[7] Through 1973, anywhere from six to eight operas were performed each season, with singers often taking on two and three good-sized or even leading roles.[8] For just one example, but a significant one, in 1972, bass-baritone Donald Gramm sang alternately General Boum in Jacques Offenbach's *The Grand Duchess of Gerolstein*, Golaud in Claude Debussy's *Pélleas et Mélisande*, and Leporello in Mozart's *Don Giovanni*—a daunting assignment. Baritone Richard Stilwell sang both Pélleas in the Debussy opera and Prince Paul in *Gerolstein*.[9] Other singers assumed similarly taxing responsibilities in the early and middle years. In 1957, mezzo-soprano Regina Sarfaty Rickless sang Suzuki in *Madame Butterfly* as well as Baba the Turk in *The Rake's Progress* and Dryad in *Ariadne auf Naxos*, plus a role in *The Tower*.[10] Such high-level vocal doubling is relatively rare today, although not completely unknown in Santa Fe, but no lead singer takes on another starring role except in a very unusual emergency.

By 1974, the company had settled down to presenting five programs of opera in repertory each season.[11] This might include a double or even triple bill. In 1980, Crosby had the blithe confidence to put on Arnold Schoenberg's *Erwartung*, *Von Heute auf Morgen*, and *Die Jakobsleiter* in one evening. That season also offered *La Traviata* ten times, *The Magic Flute* eight, Pyotr Ilyitch Tchaikovsky's *Eugene Onegin* seven (as it was a rarely mounted work, Crosby counted on audience curiosity to fill seats), Richard Strauss's *Elektra* five, and the Schoenberg trio four times, for a total of thirty-four performances over seven weeks.[12] Given the much smaller company in 1957 and the limited facilities of the house, twenty-eight shows was an amazing success and a tribute to everyone's energy and efficiency—especially given that today's computer-assisted conveniences in lighting and stagecraft were not then available, and the opera had no stage elevator. Lighting rehearsals went on through the night many times, while sets were wrestled up and down stairs.

Curtain time was 9:00 p.m. during the first season and remained so until just before Crosby's departure.[13] He believed firmly that evenings were not dark enough for proper theatrical illusion until then, even with daylight hours growing shorter in August. Several memos in the opera archives refer to the suggestion that earlier curtain times be considered, sometimes from staff members, sometimes from board members, occasionally from an audience member. Crosby quashed each with a degree of grudging politesse and what must have been long-suffering patience. Today, operas in the first half of the season begin at 8:30 p.m. and in the second half of the season, at 8:00 p.m.—a change that has pleased the audience and made longer operas more palatable. Crosby, an inveterate night owl, would doubtless find the practice untenable still, and not only for visual considerations. During a somewhat rocky morning rehearsal in 1992 for *Der Rosenkavalier*, he told the three female principals in the opera—Ashley Putnam as the Marschallin, Susanne Mentzer as Octavian, and Cheryl Parrish as Sophie—not to worry about some trouble they were having in the famous final trio. "It will be past midnight when the trio comes, so everyone will be fine," he reassured them.[14]

Throughout Crosby's tenure and even today, his concept of an artistic slate remained and remains true.[15] A classic tragedy or comedy would open the season—Puccini's *Madame Butterfly* or *La Bohème* or *Tosca*; twice, *The Girl of the Golden West*; perhaps Johann Strauss Jr.'s *Die Fledermaus* or Emmerich Kálmán's *Countess Maritza*—followed by a Mozart work or occasionally a similar period piece. That order of service quickly became the custom for the first and second nights of each season, pleasing the tradition-loving local audience and bringing in revenue to support more unusual pieces later on. Unusual meant a Richard Strauss opera, which sometimes was an American or world premiere; an American or world premiere that wasn't Strauss; and often a contemporary German or American opera, again sometimes a premiere.

In 1987, for example, thirty years after the opening season, the repertoire was *Madame Butterfly*; *The Marriage of Figaro*; George Frideric Handel's *Ariodante*, in one of the company's most lush and successful productions ever; Richard Strauss's *Die schweigsame Frau*; and Dmitri Shostakovich's *The Nose*.[16] In Crosby's final 2000 season, thirteen years later, the repertoire was *Rigoletto*, by Verdi; *The Marriage of Figaro* again; Rossini's rarely heard *Ermione*; Richard Strauss's *Elektra*; and *Venus and Adonis*, by Hans Werner Henze.[17] (A close Crosby friend, Henze had six of his operas done in Santa Fe over forty-four years.[18] No other modern composer was so generously treated, except Stravinsky.) From 1978 through 2000, a Richard Strauss opera was performed every year.[19]

To Hans Werner Henze: April 5, 1993

Since we last saw each other—Munich 1987—I have been subject to considerable pressure to produce operas by American composers. In fact, I have been criticized publicly for producing too many works by German composers (mostly recently von Bose, Rihm and Matthus) and other non-Americans such as Weir, Penderecki and Sallinen. . . . I regret this situation. My decisions have always been made on the basis of quality, and not national origin.

It is time for The Santa Fe Opera to present another work

by Henze—no doubt about that. I shall keep trying, and in the interval beg your kind and sympathetic understanding. Surely you must realize how much I appreciate your work, having produced five of your operas, and how I cherish your friendship. Be patient with me as I try to keep going in this prejudiced place.

As we've seen, Crosby believed he could train an audience to like any opera, especially when the early observer pool was so full of persons who hardly knew the difference between Puccini and Stravinsky. The increasing number of out-of-town visitors, many more sophisticated, helped the process. In 1957, *The Rake's Progress* played to 60 percent of capacity. In 1960, the production played to 80 percent in a larger theater. In 1962, it was closer to 90 percent, and in 1966 and 1970, both in larger houses, it sold out.[20] Crosby was delighted, not only at the ticket income but at the correctness of his predictions—that, over time, the audience would take all kinds of works to its collective heart.

That didn't mean that Crosby never made a mistake or misjudged a possibility. One memorable season, 1984, went down in company annals as especially unfortunate for the effect it had on critical and audience reaction that season—and the next year's ticket sales.[21] Crosby wanted to mount two tuneful and lush but turgid Germanic one-acts as the opening performance and major finds of the season—Alexander von Zemlinsky's *A Florentine Tragedy* and Erich Wolfgang von Korngold's *Violanta*. That was the same year that the slate also included Richard Strauss's "domestic comedy" *Intermezzo*, Henze's *We Come to the River*, Domenico Cimarosa's *The Secret Marriage*, and *The Magic Flute*. Unfortunately, audiences and critics did not take to the double bill, and the rest of the season caused some puzzlement—although critical reaction to the Henze opera was strongly positive—and when 1985 came around, ticket buyers were wary. After a 97 percent sales record in 1984, the number dropped alarmingly to about 77 percent the next season. Crosby, still sure he had made a properly supported artistic decision, was surprised and disappointed that after nearly three decades, he no longer had an audience eager for anything he had to present. He was also distressed that the artistic capital he had accrued could be disbursed so quickly. Because he felt that the 1984 season was exciting and the opening pair of works a near-perfect repertoire mix, he was annoyed. But he held his ground. The 1985 season went unchanged from its original plan, even after the mixed response in 1984.[22] Offenbach's *Orpheus in the Underworld* and the popular Mozart opera *The Marriage of Figaro* were crowd pleasers, but Henze's *The English Cat* and John Eaton's *The Tempest* offered more challenging fare. Richard Strauss's *Die Liebe der Danae* was an immense, long work of creative complexity that delighted fans of the composer or of rarities—but there was still a big exodus from the theater after the first act, each night of performance.

The 1957 opening night foreshadowed another company custom that remained true throughout Crosby's tenure and today: show-casing American singers. The soloists were young, lithe, eager, and able to switch between roles with assurance—a comedy one night, a supporting part the next, then a tragic role, and so on. Americans dominated the stage until 1966, when the Norwegian tenor Ragnar Ulfung, singing Tamino in *The Magic Flute*, began a decades-long presence with the company. In 1967, Jose van Dam and Maria Kouba were European discoveries.[23] Over time, there were other European and Canadian artists, and now and then an antipodean; but they were rare in the context of overall casting. They remained an appreciated minority. Major international stars such as Elisabeth Söderström, Eleanor Steber, Tatiana Troyanos, and Marilyn Horne were rather unusual during the Crosby years. A number of young Santa Fe Opera debutantes did go on to become of stellar international note, including Kiri te Kanawa, Frederica von Stade, Bryn Terfel, Patricia Racette, and Susan Graham—and today, the company tends to bring in more European artists than it did during the first half or even the first two-thirds of Crosby's tenure.

For the first season, Crosby depended greatly on his own ears and contacts for singers. Mezzo-soprano Rickless recalled,[24]

When he approached me at Juilliard . . . he came to me and asked if I'd be interested in being in an opera company he was starting. I said, "Where?" He said, "Santa Fe, New Mexico." I said, "Where's Santa Fe?" I was born in Brooklyn, I went to Juilliard, I'd had two summers at Tanglewood. That's what I knew from. He said, "I'm familiar with the area; I went to school there; and I think it will work." I said to him, "John, when you have a contract, come back and we can talk about it."

Then about four months later he came up to me and said, "Regina, here's a contract." I took it to my teacher, Florence Page Kimball. We looked at the contract. Five operas, five parts, $100 a week, room and board somewhat provided because we all lived at the ranch. I said, "This is the only job offer I've had so I might as well consider it seriously."

When Rickless arrived, though, she found challenges that still affect singers in Santa Fe.

Not a person mentioned the altitude or the dryness, not one word. We all arrived. Suddenly we're coughing, we're wheezing, we can't make things in one breath. Little by little I adjusted. . . . We rehearsed on the grass in the sun. There were no rehearsal facilities. The house was not done. Only if you're young can you survive it. We survived and all did very well.

Adapting to Santa Fe's climate and location remains a challenge for all participants today. Altitude and aridity have not changed, although housing and amenities are much more comfortable. Crosby appreciated the difficulties singers faced, but he also expected them to adjust and make good relatively quickly. Most did, and they still do. It helped then that apart from a few production personnel and some orchestra members who were in their thirties, most opera employees were in their twenties that first season and intensely energetic.[25]

It should be remembered that the maestro, even though he was the final court of decision, did not make every casting or orchestra member decision on his own over the decades. Crosby was very much the king of the hill, but there were trusted advisers around him at equal and lower levels, to whom he listened and with whom he often agreed. The orchestra members, for example, then as now, were assembled from reputable symphonies, universities, conservatories, and opera companies and closely trained under Crosby's critical ear—but they came in as much on the recommendation of the opera concertmasters and first chairs as by Crosby's own decision. For singers, as the

A convivial moment: Hindemith and Stravinsky in conversation, 1961. One singer saw the maestros passing a flask back and forth on a cold evening. Knowing Stravinsky's fluid preferences, the liquid was probably the finest Scotch. Photo by Tony Perry. Courtesy The Santa Fe Opera.

years went on, he came to trust and listen to such highly savvy judges of voice as Richard Gaddes, Matthew A. Epstein, and Brad Woolbright, as well as some agents and other general directors. He was scrupulously fair when it came to giving musicians, whether singers or orchestra members, every chance: once, when a question arose as to whether a certain soprano could still manage Strauss's Salome, scheduled for a future season, Crosby flew to Italy to hear her in Wagner's *Tristan und Isolde*. Deciding that the voice would not be able to handle the role readily enough when Santa Fe was going to mount the production, he paid off the singer's contract in full and found another Salome.

Now, just as when it began, the opera's commitment to ensemble performances remains exceptionally vital—but in the 1980s, the music world had a saying that Santa Fe presented American artists on the way up; a few favorite singers faithful to Crosby on the long plateau of their dependable ability; and, finally, performers on the way down.[26] But if a favored singer decided to accept an offer elsewhere, the founder was furious— even if he'd kept the singer too long on a string without making a definite offer, or if he'd failed to act in a timely fashion, leaving only a few months from contracting to performing.[27] Just as he wanted his administrative staff to stay with him, he wanted his singers to be faithful.

Crosby drew heavily on his Yale and Columbia connections the first season, bringing in colleagues from the theater departments of both institutions to handle production and stage management. During the first decade, emphasis was on intelligent staging and lighting and careful costume creativity, with minimal sets. After all, that not only fit budgets and locale; the larger setting was perfect on its own. As Howard Taubman noted in the *New York Times*, "After all, a flat or a backdrop is a poor thing compared with the vaulting Jemez."[28]

It took little time for Santa Fe to become noticed by the musical world.[29] *Opera News* wrote, in the autumn of 1957, "By the end of the two month season, Santa Fe had joined the ranks of important festivals." Just two years later, a July 2, 1959, memo from a fundraising and public relations consultant noted how quickly the company under Crosby had become well known and respected. "Nothing since the foundation of Tanglewood has garnered as much editorial and musical attention in the U.S. as Santa Fe," the memo noted. Besides consistent support from the *Santa Fe New Mexican* and *Albuquerque Journal*, favorable national press had included the *New York Times*, *Time, Newsweek, Theatre Arts, Herald Tribune, Holiday, Readers Digest*, and *Harper's Bazaar*. Santa Fe was going artistic places with flair, and the world was noticing.

Stravinsky's presence firmly enhanced the company's artistic legitimacy, to a degree that cannot be overstated. His movements were news not only because of his artistic power but because of his Russian background. During the Cold War, he was often asked about the Soviet system and what it meant for the arts. That he attended The Santa Fe Opera in 1957, 1959, 1960, 1961, 1962, and 1963[30] showed how pleased he was with how his works were treated and produced. Northern New Mexico and Santa Fe were also beloved by him for their own beauty, and Mirandi, of course, was a close and dear family friend. Vera Stravinsky enjoyed the area as much as her husband did, and Robert Craft was a constant presence along with his mentor. Crosby was devoted to the maestro—the only title he ever used with him—and did everything in his power to satisfy the composer.

Despite his fame, Stravinsky remained plainspoken and personable in Santa Fe. In 1957, he attended every rehearsal of *The Rake's Progress*, sometimes sitting in the house and sometimes onstage. One evening, he was presiding from a big wicker chair, wearing two pairs of glasses on his head and wrapped in blankets against the cold. A pair of singers were mortified when they backed into him and landed on his feet, but he reassured them. "Don't worry, darlings. I know I'm in the way, but I have to be here," he said. Perhaps that was the night when choristers filing offstage found Crosby waiting for them with a stack of paper cups and a bottle of Cutty Sark, giving each

One of the most famous Santa Fe Opera images: John Crosby and Igor Stravinsky watch a rehearsal, 1961. Note Stravinsky's two pairs of glasses and both men's attentive focus on the stage. Photographer unknown. Courtesy The Santa Fe Opera.

a nip to take off the chill.[31] Another night, when a flat blew over, Crosby leaped to help repair it. Partway through the process, he realized that the person behind him handing nails over so competently was Stravinsky.[32]

The relationship with Stravinsky was mutually beneficial. Besides performing all the master's musico-dramatic works at least once, the company also arranged local performances of *Symphony of Psalms*, *Cantata*, and the Mass—and after the maestro's death, the American premiere of *The Flood*.[33] Stravinsky conducted some of his own works during his various visits, including *Oedipus Rex*, *Perséphone*, and *Renard*. His conducting could be idiosyncratic, especially after the singers and orchestra had rehearsed so much with Craft. This led to interesting experiences when he was on the podium, with singers' eyes glued to his hands more closely than absolute stage illusion would consider ideal. Tempos were always slower under Stravinsky, which gave singers and dancers and orchestra players reason to concentrate even more than usual. If someone proposed a reading that was different from his original intention, he would listen politely and then, even more politely, say that he preferred the interpretation and directions in the score.[34]

During his times in Santa Fe, Stravinsky worked on many notable compositions, including partially rewriting the harpsichord accompaniment for the graveyard scene in *Rake* for the piano; the orchestral interludes for *Movements for Piano and Orchestra*; the *Sermon, Narrative and Prayer*; *Noah and the Flood*; *Abraham and Isaac*; and the *Orchestral Variations*. For him, the atmosphere was both relaxing and conducive to work.[35]

```
To Board chairman: January 14, 1963

I am very happy to be able to tell you that everything has
worked out with regard to the Papal honor for Mr. Stravinsky.
On January 19th, the Archdiocese of Santa Fe will announce
that His Holiness Pope John, XXIII, has made Igor Stravinsky a
Knight Commander with Star of St. Sylvester . . . although the
Archdiocese of Santa Fe has had a few Papal Knights among its
membership, it has not had a Knight Commander or Knight
Commander with Star, and this I understand is quite important.
```

When Stravinsky died suddenly on April 6, 1971, in Venice, Crosby immediately sent a telegram of sympathy and support to his wife and to Craft. On April 28, Craft sent back a memorable reply.

Stravinsky had an affection for The Santa Fe Opera far greater than he had for any other musical organization in the United States, and not simply because his works were performed there (and performed out of all proportion to the showing of any other company), but because he was happy there and he composed there, and he liked the whole nature of the company. I know that you deeply mourn him, but you also can be very proud.[36]

Santa Fe Was First: The Apprentice Programs

It is impossible to imagine the American operatic landscape today without apprentice programs for singers. Virtually every company from the Metropolitan Opera down to smaller regional companies boasts them. All of those programs, and the young people who pass through them to further work in the opera and music fields, owe thanks to John Crosby. So do the hundreds of theater craft specialists who have experienced the benefits of Santa Fe Opera's landmark technical apprentice program since 1965.

When Crosby began The Santa Fe Opera Apprentice Singer Program in 1957, it had only eight chorus singers and three extra local vocalists.[37] The singers benefitted by being able to work alongside equally young and dedicated soloists, learn from the production crew and resident conductors, and interact with international stars, including Stravinsky. In 1960, Crosby codified the program further under the guidance of noted director Hans Busch, although he always gave Sachse most of the credit[38]—even though Sachse's health made it impossible for him to become personally involved, as originally planned.[39] Another important influence on the program was John Moriarty, American operatic veteran and longtime head of Central City Opera, who worked at Santa Fe in early seasons and contributed greatly to honing performance and musical values. Crosby's vision was firm from the first. "He saw the value of training young artists in a fabulously concrete and beautiful way, a responsible way, and that program is still among the best," noted public relations executive Mary Lou Falcone.[40]

Crosby had both a practical and an altruistic reason for beginning an apprentice program. He gained a chorus for the company's operas, as well as singers for comprimario roles, at bargain prices. Yet, as he wrote on May 19, 1967, to an official at the American Guild of Musical Artists,

> My own personal experience in the field of opera when I was a youngster rather soured me with regard to what might be called "alleged apprentice programs" in which a great amount of work was extracted from young people with a minimum of training and help offered, and an extremely poor caliber of instruction provided. Perhaps it has been with these personal experiences in mind that I have always wanted to feel the Santa Fe Opera Apprentice Program was in every way meaningful, helpful, and honest about the service it expects from the Apprentices and the instruction with which it provides them.

In the earliest years, Crosby recruited the apprentice singers himself through applications and personal knowledge of their capabilities. As the program grew, audition tours were added to the annual slate of work. Crosby did them for many years, usually accompanied by a colleague. In 1964, for example, from January 21 through February 25,[41] he and a colleague heard singers in Cleveland, Chicago, Kansas City, Denver, San Francisco, Los Angeles, Albuquerque, Tucson, Dallas, Oklahoma City, San Antonio, New Orleans, Baton Rouge, Mobile, and Memphis. The approach was like an airline's hub-and-spoke concept. By going to major cities with major conservatories, he also could draw in applicants from nearby colleges and universities. This approach was used throughout the 1980s and 1990s, and as the program grew in stature, there were ever more initial applications to wade through before choosing the fortunate, relatively few who would actually audition in person.

John Crosby meets with apprentice singers, circa 1967, in the Sombra, both a gathering place and rehearsal hall for the cast and orchestra. Photographer unknown. Courtesy The Santa Fe Opera.

Especially in the first decade, Crosby took singers into the apprentice program rather indiscriminately. He sometimes went easy in the audition process, as one staff member found out when he began helping Crosby with the circuit. Daniel Rice, head of the rehearsal department for many years—and at times, the apprentice program—realized why he had been having trouble with apprentice quality during the summers. It was an interesting lapse in the founder's usual habits.

[Crosby] said the most depressing thing to me. He said, "Now don't work yourself to death when you have to go to these six or seven cities and you have to remember all 800 people. Just choose about 20 really good people and then choose the other people to make the stage look pretty." And I thought, Jesus Christ, this is why I've had so much trouble sometimes. He would bring these apprentices in and some of them couldn't do their cover assignments; they were awful. . . . When I started doing it I made sure we had pretty good covers, people who could do the roles. With so many good singers, why just dress up the stage?[42]

Nonetheless, dressing in and of itself was actually a crucial matter. Crosby might bring along on the audition trail a costume list for an opera such as Richard Strauss's *Der Rosenkavalier*, and as he listened for potential covers or people able to sing comprimario parts, he also would gauge their height, weight, and physical characteristics. If he had two equally good candidates of which one could fit the costume and the other could not, the choice was clear.[43] He maintained elaborate charts, with lists of which apprentice singer would sing what and cover what, and he evaluated the singers in order of quality—soprano one, two, three, four, and so on, from highest capacity to lowest.[44] The same held true for other voice types. Crosby always watched for people who might have abilities that could flower in a year or two. He always saved a few places for such people, and if their work was satisfactory, they would be brought back for successive years and nurtured as they grew. He was proud that so many young performers went on to notable positions in the field and in music education, even if they did not always attain the highest professional levels on the world's stages.

Not every singer who is great today came into the program, and the files show that many now-famous artists were advised to wait a year or two before reapplying. In a letter of December 18, 1992, to now internationally noted baritone Nathan Gunn, Crosby wrote,

> We are not able to offer you a contract this year, and believe it would be best for you to wait for two years before auditioning again for our program. In the interval, I hope you will be able to work on your vocal technique which needs to be developed further before an Apprenticeship at Santa Fe would be appropriate for you. I will be glad to hear you in the Apprentice auditions in the Fall of 1994.

Anyone who has been through or observed the program, or even simply attended the opera, realizes that apprentices have exposure to tremendous assets, although they also work hard. Early on, the program offered plenty of opportunities beyond that of filling up the stage, as it still does. On February 25, 1971, Crosby wrote to AGMA, pointing out that for the 1970 season, forty-two participants—fourteen second-year apprentices and twenty-eight first years—had taken part, at an average company cost of $2,248 per individual. Over a ten-and-a-half–week season, each apprentice had experienced slightly more than eighty-four hours in the study of body movement, fencing (twenty-five men only), diction, makeup (first-years only), dance instruction, acting, musical coaching, private voice lessons, class voice lessons and master classes, and repertoire staging. Musical rehearsals, staging rehearsals, and costume fittings occupied 219.5 hours for each apprentice. Besides this training, apprentices had the privilege of working with professionals at every level and gaining experience by working with one another while performing. A dollar value would be impossible to assign to those benefits.

No age limits are imposed today, but most apprentices are in their mid- to late twenties or possibly their early thirties; in the early seasons, most were in their early twenties and had little experience. As in the past, the program is open to singers who have not yet performed six different roles with professional opera companies under a regular AGMA artist's contract and have not been engaged more than once as apprentice artists under AGMA status. Formerly, apprentices could not return for a third year after being in the program for two years; exceptions are made today.[45]

One thing that has changed with the times, obviously, is compensation. In 1959, apprentices received $24 per rehearsal week and $50 per week during the performing season, plus transportation and a reduced rate at the Montezuma Hotel in downtown Santa Fe for double lodging.[46] They could partake of an inexpensive lunch each rehearsal day at the ranch. Saiz, then in charge of the commissary, made sure there was plenty of food: "I had a pot of good hot or cold soup, cold cuts—beef, turkey, cold chicken, ham, cheese, [gelatin] salad, cottage cheese, lettuce, tomato, condiments, sliced bread. For dessert you'd think we owned an ice cream factory the way they ate it. [John] wanted to be sure these kids were healthy and able to perform. Their appetites were humongous."[47]

In 1970, a first-year apprentice chorister made $80 per week and a second-year, $90.[48] Except for salary, which today begins at just under $615 per week,[49] the benefits list is strikingly the same, with the addition of auditions each summer for agents, general directors of other companies, and other opera executives—a major plus. Apprentices still pay a portion of their stipend for lodging.

"The idea that John Crosby had was that apprentices should come here for their first professional engagement, rent living quarters, [and] pay for their provisions," explained David Holloway, current head of the apprentice program and an apprentice in 1966 and 1967, who enjoyed an international career as a baritone.[50] "He wanted them to take that experience from the program. We have tried to stay faithful to that premise." But as Crosby often said about other aspects of the company, the tail could never wag the dog. The apprentice program existed to serve and buttress the company, not the other way around, and it still does.

Scores of apprentices have gone on to notable careers in opera and concert, as well as in teaching. Among them, listed by their current voice types, are sopranos Roberta Alexander, Jennifer Black, Judith Blegen, Leona Mitchell, Catherine Naglestad, Susanna Phillips, Ashley Putnam, and Celena Shafer; mezzo-sopranos Eudora Brown, Beth Clayton, Michelle DeYoung, Deborah Domanski, Joyce DiDonato, Emily Fons, Clarity James, Jennifer Holloway, Marlena Kleinman (now Malas), and Susan Quittmeyer; tenors William Burden, Charles Castronovo, Vinson Cole, Richard Croft, Michael Fabiano, Keith Jameson, Brandon Jovanovich, Chris Merritt, Dimitri Pittas, Carl Tanner, Neil Shicoff, and Darren Keith Woods; baritones Daniel Belcher, Patrick Carfizzi, Brent Ellis, David Gockley, David Holloway, Corey McKern, Jonathan Michie, and Sherrill Milnes; and basses and bass-baritones Mark S. Doss, Samuel Ramey, James Morris, and Terry Cook.[51]

Despite the pluses, being a Santa Fe Opera vocal apprentice isn't easy. The work is grueling, the schedule is generally only posted daily, and the sheer amount of singing and stage work required is phenomenal. Even so, the competition to get in is ferocious. Watching and hearing the apprentices in any chorus opera is sheer delight dramatically, as well as sonically. When a big choral number comes up, one is nearly overwhelmed by the musicianship of the singers as well as their healthy, enticing vocal sound.

Unusual challenges for apprentices can arise when a season is being put on, and Crosby was sensitive about them. He wrote on July 30, 1993, to the technical director, saying that the chorus master has advised us that some of the members of the chorus have fainted in the chorus dressing rooms due to the high temperatures. . . . [He] understands the fresh air ventilating system for the dressing rooms is not used on certain nights when certain artists are performing who prefer not to have air, and . . . understands that the system cannot be operated for select dressing rooms only. If all this is so, I wonder whether there may be some means of damping the flow to the principal dressing rooms in order to maintain good flow to the chorus dressing rooms.

Like the vocal apprentices, technical apprentices worked and work hard; perhaps, hour per hour, even harder. In the 1970s and 1980s, scuttlebutt had it that Santa Fe Opera technical apprentices were worked to the bone, survived on little sleep, and in general were treated like indentured servants. Of course, that is life in the theater. Whether one is working in repertory theater, summer stock, black box experimental, opera, or musical comedy, there's never enough time in the day to get everything done, and schedules exist to have more tasks added to them. The opera still warns technical apprentices, and always did, that the season's work is tremendously rigorous physically and mentally, and that twelve-hour days and six- or seven-day workweeks are typical.[52] The show must go on, and it cannot be put on without the backstage crews and their technical wizardry.

To the production director: July 14, 1992

In view of the problems which the Costume Shop is experiencing I just want to be sure that you know how deeply concerned I am that the costume staff not be subject to excessive hours at work, and particularly late evening work. . . . I hope this can be avoided, but do please let me know if there are problems so that you and Brad and I might discuss possibilities for rewarding anyone who has been subject to excessive hours.

Nonetheless, Crosby always watched out for those apprentices, realizing that overloading them too far would be both cruel and counterproductive. On July 14, 1992, for example, he voiced his concern about the excessive night hours worked by costume shop apprentices to the technical director. That benevolence did not extend to letting apprentices use the opera's washing machines for personal laundry, however. In a June 13, 1972, memo, Crosby pointed out that the use of machines for personal clothing by costume shop personnel, in conjunction with the regular heavy laundry schedule, was causing maintenance problems. He dismissed the costume shop head's excuse that hours were too late for workers to use the city laundries, noting drily, "I believe laundromats are open on Sundays."

Even if Crosby could be curmudgeonly at times, it was worth it, said Production and Facilities director Paul Horpedahl, who was an apprentice in 1978. "The all-encompassing art form of opera, the words, the music, the orchestra, the dance, the scale of productions" that attracted Horpedahl, is what also drew, and draws, technical apprentices today. In addition, there is "the accessibility to the directors and designers, the ensemble nature of the company. Even as an apprentice, that etched its way into my brain," Horpedahl said.[53] Today, former Santa Fe Opera technical apprentices have been infused into every aspect of the theatrical world in the United States, even as vocal apprentices have been infused into teaching and performance.

```
To orchestra manager: April 18, 1972

I recall our gong for Butterfly is not good—it flats at the end
of its ring.
```

In the first decade of the company, Crosby also tried to establish apprentice situations for student conductors, composers, instrumentalists, and dancers. All such programs lasted only one or two or three seasons, both because of monetary considerations and because the logistics of managing more than two programs proved to be beyond the company's resources. The results unfortunately did not justify the energy expended.[54]

One aspect of the apprentice programs that few discuss publicly involves summer romances. Anyone who works in theater knows that when you put people into the hothouse atmosphere of intense dramatic and musical preparation, infatuations bloom and affairs multiply. With his Olympian overview, Crosby certainly knew this, and he didn't shy away from discussing it internally. One letter from February 19, 1990, to several employees, dealt with AIDS/HIV awareness and prevention.

> The Executive Committee of The Santa Fe Opera has agreed [on February 15] that it is appropriate that we institute a lecture or lectures on the subject of AIDS for all Apprentice Technicians and Singers at the beginning of the summer, more specifically in the week of June 4. . . . The Executive Committee also approved my recommendation that condom dispensers be installed in all employee lavatories and not in public lavatories.

Today, about 1,000 applications are received annually for the singer program and 600 for the technical program.[55] Initial singer apprentice rounds are now submitted by professional-quality recordings; final rounds for the 2015 apprentice roster were heard live only in Los Angeles, Albuquerque, New York, and Chicago.[56] From 1957 through the 2014 season, more than 2,300 singer apprentices and 2,800 technical apprentices had passed through the portals[57]; the 2014 season featured 43 singing apprentices and 75 technicians, all of notable caliber and many with solid performance experience behind them, both in school settings and in other apprentice programs, not to mention professional gigs.[58] These numbers would have made Crosby proud. (From the beginning, Crosby made sure that apprentices did not have to take on supernumerary responsibilities in addition to their vocal and dramatic assignments. Over the years, community volunteers have filled such "spear carrier" positions—and in at least one year, 1973, inmates from the New Mexico State Penitentiary served as supers during the season.)

Buildings and Grounds: Prefiguring the Future, 1957–1967

With the premiere season successfully finished, it was easy to predict progress for the future. Crosby's theoretical model had proved itself. Now he could begin to unfold further goals for his company. They had been in his mind from the beginning, even when he seemed focused only on the demands of building the theater and navigating

Nancy King (later Zeckendorf), Vera Zorina, and Louellen Sibley in Stravinsky's *Perséphone*, 1961. The work also was performed by the company in 1962 and 1968. Photo by Tony Perry. Courtesy The Santa Fe Opera.

the first season. They were based in his conviction that careful, slow development of artistic activities and their administrative support must go hand in hand with the physical growth of the company's theater and infrastructure. No growth would be undertaken until the time and the profit margin were right. Going too fast was not only economically precarious; it was artistically foolish. As noted American opera impresario—and former Santa Fe Opera baritone apprentice and box office manager—David Gockley observed, Crosby's approach to growth and change was "slow and deliberate."[59]

On the other hand, Crosby was not one to ignore obvious signs of success. With 12,850 attendees and more than $40,000 taken in at the box office the first year, it seemed possible that the company could sell more seats in coming seasons. Laurence Crosby, proud of his son's success, agreed to continue funding assistance, and the seating capacity was expanded, from 480 to 750 for 1958.[60] Growth thereafter was slower, yet still, by 1963, the company had expanded seating capacity to 846.[61]

At that point, renovation of the original theater was necessary if the capacity was to be further increased. It duly followed in the fallow period after the 1964 season. A loggia with new public restrooms, crowned by a balcony seating area, brought accommodation to 1,153.[62] Further additions in 1966 brought the seat count to 1,210. After the horrendous 1967 fire, which completely gutted the facility, the new theater was built to seat a generous 1,889. By the time the current house was built and opened in 1998, with 2,128 regular seats, plus standing room for 106,[63] it had long been needed. Each iteration of the theater was successfully completed in nine to eleven months, from the end of one performing season to the beginning of another—amazing accomplishments that bore witness to Crosby's skills as a planner and project supervisor, not to mention a money man. He would not move on reconstruction for any of the theaters until he knew the money was in hand or at least forthcoming in definite pledges.

Following the 1964 season, changes to the theater—besides the new loggia, balcony seating, and box office—included improvements in the orchestra pit, expanded to seat seventy-five; the stage roof, which was moved out twenty feet and doubled in area; and relocation of the bar to a more advantageous location for the sale of intermission refreshments. The total renovation cost eventually came to $225,000, which included a new lighting control board and architect's fees. In 1966, the tenth season, 27,800 patrons came. Some 40 percent were from Santa Fe and Los Alamos, 25 percent from Albuquerque, 10 percent from other New Mexico locations, and 25 percent from out of state. Opera workers counted license plates in the parking lot to collect those statistics, and the information was then matched to ticket sales records.[64] Crosby knew exactly how long it would take to empty the parking lot after a performance, and he helped direct traffic himself when necessary. He loved to help with that process, even up to the year of his retirement. He would proudly watch his parking crew wave the full lot's worth of cars onto the highway in little more than twenty minutes, almost invariably with no hitch or accident.

To a correspondent: August 16, 1965

I have looked into the matter of the incident in the parking lot August 6th. The attendant involved is a young man from Santa Fe, who has been employed by us for three years. He comes from a good Santa Fe family, and has, in the past, been considered one of our most responsible and devoted helpers. Unfortunately, the driver of the vehicle which he was attempting to control, drove over one of his feet, and a loss of temper ensued.

Due to the attendant's long record of fine service to the Opera, I feel it would be improper for us to dismiss this young man at the present time. Let me assure you that I have taken steps, however, to see that such an unfortunate incident does not occur again.

As the theater was expanded over the eight years from 1957 through 1964, Crosby Development Company drew on Laurence Crosby for more than $360,000 beyond his original $200,000 investment. Of this, improvements to the theater totaled $177,309; improvements to the ranch buildings accounted for more than $48,000. General maintenance and repair costs for the whole facility came to more than $7,600. Taxes, insurance, legal costs, and office expense totaled $26,800. Crosby Development Company's only income for those eight years was rent paid by the Opera Association of New Mexico of $300 per month, totaling $25,200. The $338,000 excess of expenditures over income was covered by Laurence's investment in Crosby Development Company.[65]

By 1961, the fifth season, Crosby was speaking boldly about the company's success and the city's taking it to heart. "If Santa Fe can do it, anybody can do it," he said. "It's not the size of the city that is the determining factor. It's the determination of the city to have opera. Santa Fe with its population of only 35,000 has proved the point beyond argument."[66] The opera's luster and influence were beginning to exert an off-season impact on Santa Fe. The existence of The Santa Fe Opera increased year-round tourism and business growth and helped convince St. John's College of Annapolis, Maryland, to open its second site locally rather than in California.[67]

Also in 1961, Crosby's beloved Yale professor Hindemith led his *News of the Day* in its American premiere, in English.[68] When asked why the piece had not been done before in this country, he replied, "No one asked me." Shades of Stravinsky. All those days of classes at Yale had paid off, and Crosby was now able to repay what he saw as a welcome debt to Hindemith. Crosby was especially happy to bring his teacher to Santa Fe in 1961 because he had tried to do so for years, but Hindemith's health and schedule had not permitted it. Unfortunately, the weather gods were not favorable on *News of the Day*'s opening night. In act 2, a deluge erupted, and rained-on audience members fled to their cars or huddled in raincoats and umbrellas. The undaunted Hindemith kept conducting, with someone holding an umbrella over him, but the furious downpour soon forced the orchestra from the pit, and the show stopped. Aileen Crosby, determined to support the conductor to the last, reportedly

Gathering the flock: Carolyn Lockwood, lower right with hand raised, calls the company together in either Berlin or Belgrade during the 1961 postseason tour to Europe. Crosby stands in the center of the picture, very much the operatic executive. Photographer unknown. Courtesy Gene Kuntz.

remained in her front-row seat even when water rushing down the theater rake rose above her ankles.

During the 1961 postseason, The Santa Fe Opera was the only American company invited to the tenth annual Berlin Festival—the organization's first and so far only main-stage tour performances (although apprentice tours take place throughout New Mexico and the Southwest today).[69] Performances took place in Berlin and afterward in Belgrade, to great success and to Crosby's pride; the tour was supported by the U.S. government. The Berlin Festival was delighted that The Santa Fe Opera was coming with Douglas Moore's intriguing piece of Americana, *The Ballad of Baby Doe*, and Stravinsky's imposing *Oedipus Rex* and *Perséphone* on a double bill. An exact replica of the Santa Fe theater—complete with a backdrop view of the Jemez Mountains—was built on the large stage of the Theater des Westens.

Unfortunately, as Carolyn Lockwood recalled, only three people in the company, including herself, spoke German—and the Berlin Wall had just been erected. "The worst thing was the [Berlin] wall went up, and all the stagehands came from the east of Berlin," she said. "The only thing left were a few drunks backstage." All kinds of annoying theatrical machinations occurred. Once a grand piano needed for a rehearsal was suddenly moved completely out of the theater. Lockwood refused to be stymied. She could hear a rehearsal underway on the third floor, so she and a few stalwarts "went up and swiped the piano. And Stravinsky came in at the same time—we spoke German together—and said, 'You tell them. . . !' He had a colorful vocabulary."[70] Fortunately, things went better in Belgrade, and the company returned to the United States with political and professional success in its pocket.

Following the tour, at the beginning of the sixth season, the Opera Association of New Mexico gave Crosby a silver cigarette case to acknowledge both the tour and the previous season's success. Unfortunately, the European tour had upset Crosby's balance of artistic costs with adequate budgeting. Even with government underwriting, the tour had eaten into the company coffers. With less than $50 in the bank, more than $38,700 looming in accounts payable, and more than $77,000 due in notes payable, even the Crosby family's funds couldn't close the gap. But somehow, the seventh season went on with special support from the three ad hoc guilds of the opera, which raised more than $20,000 during that fiscal year through fundraising teas, parties, and fashion shows.[71] They prefigured today's well-established and influential guild structure, which provides sturdy monetary and public relations support for the company.

The years 1962 through 1967 featured many artistic highlights in the constantly improved theater. A 1962 Stravinsky Festival included all the vocal works the maestro had composed for music theater. Composers Milton Babbit and Carlos Chávez and critic-composer Virgil Thomson spoke at a lecture series on Stravinsky, and nine young American composers attended seminars during a one-time composer-in-residence program. In 1963, Santa Fe gave the American premiere of Alban Berg's landmark *Lulu*, which was unfinished when he died. Harold C. Schonberg of the *New York Times* commented, on the company's decision to mount the controversial work, "It remained for The Santa Fe Opera to do the honors, diving in where the big companies had fastidiously picked up their skirts and circled away."[72]

The Fire

The eleventh season opened propitiously on July 1, 1967, with *Carmen*, followed shortly thereafter by *La Bohème*, *The Barber of Seville*, and two orchestral concerts.[73] The American premiere of Hindemith's *Cardillac*, conducted by Robert Craft and with acclaimed American baritone John Reardon singing the title role, was on July 26. It was the eleventh performance of the season. Crosby later remembered what happened that night after the postshow party.

About 3:00 a.m. our technical director, George Schreiber, woke me and told me the theater was on fire. We ran to the back of the theater: the stage was ablaze and the roof was falling down, as its steel beams had melted from the heat. I hurried over to the south side of the backstage area to get a view of the balcony, which was not on fire, but as I looked at it in one instant flames erupted simultaneously all along the wood top of the railing in front of the first row of balcony seats. I thought gasoline must have been poured on the railing, but learned later from our acoustician that this spontaneous combustion was caused by the transfer of the intense heat from the stage due to the acoustical design which projected sound, and would therefore also project heat. The entire balcony was gone in about thirty minutes. My lungs were filling with smoke and all I could do was to roll down the hillside to the arroyo where the air was clear. By 5:00 a.m. our staff had assembled and planning began for the salvage of our season. With the exception of costumes for *The Barber of Seville*, which were at a local dry cleaner, everything was lost: music, musical instruments, costumes, stage properties, scenery, etc., etc.[74]

Another memory of the fire came from acclaimed stage director Bruce B. Donnell, then an apprentice technician. He had worked *Cardillac* and gone to the party, then gone to bed in a building fondly known as "the chicken coop." A friend woke him in the early morning with news that the theater was on fire. Thinking it a prank, Donnell refused to leave his bed. Urged again to wake up, he left the bunkhouse and walked up the hill toward the house. Then he saw flames shooting above the brow of the hill. He crested the rise in time to see the balcony ignite.[75] Witnesses heard what sounded like gunshots — cans of hair spray exploding. One despairing board member called the blazing bench seats "evil farolitos."[76]

John Crosby inspects the carnage on the morning of July 27, 1967, after the theater-destroying fire. He and the company immediately set out to make the season go on in the local high school gymnasium. Photo by Alan Stoker. Courtesy The Santa Fe Opera.

The opera house was destroyed, but the white petunias survived, with a light coating of ash. Balcony staircases, left and right, lead off into nothingness. Photo by Alan Stoker. Courtesy The Santa Fe Opera.

The local volunteer firefighting crew had no need to guess where the fire was. The flames could be seen for miles away. They fought the conflagration nobly, first with three 750-gallon pumper trucks, then by mining the opera's wells. But when the electricity went out, the water supply was lost. The firemen then emptied the swimming pool and a small cistern, but it was a hopeless task at that point.[77]

Even as Crosby tearfully watched the debacle, he was dictating plans to staff members concerning how performances could go on. His hair began to turn white after that night, Crosby recalled later—but at least no one was injured in the inferno. When he heard about the tragedy, major donor Marshall McCune drove to the smoking ruins and gave Crosby a check for $90,000 to help with immediate needs.[78]

The cause of the fire has never been determined. Some suggested defective wiring, which seems unlikely given the previous years' safety record. More than a few speculated that a disgruntled former employee was to blame, as cans of dry-cleaning fluid had been stacked up in the costume shop, where the fire began. Others whispered that Crosby was the obvious suspect. By burning the theater, he could collect insurance money and erect a new and improved house. Given how difficult that mammoth undertaking turned out to be, that he was in an exhausted sleep when alerted at the Ranch, and that a company party had been going on after the show, the theory seems untenable. In any event, no one ever was accused of setting the fire, and it remains an unsolved mystery to this day.[79]

The fire was over by dawn, with the theater gutted. Besides costumes, scores, and props, three pianos and other instruments were incinerated.[80] Crosby's memoir was incorrect in one particular: the *Cardillac* sets were onstage and destroyed, but the other sets survived and could be adapted to a new performance space. Word of the debacle quickly spread locally, nationally, and internationally. Fans and fellow opera heads phoned and telegrammed their sympathy and support.[81] Two board members woke up a member of the school board early that morning and persuaded him to let the opera construct a temporary house in the gymnasium of Santa Fe's downtown high school. Sweeney Gymnasium would become Sweeney Opera House. Another board member sent his private plane from Texas with orchestra scores, music stands, and stand lights loaned by the San Antonio

Symphony. Replacement scores for Henze's *Boulevard Solitude* were rushed by air from Germany. Locals rallied and helped in many ways, with prominent coverage and support from the *Santa Fe New Mexican* and the *Albuquerque Journal*. A costume construction shop was set up in a patron's house, and clothes were borrowed from community members to set the remounted operas in modern dress. Crosby was everywhere—on the phone with vendors and friends of the company, talking with singers, coordinating matters, even helping assemble music stand lights in the gymnasium. Within 36 hours, a theater had been constructed, lights hung, and *Barber* went on that Saturday to a house of 1,300 people. Critics there to report on the transformation included writers from the *New York Times*, *Musical America*, and the *Dallas Morning News*.[82] The company never played *Cardillac* again, but *The Marriage of Figaro* and *Salome* opened in Sweeney, and *La Bohème* and *Carmen* were revived, as well as *The Barber of Seville*.

The show went on, but the company was badly hurt by the fire. The season posted a deficit of $200,000. Although the theater was insured, the amount was far less than the nearly $2 million needed for a new building. As it turned out, even with vigorous fundraising, the 1968 season suffered an additional deficit of $425,000, which hung around the company's neck for several years.[83]

The Second House

Even as Sweeney Opera House was being constructed, Crosby was planning a new theater that would include improvements he had been considering for years. McHugh and Hooker were again retained and began work at once. McHugh later wrote, "The basic concepts of the new theater were developed in a sort of white heat of creativity—in about five days of highly vocal and busy sessions. Drawings were made freehand with felt-tipped pens. The later detailed working drawings varied little more than a pencil width from these original sketches."[84]

To *Time Magazine* music critic: August 31, 1967

Thank you for the beautiful story in Time Magazine and all the work you had with it. It will help us now in our efforts

Opening night number 2: the act 1 finale of *The Barber of Seville* in Sweeney Opera House, July 28, 1967. Photo by Alan Stoker. Courtesy The Santa Fe Opera.

to rebuild the theatre. And what pleased me most what that the importance of CARDILLAC did not get lost in the story of the fire.

I'm glad you saw the theatre before Thursday morning and could realize its real raison d'etre. Now we are busily planning with the architect and acoustician, and I feel confident that by next season we will be able to look back upon this as just a badly concocted opera libretto.

To get the work done in time to open the season, workers were scheduled in two shifts, from 6:00 a.m. to 10:00 p.m. daily, and they just made the goal. Final details of the construction were finished on June 24, 1968, with the opening night just days away on July 2.[85]

For the 1968 rebuild, the theater was projected to cost $1.8 million, and it came in at $2 million.[86] Stravinsky offered his name as honorary chairman of the fundraising campaign, and Goddard Lieberson of Columbia Records was national chairman. Crosby, who in later years did not much care for being directly involved in fundraising, was here active in every aspect of the campaign. He wrote Frank Magee on September 10, 1967, that he had half a million in hand and was considering applying for a $600,000 grant to help close the gap—"but the last inches are going to be hell." The board's own personal goal was to give or get a total of $800,000.[87]

> To a potential donor: September 20, 1967
>
> I expect you have been informed of the fire at the Santa Fe Opera which entirely destroyed our Theatre July 27th. The Company continued to perform the balance of our season in a local high school gymnasium. . . . I estimate the Opera Association of New Mexico will need approximately $2,400,000 to carry operations on from now until December 31, 1968. Since the fire of July 27th, the Opera Association has received approximately 1,000 gifts, and the total of gifts and pledges since July 27th is approximately $1,200,000. We seem to be, therefore, approximately halfway towards meeting our needs.
>
> The total need ($2,400,000) includes construction of a new theatre, which we estimate will cost $1,755,000. In addition to this we have an extraordinary deficit of approximately $200,000 for General Operations in the year 1967 and an estimated deficit for 1958 of $425,000.
>
> I would be very grateful for the opportunity to call on you and give you further information about The Santa Fe Opera.

Crosby and McHugh were determined that no future fire would be able to decimate the new opera house.[88] The imposing theater was built of concrete block and reinforced concrete, stuccoed and painted a rose-adobe color. The return of redwood trim was Crosby's touch, but it, like all materials used, was fireproofed. A new 76,000-gallon water tank was constructed, from which water could flow by gravity to feed fire hoses. The pit was enlarged, mostly horizontally, to 1,200 square feet, from about 800. (Crosby believed that the conductor should be no more than sixteen feet from the edge of the stage.) The reflecting pool was removed to provide room for more seats—something that did not completely please Crosby, who liked having the pool between the audience and the players as a barrier. But leaving it out meant more seats and, hence, more needed income.

Anchor footings went down ninety feet. The drop from stage level to the lowest level was thirty-eight feet, with ten times more backstage space than the first theater had had. Crosby himself paid for three new rehearsal halls, and Aileen and Laurence Crosby gave generously as well.

Crosby also made sure the backstage area was appropriately enlarged. At just over 41,000 square feet, it was ten times bigger than in the original petite house. Technical workers and their fiefdoms occupied side structures attached to the main building. A hydraulic lift was added to facilitate set changes and spare workers' backs.[89]

Along with the construction, further land transfers took place. In the past decade, the Opera Association of New Mexico had bought various acres from Crosby Development Company from time to time and been gifted with some occasionally. Now the association bought seventy-six more acres from Crosby Development Company, at the bargain price of $65,338—just $860 per acre. Combined with the earlier transfers, the association now owned all the opera grounds and the parking areas, although Crosby Development Company continued its ownership of the theater; Crosby was taking no chances on being outmaneuvered by the board. (Crosby became owner as a private individual in 1971, when Crosby Development Company was terminated.) By August 31, the end of the 1968 season, bank borrowings totaled $550,000, with $250,000 of it on a ten-year mortgage guaranteed by a number of patrons and donors.[90]

Despite financial worries, the 1968 season was a triumphant one. Eight works were mounted. *Madame Butterfly* opened the house, as it had in the original theater. *The Magic Flute*, *La Traviata*, Gaetano Donizetti's *The Elixir of Love*, *Der Rosenkavalier*, the United States premiere of Henze's *The Bassarids*, the world stage premiere of Schoenberg's *Die Jakobsleiter*, and a return of the Stravinsky *Perséphone* all had equal pride of place.[91] But money and time were in such short supply that the Stravinsky was played in concert form, and *Rosenkavalier* and *Traviata* had to return to the company's earlier practice of being played against minimal—to the point of bareness—sets.[92]

The next few years were a challenge to the company. Besides theater reconstruction costs, the opera—like other arts organizations—was bruised by the 1969 recession. Fortunately, in 1972, the Ford Foundation announced a series of major grants to assist arts organizations nationally. For The Santa Fe Opera, the foundation offered a three-to-one match.

Some $727,600 would pay 50 percent of net current liabilities of the opera if the company raised a match of $334,660 by September 30, 1972; an additional grant would provide $131,000 per year for four years, totaling $392,940.[93] Crosby again transcended his dislike of personal involvement in fundraising and led efforts to raise the amount that would be matched and save the opera, which it did.

With the new house soon came two men who would play tremendously influential roles in the company's life. The first, in 1968, was the young Charles MacKay, a native New Mexican, who had begun working with the company at age fifteen and who had attended the company's first youth night,[94] and in 1969, Richard Gaddes arrived. Crosby had met him during a trip to London in December 1968 and would soon bring him to this country as artistic administrator.

From left, Charles MacKay and Richard Gaddes celebrate winning a race at a July 4, 1976, company picnic. The winning ribbons worn by the men—later the company's third and second general directors, respectively—were made by designer Dona Granata. Photographer unknown. Courtesy The Santa Fe Opera.

When Gaddes and Crosby first connected in London, Gaddes was working for the agent Basil Horsefield.[95] His previous résumé was stellar. He first worked for insurance brokers in Newcastle-on-Tyne, England, then became a student at Trinity College of Music in London from 1960 to 1964. There he took a licentiate and graduate degrees, also teaching at the London School and Trinity from 1964 to 1966. With a colleague, he also began a lunchtime recital series for young musicians. He was with Horsefield from 1966 through 1969, when Crosby brought him to America. Crosby clearly valued and wanted to keep Gaddes. A long-term visa application was submitted April 24,

1969, and the petition included letters of support and testament to Gaddes's abilities from the Covent Garden, Sadler's Wells, and Glyndebourne opera companies. On January 13, 1971, Crosby wrote to the Immigration and Naturalization Service, "I hereby confirm to you that Mr. Richard Gaddes is employed on a permanent basis by the Opera Association of New Mexico as Artistic Administrator for The Santa Fe Opera."

Gaddes became Crosby's most trusted and responsible associate until he left the company in 1978 to oversee Opera Theatre of St. Louis, which he had helped part-time to found in the previous two seasons.[96] Gaddes later returned to Santa Fe as a consultant and became associate general director in 1995 and then the company's general director on Crosby's retirement, a position he then held for eight years. Arguably Crosby's closest male friend and colleague, he declined to be interviewed for this study.

To Richard Gaddes: June 2, 1976

Congratulations again for your fine achievements with the new company at St. Louis. You deserve to be proud. . . .

Please be careful to provide ample funds for your next season for administrative and office assistance. Second seasons are often very very trying. The glamour of the "first" year is gone. Costs will go up tremendously, because so much has been forced through at no cost or little cost in the first year.

You spoke of the possibility of some arrangement for use of my office at New York, and I have a suggestion for you now: I believe that a minimum sum of $2,500 would be appropriate for a base rent on the assumption 40% of your time would be devoted to St. Louis over the next winter. I am estimating a total operating expense for the office next year of $37,300 (12 months). Santa Fe meets $24,000, so my loss is about $13,300. The office supports three executives. . . . Accordingly, your account for $1/3$ of the cost and 20%—$1/3$—$37,300 is $2,500 in round numbers. That would in my opinion, be a fair rental for St. Louis to pay to me. It would not include direct office expenses for postage, telephone, copier rental, etc., nor secretarial support. . . .

Although it may appear the numbers add up to quite a sum. . . . I doubt that St. Louis could obtain the facilities available on the

A magisterial John Crosby stands with his trusted right-hand man and company artistic administrator, Richard Gaddes, at a 1975 Apprentice Artist reception. The cocktail in one hand and the cigarette in the other were nearly permanent Crosby appurtenances. Photographer unknown. Courtesy The Santa Fe Opera.

first and second floors of 48 East 63 Street on a part time basis elsewhere for anything like that amount.

MacKay, a native New Mexican, first was an additional French horn player and pit boy and then became an office staffer in February 1970. He moved up the company ladder with notable speed until he, too, left in early 1979 to work at the Spoleto Festival.[97] When Gaddes left Opera Theatre of St. Louis in 1985, MacKay became his successor, and years later, when Gaddes retired as Santa Fe Opera general director, MacKay succeeded him there on October 1, 2008. Thus The Santa Fe Opera's only three general directors form a direct line of succession and experience.

For the next three decades, the 1968 theater served the company well. Crosby knew that demand would continue to increase, in large part because of Santa Fe's growing reputation as a place to be and visit—a process the opera had played a major part in establishing. He also knew the value of repeating repertoire staples, to provide artistic reassurance to new operagoers who might know the names of a few works but not be familiar with more esoteric fare. From the thirty-two seasons of 1969 through his retirement season of 2000, *The Marriage of Figaro* was presented in ten seasons; *The Magic Flute* nine; *Salome* seven; *La Bohème*, *Così fan tutte*, and *La Traviata* six each; *Madame Butterfly*, *Die Fledermaus*, and *The Grand Duchess of Gérolstein* four times; and *The Rake's Progress*, *Le Rossignol*, *Tosca*, Richard Wagner's *The Flying Dutchman*, and Mozart's *Don Giovanni* three.[98] Operas presented twice included *Ariadne auf Naxos*, *Der Rosenkavalier*, *Intermezzo*, *The Barber of Seville*, *Carmen*, *La Fanciulla del West*, *Lulu*, and Poulenc's *The Dialogues of the Carmelites*. Single-mounted rarities included *Ariodante*, Krzysztof Penderecki's *The Black Mask*, Leoš Janáček's *The Cunning Little Vixen*, a dual bill of Richard Strauss's *Feursnot* and *Friedenstag*, Ambroise Thomas's *Mignon*, Virgil Thomson's *The Mother of Us All*, Gluck's *Orfeo ed Euridice*, Benjamin Britten's *Owen Wingrave* and *The Turn of the Screw*, and Claudio Monteverdi's *L'Incoronazione di Poppea*. There also were several world premieres and commissions: Heitor Villa-Lobos's *Yerma*, Luciano Berio's *Opera*, Eaton's *The Tempest*, Carlisle Floyd's *Wuthering Heights*, George Rochberg's *The Confidence Man*, Tobias Picker's *Emmeline*, David Lang's *Modern Painters*, and Peter Lieberson's *Ashoka's Dream*.

To Deputy Warden, New Mexico State Penitentiary: August 31, 1973

I have pleasure in enclosing the Opera Association of New Mexico's check in amount $565.00 in payment of the men who acted as supernumeraries in our productions of *La Boheme* and *Der Fliegende Hollander* this past season. The name of each man is listed below, together with a note of the number of services and the amount each should receive.

The Third Theater

Whereas the first theater had been put together in a white heat, as was the new house after the fire, the company's current house was carefully planned and considered over a decade, beginning with a detailed facilities plan in 1988.[99] That master plan looked at the entire company acreage, including items that have yet not come to fruition, such as a hotel on the opera property and onsite apprentice housing, and some that have, such as more vocal studios and rehearsal facilities, an expanded and improved cantina, and Stieren Orchestra Hall, which provides for costume storage as well as for staging and orchestral rehearsals and benefit events.

The idea for the third house came straight from Crosby. The board saw no special need for a new building; the second theater still seemed more than adequate. But if the founder wanted a new theater, it would be done.[100] Fundraising planning started early for the new structure. Originally the new theater was to have been built over two winters, but when full funding was not in place by the fall of 1996, Crosby declined to permit construction to begin.

His fanatic attention to detail and his rigorous control of scheduling and finances, including any necessary bank borrowings, famously involved apparent minutia of the new house—for example, whether plans paid adequate attention to storage space for toilet paper and program books. "I need 65,000 programs for the season," he said. "There are 40 programs per box. That makes 1,625 boxes. Each box is 9 by 12 by 12, taking up 3/4 cubic feet of space. Therefore, I need 1,219 cubic feet of space for program storage."[101] The same discussions took place regarding the storage for toilet paper, although it was understood that that material would be regularly replenished throughout the season. Following along on that, he also considered how much water would be needed to flush the toilets at intermission and what that meant for the pumping schedules of the company wells. During the planning, he even timed how long it took for one woman to enter the line at the women's restroom and finally exit. From that, he calculated how many facilities should be built in the new complex. (For once, he underplanned. A consistent complaint from operagoers since 1998 has been insufficient toilets—a lack the company intends to address via a current building fund campaign that has raised nearly $35 million.)[102]

Several architectural firms were interviewed for the project, and the distinguished firm of James L. Polshek & Partners, now Ennead Architects, was chosen to design the new structure. With his usual care, Crosby researched the firm. In a letter of April 25, 1988, a decade before the new theater opened, he noted to staff members that his friend Schuyler Chapin, former general director of the Metropolitan Opera and then involved with Carnegie Hall, had spoken very highly of Polshek's involvement with the renovation of Carnegie.

James Polshek, the principal design partner, remembered his interviews with John Crosby as fascinating—including, after a telephone interview, a personal talk with Crosby in Santa Fe.[103] Polshek spoke then to Crosby about his belief that when it came to certain cultural institutions, architects should be preservationists as well as creators. The company's current site and theater placement would be preserved, not destroyed for the sake of change or architectural ambition. The new building would be expansive and noble, but first and foremost, a house for the production and enjoyment of opera.

In addition, Polshek recalled,

We talked about the landscape. He was very concerned with physical phenomena, particularly climatic phenomena, or water rushing through the arroyos and wind and rain blowing in on the violins—things that really became quite fundamental in the design. He understood the peculiar, very special way in which water and land interacted in that mythic place. I knew that we had a person that would respect what we did and that there would be a dialog between us. We grew to have a very warm, albeit silent relationship.[104]

Polshek said that one of his favorite memories of Crosby was of an evening during a rehearsal close to opening night in 1998, when Crosby walked around the entire theater with him, then guided their steps to the Opera Club. There he ordered two glasses of champagne and toasted the architect "with the smile of a very young person who was quietly pleased"—an acknowledgment that made up for more than a few challenging times during the decade-long relationship.[105]

Indeed, Crosby was hardly easy to work with. He knew what he wanted and what was needed, and he would not settle for anything less. As Polshek put it, "He was a nitpicker beyond any I ever dealt with."[106] As he could and did in orchestra or AGMA negotiations, Crosby would walk out of architectural meetings if he was dissatisfied with the way things were going or felt outgunned—rare though that could be. Of some thirty-five meetings in Polshek's office, Nancy Zeckendorf noted, "John threatened to walk out about thirty times. He never made it to the door and he always got his point across."[107] On the other hand, Crosby backed the firm's design through many complaints, including from several people who worried that the arching stays and cables that held up the roof were going to be white, not adobe colored. He understood Polshek's concept that the white would represent the Native American concept of Father Sky, while the adobe-colored building itself would represent Mother Earth. They would come together against the backdrop of the New Mexico horizon.[108] In effect, Crosby deferred to Polshek on aesthetic matters, the same way he tried to do for directors and designers.

Crosby at first wanted to leave the roof partially open to the elements, as the first two houses had been. To him, it was a connection

John Crosby happily celebrates the placing of the Igor Stravinsky bust on the Stravinsky Terrace during the construction of the 1998 theater. Photographer unknown. Courtesy The Santa Fe Opera.

with the past and had sentimental associations with the company's early days, his then-colleagues, and his parents.[109] But as it was pointed out to him, times had changed, and people paying big money for a ticket did not want to be drenched—and that for a project costing some $20 million, a roof was a necessity. After all, it would be enough that the theater sides were open, which would permit the New Mexico sky to be seen by the audience. He also could comfort himself with the thought that wind and rain would doubtless pour in from time to time. (Discussion did take place at one point about finding some way to close the new structure's sides with moveable panels during bad weather, but acoustician Purcell spoke against the idea. He pointed out that the effect on the acoustics would be both unpredictable and probably detrimental.[110])

The 1998 renovation, besides providing a gorgeous new house, added some highly needed backstage amenities.[111] A new computerized lighting system was installed. The ten catwalks above the stage were given ample head room for technicians working there—no more head-banging experiences for those hanging lights or working a show. A backstage audiovisual system linked pit and backstage personnel at all points and could be used for specialized sound effects such as wind, rain, thunder, or explosions. Reflective plastering in the orchestra pit and the installations of special steel panels above the stage helped both singers and orchestra hear and perform better. The heaters over the orchestra pit were a major concern, in terms of keeping the players happy and comfortable and keeping their instruments in tune. The first installation made too much noise when in operation, and Crosby, fuming, demanded a new and silent set be installed.

In the house proper, under the two soaring roofs connected by a clerestory window, all the seats were upholstered, and they were now wide enough to accommodate larger patrons. An elevator, the company's first in the front of the house, connected all the levels of the new structure. Wheelchair seating was made available in all ticket price sections. In a nod to accumulating income, more refreshment stands and a larger gift shop were planned to attract and quickly serve more visitors. Finally, emergency generators were put in place so no power interruption could stop a performance. The roof was configured to harvest rainwater into storage tanks to be used for watering the grounds.

To: Polshek and Partners, Architects: January 18, 1996

The subject of the reflecting pool in the orchestra pit continues to worry me. Now that I have a better idea of your plans (cross section 1-17-96 and A 407) I would like to make some comments.

1. I understand and appreciate very much the artistic appearance which you wish to achieve with the water. (The technical director) has also described this to me, as per his understanding of last winter.

2. Is it necessary for the water to flow over the sides of the pool to achieve the effect you wish? As we discussed, I have real concern about the overflow on the orchestra pit side, and I have some concerns for the overflow on the audience side because of the fact that adults and young persons can be careless about putting wrappers, etc., on ledges, nooks and crannies. And what will happen if patrons brush by the pool while entering the first row to take their seats? Will they get wet?

3. We are greatly concerned about costs, and therefore the detail work for the overflow and collecting trough(s) as well as plumbing and pumping are worrisome in this regard.

4. We must think about winter shut down, and protection of troughs, etc., from accumulation of snow which can melt/freeze and crack masonry. (We cover all the drinking fountains and cigarette receptacles over the winter in the present theatre for this reason.) Our water is very "hard"—much calcium or lime, which gives us problems over the years with delicate or small metal orifices in plumbing.

I hope we can find a solution which will satisfy your artistic objectives and also address my concerns.

Let me describe the problems with the original reflecting pool next to the orchestra pit in the old theatre (1957–67). That pool had no filter and no automatic plumbing. It was filled by a hand held hose and drained by removing a short pipe which was coupled to a drain and served as an overflow when in place. There was no filter and no recirculation system. That pool was very simple and certainly did not achieve the fine artistic objectives which you have given us with your design, and which are so desirable. But the old pool has left me with some memories. These are:

1. The old pool was too deep (3" or 4" of water) so water was wasted in cleaning and filling, and the chamber for the water was just a flat bottom and vertical sides, so there was no particularly special effect from the water; it was "just there."

2. Maintenance consisted of three things:

   a. Skimming off moths which are attracted to the pool by the reflection of light during performances.

   b. Flushing out the fine sand which accumulated on the flat bottom (sand carried in the air on breezy days).

   c. Removal of occasional spots of algae: the shallow water warmed up in the sunlight (direct sunlight fell on the pool in the old theater because the stage roof was very small). But occasional algae will continue to be a problem as shallow water will reach air temperatures.

3. The maintenance procedures were:

   a. Skimming off moths on performance days.

   b. Emptying the water once a week, and sweeping out the sand and scrubbing off the few spots of algae.

I look forward to discussing the plans for the orchestra pit reflecting pool further with you.

The height of the pit rail is 2"–6¼" above the existing seating slab at the existing first row of seats. This height was modified (reduced) a few years ago for acoustical purposes.

In his attention to customer comfort, Crosby was concerned that the architects work to take into account how warm certain areas of the theater could become during performances. In an August 19, 1992, letter, he notified Polshek's contact about how thermometers had been placed on the back inside wall of the balcony and the back interior wall downstairs behind the standing room area, so that temperatures could be taken after each opera began for several nights. The results showed as uncomfortably warm, and Crosby asked that the architects take this fact into account in their design.

Land and Water

John Crosby was focused on the art and craft of presenting opera. But he also was fanatically devoted to land and water. He loved the land on which his creation stood, as well as the acres around it, with the abiding ardor of his English and Irish ancestors. Land was to be preserved, nurtured, and cared for. He equally loved and respected water, and its life-giving power, with the fervent dedication of a Northern New Mexico acequia master. To him, wasting water was unthinkable, a misuse of a precious resource in the desert, and not to be tolerated. Perhaps his keen focus began to develop at the Ranch School, where environmental respect was stressed long before the term and practice became generally known, and buttressed further during his summers at Bishop's Lodge, where he trekked into the backcountry and became further exposed to the beauties of New Mexico's mesas, mountains, valleys, and high meadows.

To a groundskeeper: September 8, 1986

The little water well at the East end of my property is not working. . . . For your reference the hour meter at the well is reading 932.8 hours as of this morning.

You will have to leave the big well on until you are sure that the little well is fixed. I have turned the automatic sprinkler system off, and I have closed off and back drained the water line to the channel at the West end of the swimming pool.

I have set the thermostat for the swimming pool at 34¼, but water will have to be added to the pool daily for a while until the water cools down somewhat.

Please bring the jeep, tractor and grader into the Opera for Winter storage, and be sure to check the anti-freeze in both the jeep and the tractor radiators.

The four wooden chaises around the swimming pool should be
stored at the Opera for the Winter and repaired and re-painted
as necessary. The cushion and pillows of the four chaises should
be placed in the bedroom of my office building at the Opera and
brushed or vacuumed clean.

The one chaise on the porch by my bedroom at the cabin should
be left there, but the cushion and pillows should be removed and
placed in my bedroom at the cabin.

His environmental awareness could be seen even in the first season,
when he would rise early in the morning at the ranch and clump off
to water the just-planted birch saplings, passing by the breakfasting,
laughing cast without a glance, intent on his task.[112] He knew where
every planting was and how it was doing, whether it was the precious grass lawn or the water-hungry flowers in beds and baskets. His
famous concentrated silences did not keep him from being friendly
with the grounds crew and opera maintenance staff, many of whom
were from Tesuque and Chimayó families he had come to know
during his earlier years in the area.

Crosby knew all about the company's water rights, the depth and
capacity of the several wells, and how much water was needed for an
off-season day versus for a performance night. On August 2, 1963,
during the season, he wrote in a memo,

We must try to control the use of water so that the pump systems
are not required to be supplying water to the Theater for filling
the reflecting pool and watering the garden simultaneously along
with the use of water at the gardens around the Ranch. . . . I suggest that we allow your crew the hours of 8 a.m. to 12 noon for
the above use of water, and accordingly [we] will not turn on any
sprinklers at the Ranch until 12 noon daily.

On May 30, 1965, he sent a detailed and in part wry letter to the
construction contractor and architect McHugh, after the extension of
the theater roof and the building of the loggia and balcony. The letter
is a mix of construction instruction about both buildings and land, as
well as water, eventualities. He and staff members had observed conditions that day, a Sunday, during a two-hour storm, with rain blowing

in different directions and at different intensities. Among other things, he noted, "The forward projection of the balcony deck beams collect water at the forward lower corners, which spouts off in a stream comparable to that of a male infant urinating. This stream falls in Row J of the orchestra seating in line with each beam." Crosby always could be trusted for the mot juste.

An April 11, 1994, memo demonstrated his concern for a balance between overwatering and too-scant watering. While a planter in front of North Hall was quite lovely, with its various annuals, the maintenance staff was letting hoses run far too long, he wrote. It was "not uncommon to find hoses running with two inches of water above the earth in this planter." This meant a loss of more than five hundred gallons per overwatering occurrence—enough to give Crosby a headache or lead him to provoke headaches in others.

On June 25 of that year he also complained in writing that toilets had run all night after outside groups had used the theater, wasting significant volumes of water. The toilets were twenty-five years old and had poor fittings, he acknowledged, and would soon be replaced with 1.5 gallon low-flush models, but in any event, he insisted that closing inspections of the public lavatories should follow all special events or rentals to outside groups. "If two W.C.s run for 12 hours 'overnight' from June 1st to August 29th, approximately 380,000 gallons of water would be wasted which is just over one acre-foot," he stressed. "I think we have the opportunity to achieve very substantial savings since we now know that the situation in recent past years was fairly devastating."

Water came up again on July 5, when a rodent caused a well to malfunction.

Concerning the problem of the mouse getting into the electrical controls for the cistern well, I suggest that as soon as possible [we] wrap some tin sheet metal around the wooden post on which the electrical controls are mounted. That should prevent mice and other rodents from climbing up the wood post to the controls.[113]

To a friend: July 2, 1985

We had a successful opening night, but after the performance all the lights went out on the north side of Santa Fe because,

according to the Electric Company, a rat crawled into a
transformer. Hence the party afterwards was by candlelight,
which was amusing.

Crosby was proud of the wetlands water reclamation project the
opera began to put in place in 1995 so that nonpotable water could be
treated to become greywater, which in its turn could be harvested to
irrigate plantings.[114] The system was completed in 1998, and his obsession continued in a September 24 letter that year about the possible
acquisition of a new 250,000-gallon water tank.

> I have made some calculations on my own on the basis that there
> are 7.48 gallons per cubic foot and that the area of a circle is $\pi r2$,
> and assume the volume would be the area of the circle times its
> height. That indicates to me that a 250,000-gallon tank would
> have to contain 33,423 cubic feet, and if the diameter of a circular
> tank was 50 feet (radius 25 feet) its area would be 4,472 square feet
> [actually 1,963 square feet] and it would have to be 17 feet tall to
> contain 33,423 cubic feet.

Crosby was as concerned with land as he was with water. That was
true whether it was his land, the Opera Association of New Mexico's
property, or land owned by others, when its use interfered with the company operations. He objected strongly when Tesuque pueblo opened its
flea market just north of the opera grounds in the early 1980s. Not only
did trash blow from the market over the opera boundaries, but weekend market-goers would frequently invade the opera grounds to use
the bathrooms or to picnic. He was also annoyed that the flea market
entrance was right next to the opera's northerly main gate rather than
farther up the access road from the highway. He felt the pueblo was
being given a favored nation status that it did not deserve. In 1984, when
he had received Highway Department permission for a south exit road
access, Crosby had had to pay for construction of the acceleration and
deceleration lanes there.[115] "I wish the Highway Department would be
consistent in its approach to the Flea Market and make the Flea Market
build its own proper access," he wrote, in a temper, on February 27, 1984.

John Crosby, showing rare laughter, prepares to cut the twentieth anniversary cake during the company's 1976 season. This also was the year of his fiftieth birthday. Note the flaming sword Crosby holds, as well as the uniformly celebratory expressions on the faces of those looking on. Photograph by Ken Howard. Courtesy The Santa Fe Opera.

To his attorney: February 7, 1984

The matter of the highway signs in the area of the Opera worries me. The present signage is inadequate as a visitor to Santa Fe would have some difficulty finding the opera.

I continue to be sad that we are now identified as a "roadside business" and no longer merit an historical marker on the northbound lane.

I do feel quite strongly that we will have to make an effort to gain the cooperation of the Highway Department and in sufficient time for appropriate new signage to be in place, hopefully during the month of May, so that all this is in order before June when we all become so busy with preparations for the season.

I suppose I sound fussy about this, but we have a great many good tourist visitors coming to us and we do have a pretty fair international reputation, and so I hope these facts can bring us effective and forthright cooperation from the Highway Department, which I would hope would consider us to be an enterprise of real value to the state and the local community.

Crosby's love for the grounds was hands-on. He not only watered trees and flowers himself; he graded the roads himself and plowed them in winter. Only he and a trusted maintenance employee were allowed to use the tractor/grader, which he cherished. In an October 10, 1972, letter, he noted that the current tractor was a blue, new, Ford model and was insistent that it be properly registered—and taken care of with regular maintenance. It replaced a 1963 International Harvester Farmall Club Tractor with accessories that included a hydraulic lift, grading blade or snow plow, furrow plough, sickle mower, rake, and gang mower. (There also was a two-wheeled trailer for transporting the tractor.) That piece of machinery had cost him $1,650 in 1964, and it was used through 1967 mostly to develop the gardens around the ranch and for mowing and grading purposes. After the entrance roadway was paved in 1968, it was used for snowplowing.[116]

In the mid-1960s, Crosby measured out the areas for lawn additions and new buildings meticulously. His dedication to the grassy areas was near fanatical. Then and later, he would often repeat the story of how his parents nurtured the lawns with him "on their hands and knees."[117] He had a preferred mixture of seed to be used when seeding the grounds—clover with grass seed, so that the clover could germinate first and shield the tender grass shoots as they grew.[118] He also could not bear to see a tree want for water or be lost. When an early Opera Guild event entailed cutting down a tree to put up an event tent, he was outraged when he found out about the act.[119] Decades later, when the first special event for an outside group was held at the opera and the caterers scorched a circle in the earth and erected a tent, his rage was Olympian.[120] He displaced his anger onto an innocent staff member, who for several years—while professionally respected—was on the in-deep-trouble list.

Crosby often said he was land rich and cash poor. Certainly the original 615 acres that Crosby Development Company acquired between 1957 and 1964, including the ranch and buildings, represented a major investment that did not yield any return (except for tax relief when Crosby gave acreage to the opera) until the early 1980s, when he sold 138 acres to the developer of what became the upmarket Casas de San Juan subdivision south of the opera grounds. Even Crosby, who was in more than comfortable circumstances, had to plan carefully to meet

various needs. A January 9, 1975, letter notes that he wanted to sell enough of the Tano Road land to provide him and James with approximately $25,000 after the cost of sales. He noted,

> Jim wants to take four months off from teaching this summer to finish some research. He has sufficient funds in reserve from the recent sales to do this, but I think it is best for me to see to it that we keep one year ahead of his needs with real estate sales. . . . For myself, you can tell from the report on my father's affairs that I need to sell land to generate cash to meet Dad's expenses, as I do not have enough income from Opera rents and fees (after expenses) to come up with all of the $25,000 to $30,000 required yearly for Dad right now.

A little later, he wrote to a Santa Fe banker on July 2, 1976,

> For some time I have been thinking about the possibility of developing a good use for the property I own directly south and west of the Opera site. . . . The subject property contains about 500 acres, and there is approximately 2,500 feet of highway

frontage with two access roads to the highway. . . . it has seemed to me that [a] somewhat private condominium/resort project might be appropriate near the highway in a pleasant valley containing about 60 acres. West of that there is another valley with about 40 acres and easy access to the theatre, perhaps suited to summer housing for the apprentices in the opera company. Since I am now 50 years old I would like to have the opportunity to be active in the future plans for this property.

Retired Santa Fe Realtor Dale Scargall recalled a long association with Crosby of more than three decades that began after Aileen and Laurence Crosby died. Scargall found Crosby "inquisitive," "ultra-smart," and always soft-spoken. Their relationship was simple, professional, and for years based solely on handshake agreements.[121] As a client, Crosby knew what he wanted and counted on Scargall to provide it. After the Point properties were sold, Crosby still owned 360 acres of land. Much of it included steep hills and arroyos, but its worth gradually increased over time. He eventually, in 1981, decided to build a summer cabin residence in bottomland to the southeast of the opera complex. Two or three wells were drilled, and water was brought down from the opera pipes. The total cost was $346,708.83.[122] It was about five hundred feet west of the site of a proposed main residence, which was never built. Only after retirement did Crosby build a more formal house, and then on one of the highest points in the Casas de San Juan property. Crosby moved into the cabin, where he spent the summer months, in August 1982; it was sold in March 2000.

To board president: August 16, 1993—via Xerox Telecopier

With reference to your question concerning the square footage of my home in Santa Fe County (Section 26), I am pleased to provide the following information.

Fully built	2,589 sq. ft.
Roofed porch structure	688 sq. ft.
Open Deck:	
Flagstone	68

Concrete	192
Wood	341
	619 sq. ft.

The above does not include the concrete deck around the swimming pool, the swimming pool (40,000 gal.), pool equipment room with wood deck and planters, pool solar collectors, stable, two water well pump pits, one with above ground housing for controls, and over 2,000 linear feet of split fence railing.

Fully built square footage (2,589 sq. ft.) is on concrete footings and foundations, exterior walls are log, roofs are tin (73% of area) and gravel/tar (27% of area). Porch roofs are tin (without) insulation. Interior floors are wood (hemlock) 83%, flagstone, 10% and adobe (7%).

In selling land to others, especially for the Casas de San Juan property, he made sure to maintain control over the ridgetops.[123] He refused to let houses, ancillary buildings, or construction materials be visible anywhere from the opera and thus interfere with the theatrical illusion being produced. "There were markers on the other side of the ridge and we'd have to move them further down to be sure any new construction couldn't be seen," Scargall said. "Finally, some properties ended up almost in the arroyo." That would happen when purchasers would presume that easements and covenants did not apply to them and try to site their houses higher than they should be on the ridge side. Crosby would monitor new construction from the opera balcony and by driving the construction roads. If he discovered encroachments, he would demand that the construction be moved beyond the sight lines. In a letter of March 30, 1988, he commented that since some trees had been cut down to facilitate the burial of a water tank, a house's chimney and TV antenna were now visible from the opera. He wanted to know what steps the Casas de San Juan partnership planned to take in terms of new planting or other efforts "to improve the current situation of the visibility of the building." Crosby also insisted that infills be kept to a modest level—an eight-acre tract could be subdivided into two four-acre tracts, but nothing smaller.

He even kept an eye on what decorative plantings at Casas de San Juan might mean to the opera.[124] In a letter of June 15, 1993, he noted what kind of construction and landscaping was being done at the Casas gatehouse—directly to the south of the opera grounds. Would aspen trees that were being planted around there get their roots into the opera's water main? And what about shade in winter? Even leafless, the trees might cast enough shadow to cause icing on the opera's access road. Besides, the plantings appeared to be overdone. "I am concerned about the amount of water which will be used to maintain these plantings: the Opera really cannot spare much water given current regulations. . . . In any event, when the time comes that the Opera needs to repair its water main and/or the electrical control cables adjacent to the main, the plantings will have to be torn up." He also noted on June 19, 1983, that all other considerations aside, the gatehouse entrance was too narrow for a fire truck, with only six inches clearance on each side. His source for that measurement, he added, was dependable. It was the Tesuque Volunteer Fire Department.

To a correspondent regarding the naming of roads in Casas de San Juan: June 17, 1993

Further to my letter to you of June 11 regarding the naming of the roads which you asked me about in your letter of June 9 may I suggest the following.

The road from near the Casas de San Juan mailboxes to my property could appropriately be identified as "Camino del Valle," which translates as either "road to the valley" or "road of the valley."

I do not find this name listed in the 1993/1994 telephone book Street Guide for Santa Fe.

For the road along the east side of the ridge, and leading to it, I would suggest "Camino de la Sierra," but this name is already in use according to the current telephone book Street Guide for Santa Fe.

Therefore I believe "Camino del Alba" would be very nice, meaning "road of the sunrise," and the word "Alba" in Spanish has many poetic connotations. There is no "Camino del Alba" in Santa Fe according to the current Street Guide. In case you should be questioned, although "Alba" is feminine, the masculine pronoun "del" is used because when the accent falls on the first syllable of a feminine noun the masculine pronoun is used.

I hope you like "Camino del Valle" and "Camino del Alba": certainly the easterly road looks right at the sunrise.

Over the years, Crosby made many gifts of land to the Opera Association of New Mexico, in addition to selling some acreage to the nonprofit from time to time. On November 23, 1976, he proposed making a gift of 11.255 acres to the company for approaching year-end and tax purposes. However, the sale would include a safe easement so that nothing could be built on the bluff between an existing water tank and his road. "I would like to consider that the area south of my road be kept in its natural condition to enhance the beauty of the entire Opera complex." Three years later, as of August 30, 1979, he was planning to give 12.687 acres of land to the opera. And on December 27, 1985, he made a gift of 11.389 acres of land to the opera, land that had been appraised the previous month at $238,000, or $250,000 less $12,000 that the company had paid to drill and set up a well on the acreage. On September 29, 1975, he wrote in a memo that he planned to sell 26.29 acres to the company for just over $5,789 per acre, for a total of just over $152,000. The sale would take place the next year, and what was the best way to structure it so that he could avoid as much capital gains tax as possible? On March 25, 1983, he noted to his accountant that on December 15, 1982, he had gifted slightly more than 17 acres of land to the Opera Association of New Mexico. As a result of these transactions, by September 20, 1992, the opera owned 155.050 acres of the complex, of which 16.2 undeveloped acres were on the east side of U.S. 84/285, directly opposite the ranch complex and theater. The balance was, of course, on the west side of the highway. "Although portions of this property were acquired at different times and in tracts ranging from 76 acres down to 11 acres, all of the acreage is contiguous."

To a friend: May 25, 1970

Now really! You ought to realize that a simple musician knows nothing about politics, particularly when he is trying to keep an Opera Company operating. However, I am very grateful for your clipping the article which escaped me. Governor Cargo did designate the month of April as "Opera Month" but I didn't note any significant changes on the Balance Sheet of the Association.

Circa 1965, John Crosby labors at The Santa Fe Opera in jeans and sneakers, while Donna Quasthoff's monumental sculpture of Orpheus and Eurydice looms over him. This photo appears to have been taken during the theater remodel after the 1964 season. Photographer unknown. Courtesy Gene Kuntz.

To return for a moment to the concept of land rich and cash poor, the files do not back up Crosby's assertion of this condition. He was not immensely wealthy, but his financial situation would seem like riches to many. In April 1988, he owned assets of $757,518 with liabilities of just $34,685, so his liquid net worth was $722,833.[125] Fixed assets included his Santa Fe property of 275 acres, plus his cabin residence, together valued at $3,250,000; the New York brownstone, $1,275,000; and an annual gross income of $185,000. He projected his annual expenses at $175,000, but at least 50 percent of this comprised monies he expended on behalf of the opera and for which he could expect reimbursement.

Five years later, per his federal income tax return, Crosby's income had gone up. His professional income in 1993 was $204,843, of which $144,500 was allocable to New Mexico and $60,343 to New York. He also anticipated $22,540 in municipal bond interest.[126] He continued to acquire real estate:[127] in 1995, he bought a Canyon Road residence in Santa Fe on an 11,500–square foot tract, with a two-bedroom residence of about 1,400 square feet and a detached guest house of about 480 square feet. The price paid was a quarter of a million dollars on mortgage.[128]

In a memo of September 5, 1995, Crosby's revised statement of income showed a gross income of $444,775 after adjustments (including contributions to his retirement plan), yielding a taxable income of $334,106, which included $203,739 in capital gains. He estimated all taxes owed at $110,051.24—33 percent of his taxable income. By the time of his death, his net worth was easily close to if not more than a million dollars.

Finance versus Fancy: Keeping The Santa Fe Opera Solvent

His desk is immaculate. Except for the ledger, a few sharpened pencils and the overflowing ash tray, its icy surface gleams undisturbed. For years a small embalmed mouse, memento of Crosby's boyhood, crouched at the desk's edge, nearest the visitor. Recently it has disappeared. "I have a good time with my balance sheets," Crosby likes to say, whereupon the ledger is opened, and spread wide across the desk. "Financing can be ever so fascinating," he murmurs, staring without expression at the array of figures.[129]

John Crosby loved figures, for he could trust them implicitly. They always lined up accurately, never went back on him, and even if they offered a negative number, they still could be trusted. And when it came to figures and spending, Crosby was parsimonious. He laid out his annual estimates—the word *budget* was anathema to him[130]—on big spreadsheets with only a pencil and a calculator for help. He wrote every number carefully in its place in his tight, barely legible handwriting. Once approved by the executive committee and the board—a foregone conclusion—the numbers seldom changed. He had little patience with those unwilling to use their minds rather than machines. When staff members grumbled about not having enough calculators to go around, he sent a tart memo pointing out that people could pick up a pencil and use it on paper, just like he did.[131]

No number escaped his ken. Legend is truthful when it claims he knew how many spools of thread were bought for the costume shop and how much they cost, how many board feet of lumber went into the original theater, and how many tons of concrete were poured for the 1968 and 1998 houses.[132] He knew how much was saved by removing buttons from a set of costumes after one season and then reusing them the following summer. The amount saved might have been six dollars or so, but for Crosby, money saved in any amount was desirable and even pleasurable.[133] He kept the information in his spreadsheets, on his famous yellow pads, and in reports—but mostly in his head, in an achievement that suggests an autistic (certainly not idiot) savant ability. Asked years after an event how much something had cost, he could have an answer within seconds. He was equally fluent when it came to ticket sales figures, donation histories, and all income projections.

As obsessive as he was about money, Crosby never minded spending up to the limit of his estimate to get good results or investing capital sums where they would do good. But woe betide someone who spent money he felt was unnecessary. On June 5, 1996, he wrote about a *Madame Butterfly* production whose director had decided, late in the rehearsal process, to open the back of the stage for act 1 instead of leaving it closed as planned—which meant more production time and bother. Crosby asked rhetorically,

> Do you recall how I asked for this at the first presentation last summer, and how I was firmly told by [the director and designer] that it was not appropriate? Obviously I am very happy now that Act I will be open, but disappointed that we have to take the time and money to do this now, since we asked for it a year ago and were refused.

He further groused that a beautiful table for act 2 was being scrapped because it did not suit the height or figure of the leading lady, when the company had known for a full year who was going to perform the part. Speaking of that season's production of *The Rake's Progress*, he said, "At least Baba will come in on a sedan chair and not on a donkey. . . . I believe I will have to become more forceful at the beginning of the design process to avoid these unnecessary problems."

In the early years of the company, Crosby monitored matters so closely that he hesitated to let the rehearsal department or the apprentice artist program coordinator use the photocopier very often, because it cost five cents a page per copy. Instead, the complicated rehearsal schedule had to be typed up in multiple copies for posting and distribution every day.[134] Crosby refused to consolidate operatic acts to make evenings shorter for audiences, not only because he wanted to make sure the orchestra and singers had adequate rest between acts but because it would cut into bar sales revenue.[135] He knew about every penny that came in or went out.

Crosby was meticulous about paying people on time whenever possible, including local vendors. If the season ended with a shortfall of cash, he would send out dignified letters to those holding account balances, asking for more time to see the payments through. During the 1970s, dealing with accounts payable, Crosby and two associates would set up a production line in the business office.[136] Crosby would type a check with its double carbon slips, one yellow, one pink; the check would be put through the imprinter; Crosby would sign the checks; the different carbons would be separated from the check; and the original would be put in an envelope for mailing. The yellow carbon was filed with the original invoice, by account; the pink copy was filed by check number. When everything that could be paid at that point was paid, the session was over—usually in a matter of thirty or forty minutes. Crosby's omnipresent cigarettes would be smoking away, one often dangling out of a corner of his mouth, during the entire process.

For all his persnickety attention to monetary detail, Crosby was a fair man. In an October 31, 1973, letter, he discussed how much firewood would be needed at the ranch that winter to supplement the heating system for the offices and for the staff members who lived there during the off-season. The letter documented his decision that he and two other employees would each pay for a cord of wood, and the Opera Association of New Mexico would pay for three. The equation was based on the amount of wood each person or entity would consume; the letter is a masterpiece of simplicity and egalitarianism.

To a correspondent: June 9, 1995

Thank you for your advice concerning the plans of the New Mexico State Legislature Professional Tax Study Committee.

I have some difficulty understanding the logic that the Opera or the local symphony orchestras compete with motion picture theaters. The motion picture industry is, generally speaking, a highly profitable industry.

Annual earned revenues of the Opera provide only about sixty percent of annual operating expenses. The difference is provided by contributions and grants. If the Opera passed the cost of the gross receipts tax on to the ticket buyer, the Opera would have to consider some restructuring of ticket prices in the future.

I do not know what the tax rate might be, but for estimating purposes $4.5 million of earned revenue should be considered, and the effect of a gross receipt tax on that revenue would have to be offset by increased private contributions.

In another example, he was minutely careful from the very beginning of how much to reimburse cast members for transportation expenses. In 1961, he paid $100 per week during the season for each company dancer, plus air transport from New York to Santa Fe.[137] Two weeks of rehearsal were paid at $75 per week. The European tour that year paid $100 per week for the dancers, as well as transportation, lodging, and sustenance, per the AGMA contract. In 1962, pay for the dancers was up to $110 per week for both rehearsal and performance weeks. In addition, transport was reimbursed to $190 for Air Tourist Class New York–Albuquerque–New York. Female dancers were reimbursed for the weight of one makeup kit and one pair of dance slippers, an estimated weight of seven pounds, at $.64 per pound.

One area in which Crosby was slow to acquiesce because of both financial and artistic considerations, but to which he eventually became committed, was that of projecting simultaneous English translations of opera libretti for the benefit of the audience. As early as 1989, when many houses were using surtitles, he pointed out to a correspondent that The Santa Fe Opera offered special challenges to surtitles above the stage because of the house's construction.[138] He noted, "At the present time we are playing to sold out houses for most of our season, so, given human nature, there has not been an urgent need in mind to undertake somewhat costly projects to increase audiences, since we really cannot increase attendance. Good subtitles are costly to prepare and to present, and we would never want to think about an inferior system or operating plan." He added that, in his opinion, surtitles in the current house would only be workable for people in the balcony due to the ceiling slope, but noted that the balcony contained just one fifth of the audience, or 21 percent.

But on October 24, 1992, he noted to a correspondent, "We are looking into some new technology which may be available in the not-so-distant future and which would provide optional viewing of translations on a seat by seat basis. If this technology appears feasible it will in all likelihood be incorporated into plans which we are considering for various renovations to our theatre."

This finally came about in 1999, when seat-back translations became available at every seat in the theater. Crosby was as meticulous in this project as in any other, wanting to make sure that the screens would only be viewable by each audience member, so that the theater would not present, especially from the rear, the impression of a drive-in movie theater with cars hooked up to lighted speakers. He wrote to a donor to that system on July 6, 1998,

At last we have opened the season and the theater is finished save for some minor details. From all we have heard, the public likes the new building very much, and there seems to be a general enthusiasm for the Opera. The fund for the Electronic Libretto System is now nearing $1.4 million. $225,000.00 of that sum has been allocated by donors for the endowment of the operation of the system. . . . It seems that we should be able to complete the funding for this project if not by December 1998, at least by the spring of 1999. Your leadership gift for this has been vital to the success of the program.

Given how successful The Santa Fe Opera is today, those earlier struggles might seem petty in comparison to current revenue and expenses. But without the founder's committed control, the company would not be here today. By being a penny-pincher, he made the company sustainable—and his predecessors have followed that precept faithfully.

CHAPTER FOUR

A Successful Run

To a staff member: December 21, 1989

I know I must be a nuisance to you about things like the following so I shall be most very grateful to you for your kind attention at the appropriate time to the following request.

At such a time as you shall be ordering new stationery (letterhead) for our offices at Santa Fe and New York would you kindly change the word "FAX" to "TELECOPIER."

As the word "telecopier" has one more letter than the word "telephone" this means that the line with "telephone" will have to be moved one character space to the left so that the numbers for the telephone and the telecopier are lined up.

In the case of some of the New York stationery there are parentheses around the numbers 212 for the telecopier but not around those numbers for the telephone, so we should make that consistent, with both with, or without, parentheses.

I note some of the Santa Fe office letterhead now has the text "TELEFAX" but to be just right the correct word is indeed "telecopier."

The Man and the Myth

As an adult, John Crosby stood about five feet eight inches tall and was height-weight proportionate for much of his life, until he became more chunky with increasing age.[1] His blue eyes peered out from behind glasses early on, and he used the spectacles as shutters to hide behind, or as barriers to communication. Looking blankly out from

After the 1967 fire, John Crosby's hair began quickly to be peppered with white. Here, looking handsome in a white sweatshirt and with a concentrated stare, he rehearses the orchestra circa 1970. Photographer unknown. Courtesy The Santa Fe Opera.

the wall of the frames was a favorite trick of his. He was unconventionally handsome in his youth, with regular but not perfect features, but he was certainly attractive enough to cause flutters in many feminine hearts during the early years of planning for the opera.[2] Later he became rather more interesting looking than comely. He assumed the mantle of distinction early on, especially when in his conducting gear. In later years, his bearing was measured and magisterial. His hair was dark and curly when he was a young man but began to turn white early, after the theater was leveled in the 1967 fire.[3] In his forties and early fifties he was attractively salt and peppered. Eventually he was snow peaked.

Crosby took frequent exercise most of his life.[4] He learned to ice-skate in his youth and did so often. As an adolescent he was a fearless soccer player. He loved to swim, whether in pools or the ocean or a lake or a cove. When he was in New York, he faithfully swam at least three times a week at the University or Yale Clubs, often for an hour or an hour and a half, followed by a good sauna sweat.[5] On vacation in Jamaica, he water-skied, including learning to manage on one ski.[6] He learned horsemanship as a boy and rode whenever possible for years to come.[7] (The company grounds included a stable at the lower north end in the earlier years.[8]) But he was a conscientious horse owner. He did not like to take on more animals than he could comfortably accommodate or more than he could adequately exercise.[9]

To friends: April 26, 1969

You have done so many kind things for so many persons, and I am very grateful to be one of those. The kindest, for me, was the matter of the vacation, which was completed at Ocho Rios, Jamaica, March 23–April 7, adding fifteen days to five at Cape Cod in September and eight at Ocho Rios in December/January for a total of 28 = 4 weeks.

Thanks to you, I have found a remarkable place (Ocho Rios) where the only music is far different from opera; and nobody there knows the meaning of that word. Also, a new sport—water skiing, which IS masterable at age 42 on one ski with the assistance of two jet-black instructors of unusual capability named Cecil and Mitch. Either one would make you shudder playing the executioner in "Salomé," but we won't try to import them.

In the mix of genealogy and personalities that defined him, he could be intensely loyal to those loyal to him, but he also could be a good hater and could cherish rancor. Most vital to him was truth. He believed he was absolutely truthful in his dealings with others and expected the same from everyone—even if, at times, he found it irritating to hear. And yet, also at times, he was happy to have yes men at his beck and call.[10]

Donald Gramm, far right, and John Crosby, second from right, with two friends, presumably participants in the Apprentice Artists Program, 1976. Photographer unknown. Courtesy The Santa Fe Opera.

John Crosby riding, ca. 1980. Note the foal following on a leading string. Photograph by Michael Salas. Used by permission.

Crosby had few notable sensual indulgences that could be called bad habits. He did partake heavily of spirits, which was the custom of his time; friends of the early company years recalled regular parties at which potent highballs and drinks on the rocks were consumed in tremendous quantity.[11] He drank Scotch in his younger years, then switched at some unknown date to vodka, "with no junk in it." One of his favorite sayings was "just a thimbleful of Scotch"—but he possessed pewter jiggers made to look like thimbles that would hold an astonishing amount of liquor.[12]

To call him a heavy smoker would be an understatement. Cigarettes and Crosby went together like operatic music with a libretto. He smoked menthol cigarettes when younger; Dorals, by one account, which he kept by the carton in the ranch house refrigerator.[13] Marlboro Lights 100s were his indulgence of choice later on.[14] He realized how gripping his habit was. On the way to his father's funeral, he gave his cigarettes to a colleague so he would not find himself reaching for them in the midst of the service.[15] He chain-smoked in rehearsals, although not during performances,[16] and always when in his office or in meetings. In any informal photograph of him, he would virtually always be caught with a cigarette in hand or mouth. He got through several packs a day at the least. (Interestingly, no one asked could say how many; his regularity made counting pointless.) He was generally surrounded by a haze of cigarette smoke.

To staff: June 2, 1981

It seems to me that it will be helpful if we can give our nice, new canteen management some suggestions and hints about menus and serving procedures.

Frankly, at this time I am inclined to feel the service and menus are a little on the drab side, but I am sure some hints from you can change this.

Regarding service: a little better display of available items will help, and, connected to menus, perhaps not such a great variety as shown on the sign at the left of the counter. In this connection, perhaps the old blackboard (with chalk writing) might be more attractive and "daily specials" could be highlighted.

Service will soon have to be faster: certainly by June 11th when as many as sixty more lunch customers will be arriving, and to a great degree, all at one time (whenever a chorus rehearsal ends before lunch time).

Regarding menus: basic additions such as lemonade are needed daily, and perhaps also fresh baked cookies.

How about suggesting some weekly cycle of daily specials:

1. Roast (or broiled) chicken parts
2. Hamburger/Cheeseburger
3. A nice cold cut spread
4. Attractive wieners on a bun
5. A curry dish—rice/lamb
6. A good chef's salad, one with anchovies/scallops and one with ham/chicken.

Of course the above weekly special proposal is just off the top of my head and can undoubtedly be improved.

There should also be, along with the daily specials, some fixed (or semi-fixed) alternatives such as a fruit salad on a constant basis.

All of the above needs revision and adjustment, and further thought has to be given to quick dispensing of condiments (mustards, etc.).

Regarding service, the staff at the canteen must realize they will have sudden peaks (per rehearsal schedules).

Finally, we must bear in mind that the canteen needs to achieve a certain high usage in order to break even or just sustain tolerable losses. If attractive lunches are not produced, I feel that a number of company personnel will start bringing their own box lunches, which will contribute to the increase in our losses.

When it came to food, Crosby was abstemious.[17] He ate well but moderately, preferring standard fare such as meat and potatoes and vegetables—a roast, lamb chops, turkey on Boxing Day. He liked Häagen-Dazs's rum raisin ice cream, and lime sherbet. For lunch alone or with one other person, he preferred sandwiches for both convenience and calorie control. His letters contain a number of references to shopping lists for his housekeeper or assistant, and these include delicatessen meats, cheeses, lettuce, tomatoes, and other sandwich materials; he had meats and eggs delivered in New York by a trusted butcher. He liked good coffee and was not unamenable to fine wines with dinner.

```
To his housekeeper: October 4, 1999

I will come to New York Thursday evening, October 7th,
arriving at the house around 9:00 p.m. Please kindly shop
for the following items October 7th.


2 quarts orange juice
1 loaf Peppridge (sic) Farm bread—white
1 lb. butter
1 jar marmalade
1 Boston lettuce
2 tomatoes
2 avocados
fresh fruit
small packet of Brie
1 pt. Half & Half cream


I will telephone the butcher . . . and arrange for him to deliver
some meat and eggs Thursday between 10:00 a.m. and 1:00 p.m.

To a New York store: April 13, 1993

Enclosed please find my check in amount $558.74 in payment of
your statement of March 31, 1993.
    Please correct the charge of $25.70 March 24 which reflects:

1/4 lb. Prosciutto   $ 7.95
1/4 lb. Bologna        4.80
1 SL Calf's Liver     12.95
                     $25.70

The "1 SL Calf's Liver" was one slice of Calf's liver weighing 1/4
lb. for which you have charged me the rate for one pound. . . .
Please reflect the appropriate credit on your next statement.
```

Crosby's low, tight-mouthed, quiet voice was unmistakable across the entire campus and in virtually any overheard conversation. He spoke very softly, from temperament and training, and also to make people focus on what he was saying. Often staff members would find themselves straining to catch his words, not daring to ask him to repeat himself or speak up.[18] He would bid anyone—an employee or board member or friend—good morning or good evening in a near-mutter. He once expressed condolences to a singer who had been ill by whispering in her ear—not only for privacy, but because he preferred it.[19] He once told a joke to a staff member in the Opera Club while standing by her, not looking at her, and speaking as softly as any operatic confidant.[20] When angry he would still seldom let his voice become very loud—when it did, it was like the cannon going off in *Tosca*, company lore has it—although he might take to repeating phrases over and over for emphasis.[21] Yet he could at times be even boyishly boisterous. Dining at a staff member's one night, he was excited when the pilot light on the floor furnace went out and he had an excuse to play with the machinery. "Let's go light it!" he exclaimed in pleased tones, grabbing up matches and a flashlight and burrowing into the crawl space in his standard white pants and bush shirt.[22]

To technical production director: July 27, 1989

I think it is fair to state that anyone exercising a modest mental effort would realize that you record Act I on one tape and combine Acts II and III on another tape, rather than persisting to do it the other way around with continually incomplete recordings. I find no excuse for this.

Crosby's moods and temper are legendary, and it has proven difficult to separate fact from apocrypha. On the credible side of the ledger are several early instances, both in New York and Santa Fe, in which he invited people to dinner or went to a party, only to disappear suddenly and not reappear.[23] His later explanation was that he had not felt welcome, that he was not wanted, and that he should leave. In one Santa Fe case he did show up later that evening, three sheets to the wind and with broken bones in a hand after smashing it into a kitchen cupboard at the Ranch.[24] One longtime company designer reported three instances of notable encounters during the 1972 season, including one instance of Crosby pushing the man through a screen door, one case of Crosby breaking a car window with his fist, and another of him physically throwing someone off the ranch premises. At a later time, when the name of a staff member with whom Crosby had a love-hate relationship came up in conversation, he screamed, "That bitch!" and threw a crystal ashtray across the room against a wall. And in a *New Yorker* Profile, he admitted to having put his hand through a wall at one time.[25]

These occurrences appear to have fallen off sharply as Crosby became older. Charles MacKay himself never saw or heard of Crosby striking anyone, although, during MacKay's earlier years at the opera, from 1968 on through 1979, "from time to time there were doors slammed. But his demeanor would change [after a tantrum] and he would be conciliatory in his behavior to that person. It wasn't spoken, but it was conveyed that he wasn't mad anymore, that kind of thing."[26] Among those few who could reprimand him and bring him out of a tantrum or a blue funk were Richard Gaddes; the acclaimed pianist-conductor-composer Earl Wild, who knew him from his earliest New York years; an occasional tough board president; and composer John Kander, who had been at Yale with him.[27]

With all his temperament, Crosby, as has been noted, was "enormously shy," MacKay said. "It was a strange dichotomy. He was very, very shy, yet he put himself in the spotlight on the podium and was head of a very important opera company. He saw himself as a crusader, someone who took his role seriously and took himself seriously. John would talk about himself in the third person. 'John Crosby should not be subjected to this,' or, 'So and so should not speak to John Crosby in this manner,' or, 'John Crosby should be treated better.'"[28]

Brad Woolbright noted that "John was not a yeller. You could tell he was extremely angry as a result of a combination of his words, or sometimes he'd get red in the face. In some incidents, he would continue to repeat a remark."[29]

John Crosby, left, and Richard Gaddes share a smiling moment during an orchestra rehearsal in 1994. Photographer unknown. Courtesy The Santa Fe Opera.

In the 1970s and early 1980s, John Crosby was a major fitness buff. He often stood on his head, claiming it promoted clear thinking and relaxation. Photograph by Michael Salas. Used by permission.

Crosby's temper often flared over artistic matters with which he disagreed—especially because he generally worked on two operas at once, the opening comedy or tragedy and the season's Richard Strauss offering, and therefore was not fully in touch with how rehearsals for the other three repertoire works were going. He had seen and passed the set and costume and lighting designs at least a year before, of course, but things don't always come together on the stage exactly as planned. Sometimes he would come to a first piano dress rehearsal and, expressing annoyance at what he saw given all the money in the budget devoted to this production, he would exclaim, "Now look at this!" At that point, letters would begin flowing from his office to the director and often the designers, expressing concern or, in some cases, annoyance or downright anger. It would be frustrating and confusing for those creative personnel, who were simply trying to mount the best possible production.[30]

The memory of Hans Fahrmeyer—onetime company photographer and recording engineer, as well as companion and friend of Crosby's—was that "he was never happy with anything. I never heard him say, 'This was perfect.' You could not tell from his facial expression if he ever enjoyed anything. He loved his work, but there was a misery with it included."[31]

Crosby always had a certain reticence, although he could let his guard down. He might ask a cast member who addressed him as "Mr. Crosby" to "call me John." But years later, when waiting in a doctor's office, a friend saw him flinch when the young nurse called him back to the examining room with a cheery, "John!"[32]

To his attorney: July 21, 1983

I shall appreciate your candid opinion as to whether (a critic's) statement that the director, designer and conductor of "Arabella" are "pimps" gives any ground for action within the accepted definitions of either libel or slander.

It is possible that either the director or designer, or their representatives, may be asking me about this, so it could be helpful to me to be prepared.

Crosby preferred not to indulge in discussions about, or diatribes against, critics. He said he preferred not to read their comments, because they so often disagreed.[33] He did tend to harbor resentment against local critics, however. He referred once to a Santa Fe writer who was "A difficult man to deal with. . . . He has given our house staff problems at the Theater on occasion including, I am told, when under the influence of liquor, and at one of those times it is said he ejected the contents of his stomach by mouth in the public area flower beds."[34] On August 25, 1988, he wrote to John Moriarty at Central City Opera, noting, "I am sorry that you have such an uncalled for problem with the local critic, and believe me, I know from experience how frustrating that can be and how detrimental it is. . . . I suppose it is just wishful thinking to believe we will ever have a really responsible level of music criticism in the Press." Not only locals came in for his displeasure. Once, when angry with the distinguished critic Martin Bernheimer, he sedulously avoided him for a number of seasons. Even when he and Bernheimer accidentally collided and slipped on wet concrete one night, both falling down, Crosby picked himself up, looked through Bernheimer without a word, and stalked off.[35]

To a press agent: February 11, 1980

This is just to report on the interview with (a writer), last Saturday, 3 PM to 5 PM. . . . (He) asked me how I felt about criticism in the press, particularly about me. I tried to hold the line that I believed critics' opinions were their personal opinions, and finally I tried to prove that by showing him a few copies of some reviews of my performance. These were conflicting reviews of the same performances. Amongst these, I showed him the three of "Butterfly" at City Opera (Times, News, Post), where one critic had said it was full of passion and another critic had said it was like chamber music.

Crosby always was careful of appearances and behavior at the opera by everyone. He wrote the then press officer on July 1, 1996, to ask if it were true that a photographer for a prestigious national magazine "appeared to be under the influence of alcohol during the latter part of the evening, June 28, and just prior to or after her unauthorized appearance on stage."

At that, Crosby seemed to have problems with photographers in general over the years, until Fahrmeyer became established in the 1980s. Once the company's press representative had set up a story in a major magazine that sent a photographer to get an atmosphere shot of

Crosby in his surroundings. When the employee went to get him, she found him seated in his office dressed in a double-breasted blue jacket, with a crisp white shirt and tie beneath. To her invitation to come up to the Opera Club for the photo session, he said, "No. We're going to photograph here." She pointed out that the operatic setting as seen from the club was just right, a perfect portrait of his success and years of achievement. Crosby again declined. She persisted. Finally he stood up, fuming but without a word, to be revealed wearing shorts and his trademark espadrilles. The session was not pleasant for anyone except possibly the maestro, and the photographer remarked that it was a good thing he had war zone experience. The press representative took him (and herself) out for a much-needed drink.[36] Another press officer has told the story of how one took a photograph of Crosby in his later years. The photographer would set up, and then Crosby would be invited to attend. He would walk into the room, through the room, barely pause, and then walk on out.[37]

Among Crosby's few closer friends was Brigitte Lieberson Wolfe, known professionally as Vera Zorina, and her husband Goddard Lieberson, president of Columbia Records. (Her first husband was choreographer George Balanchine.) Crosby's love for her went back to the Stravinsky days, when she starred in *Perséphone*, portrayed the title role in Honegger's *Joan of Arc at the Stake*, and also directed several productions in Santa Fe. After Lieberson's death, Brigitte married Paul Wolfe, who worked with Crosby at the Manhattan School of Music. At a big cocktail party before one opera season opened, Wolfe recalled, Brigitta was sitting in the living room of the house. Crosby came in and the pair remained alone for some time. They were preparing to go outdoors to join the party when Zorina suddenly said, "You know, John, I love you." He replied, "You know, Brigitta, I love you too." And they both then fled the room in different directions, as if the revelation had been too much to bear.[38]

Crosby was not lacking in personal courage. In the earlier years of the company, he faced down and chased off a large group of motorcyclists who had come onto the grounds during a performance and were revving their engines in competition with the music.[39] He could deal with angry members of the public with no sign of fear. One night, a member of the audience who had dined far too well made a ruckus down front in the orchestra. He was escorted out to the parking lot, where he became obstreperous with the parking lot supervisor, who had security experience, and the cadre of young and fit parking attendants. Crosby had been observing the encounter. He came up to the group and said to the man, with authority, "You will never enter my house again."[40]

His most notable encounter with trouble came on March 27, 1984, when two burglars gained access to the East 63rd Street brownstone at night by opening a second-floor bathroom window.[41] (This followed on minor burglaries in 1981 and 1982 when no one was on the premises.) Crosby was in his bedroom on the fourth floor, spending a night at home, reading. When he heard the sounds of entry, he turned on the landing light and called out, "I'm up here on this floor." The revelation made sense in that there was only one exit in the brownstone, the front door, and letting the burglars be surprised when they found a resident would not have been prudent.

The two robbers were professionals, after loot and with assault the last thing on their minds. They tied Crosby up with phone cord and proceeded to rifle the house, stealing stamps, money, jewelry, and a silver cigarette case—perhaps even the one the board had given the founder after the European tour. They then calmly took his fine luggage, filled it with his silver dinner service and other silver pieces, left the house, and hailed a cab.

At this point, the story turns into comic opera, since no harm had come to Crosby. He managed to extricate himself from his bonds and called the police. In the meantime, the two burglars decided they were hungry after their exertions and asked the cab driver to take them someplace where they could eat. Suspicious at seeing what clearly were second-story men with heavy luggage out on the street at night, he drove them to a cafe in the Bronx where he knew policemen, including plainclothes officers, congregated. When the robbers went into the café the driver called the police, who arrested the miscreants. The next day Crosby got a call in the afternoon that his goods had been recovered, and he went to the precinct station in the Bronx to pick them up. He rewarded the attentive cabbie generously.[42]

John Crosby and his father, Laurence Crosby, enjoy the sunshine at the Opera Ranch around 1973. During the years when Laurence lived at the opera, from January 1972 through his death on January 2, 1980, he was a beloved figure on the campus, although his increasing mental confusion caused a number of minor and major contretemps over the years. Photo by Al Cabal. Courtesy The Santa Fe Opera.

The Creative Crosby: At the Shrine of Strauss

When it came to the operas of Richard Strauss (1864–1949), John Crosby was both an arms-carrying champion and a humble suppliant. He studied the opera scores intensively and knew every detail of any Strauss work he conducted, from orchestration and libretto history to performance history and anecdotes. He treasured the composer's writings and often humorous conducting hints, including the English translation of Strauss's *Recollections and Reflections*. He owned many works by and about Strauss, including the opera scores, the orchestral and solo vocal works, and scholarly studies of the composer's music. He delighted in gifts such as Strauss music manuscripts, autographs, and documents.[43]

Crosby was also an eager auditor of any biography, article, or review about Strauss. He would discuss the composer with anyone who shared his love. Such discussions were one of the few things that could lift him from one of his infamous dark-browed spells of silence. Delving into stories of specific performance occurrences, generational performance practices, and score errata delighted him. And he constantly evaluated his own work in Strauss by listening to his own Santa Fe Opera performance recordings. One of his favorite places for this study was poolside at his beloved cabin, with the sounds he loved filling the landscape. He also would listen to recordings of Strauss by noted conductors.[44] All was fuel for his steadily burning Straussian fire.

This lifelong dedication began when Crosby was about twelve and bedridden for several days with a sinus infection. The New York Philharmonic was broadcasting by radio a live performance of the Strauss tone poem *Tod und Verklärung* (*Death and Transfiguration*). "John said it was an epiphany for him. He had not heard the music before; he was a kid, you know," said music critic James A. Van Sant. "From that moment on he was absolutely riveted by the idea of Strauss. His mother took him out to a record store and bought him all the Strauss records he could find. He started listening to Strauss then and never stopped."[45]

Crosby went on to explore the composer's entire canon, eventually focusing on the operas as his favorite artistic statements. Crosby's first time actually working on a Strauss opera, as far as is known, was when he accompanied the 1955 *Salome* rehearsal under Leopold Sachse.[46] When it was time to slate repertoire for the first season of The Santa Fe Opera, Crosby had a Strauss canon in his mind for that time and for years to come. The regularity of Strauss mountings shows he had the courage of his convictions, as well as a sublime indifference to others' opinions. As we have seen, Crosby was sure he could train his local audience to love just about any operatic genre, including Strauss—and he knew that sophisticated opera-goers would be drawn to a house that served Strauss rarities as well as standard repertoire.

Events proved him right. Consistent international attention was paid to the near-annual Strauss mountings that Santa Fe devised, and fans of the composer flocked to the opera house. Out of the many seasons under Crosby's baton, only eight, six of them in the 1970s, had no Strauss work in the repertoire. That actually made financial sense. At the time, the company was experiencing six-figure accumulated deficits, and regularly committing funds for a new Strauss production was a questionable business practice. Even during such a dry spell, though, Crosby was undoubtedly considering how to manage future mountings while still keeping Strauss on the boards. As a budget move, he put on the same production of *Salome* five times over a ten-year period, from 1969 to 1979.[47]

Crosby's spiritual dedication to Strauss was selfless, and it was matched by the practical work he put into studying and analyzing the works. He was greatly helped in this by his long and warm friendship with the highly acclaimed American Strauss scholar Bryan Gilliam.[48] Crosby met Gilliam in 1980, when the young man was working in New York on his dissertation on the composer's *Daphne*. Crosby asked Gilliam to contribute program notes for The Santa Fe Opera's 1981 production of *Daphne* and brought him to Santa Fe to give lectures. The professional compatibility grew into a friendship. Gilliam would visit Crosby in New York, and, Gilliam said, "We would talk about things. When he was doing *Die Liebe der Danae* [in 1982] for example, he wanted to know about transpositions, traditional cuts," and other historical and practical information on the massive work.

Gilliam saw Crosby's sunny side. He was one of the few people with whom the founder was always genial and comfortable. "He was always open with me, had a great sense of humor; we could talk freely and openly," Gilliam said. But Gilliam also confirmed what many others said:

> He was very shy, almost painfully shy to some people. Almost unfriendly shy to some people. When I would bring friends who would come to the festival, he could hardly say three words. It always embarrassed me. A friend of mine went and bought him a very expensive bottle of port, and he gave it to him, and [John] said, "Oh, here, I'll have this put away," and handed it to somebody.

Gilliam introduced Crosby to Richard Strauss's familial descendants—the composer's daughter-in-law, Alice Strauss; her sons, Richard and Christian; and their families. Recalling the introduction, Gilliam said,

> I first introduced John to the family in 1982. It was at a nice restaurant, no longer in existence, facing Central Park next to the old Essex House. . . . John ordered two wines: a Chateau

Beycheville and a Chassagne-Montrachet. My wife, John, Alice, and I went with the white Burgundy. The Strauss boys had steak and a Michelob! He was nervous at first, but I told a few jokes and funny stories about my early trips to Garmisch and things relaxed quite pleasantly.

Later on, Crosby visited the Strausses twice at the family villa in Garmisch-Partenkirchen, Germany, in 1986 and 1988. He also corresponded at times with Alice Strauss and her son and daughter-in-law, Christian and Susan Strauss. He wrote Gilliam on October 6, 1986, "Thank you for your letter and your kind encouragement about my calling Frau Dr. Alice Strauss. This resulted in a lovely visit to the Villa September 18th. . . . Frau Dr. Strauss was most kind and showed the house, correspondence, photocopy of the "Helena" partitur (m.s.), etc. Her son Christian joined us with his two boys."

On this particular trip, besides seeing the composer's manuscript of *The Egyptian Helen* in Garmisch, Crosby examined in Vienna the score of that work that had been used by Strauss's disciple and favorite conductor, Clemens Krauss. He told Gilliam in his October 6 letter, the fall after the company's premiere of the piece,

> The adjustments which Krauss made are very striking and have given me quite an unexpected new perception of what one may — or might — do when coming up against troublesome spots in some of the rare works for which there is no tradition. Krauss's changes for Helen and Menelas were numerous, but presumably were needed to make it work for the artists available. More striking however were the changes in the orchestration and dynamics which I assume the composer was aware of since he and Krauss were so close. . . . How I wish I had seen all this before the summer!

Gilliam later facilitated a vacation for Christian and his wife in Santa Fe in 1996, a year the company performed *Daphne*. Crosby had written on February 12, 1995, to Susan Strauss,

> I will certainly let you know if I shall be in Germany next fall, but it looks rather doubtful at this time. We are working on a major

building project at the Opera [the new theater] which keeps me very busy. Please remember me warmly to Dr. Christian. The manuscript which he and his mother gave me is hanging safely under protective glass in my office. It is directly over my shoulder as I write to you now, and so it always reminds me of wonderful visits to your family at Garmisch.

Besides his Vienna and Garmisch visits, Crosby once spent hours in Munich noting "little mistakes" in his score of *Friedenstag* in fall 1988, he said in a letter of May 15, 1989. He noted also therein that the photocopy of a Clemens Krauss orchestral score of *Der Rosenkavalier*, sent to him by the director of the Strauss Institute, contained fifty-eight mistakes in notes or instrumentation in act 1 alone. That delighted Crosby, who always wanted his Strauss knowledge to be up to the latest scholarship and discoveries.

For all his apparent confidence in his ability to delve into Strauss, Crosby was not above admitting to some challenges. He confessed in

Informal maestro: John Crosby shares a joke with soprano Janice Watson and tenor Mark Thomsen during the 1996 production of Richard Strauss's *Daphne*. The photo was, famously, taken at the urging of a press representative, who realized that catching the maestro sitting onstage was a one-in-a-thousand chance. Photographer unknown. Courtesy The Santa Fe Opera.

a May 1, 1987, letter to having "a devil of a time" learning *Die schweig-same Frau* for the upcoming summer. He compared it to a small version of *Die Meistersinger von Nürnberg* and expressed great affection for its perfections and challenges. Crosby especially adored *Salome* and once commented to a cast member, while gazing toward the Jemez Mountains from the back of the stage—and drawing deeply on a cigarette—"A perfect piece. Not a wasted note. A joy to behold."[49]

Crosby loved the Strauss operas because of their richly layered musical fabric, the interplay of instruments and voices weaving into a consuming whole. Gilliam thought the orchestral complexity and theatricality of the works drew him like the vision of an artistic El Dorado.

> It wasn't so much the stories. It was the orchestration, the orchestral complexity, and his love of theater. And Strauss is so theatrical, in certain ways more theatrical than Wagner. You have the complexity in the harmonies and the motivic complexities of Wagner, then you have this kind of Italianate spirit of Mozart. It's kind of Mozart plus Wagner equals Strauss. He loved the complexity and he was a complex person. He knew the scores left and right.

Carolyn Lockwood, who knew Crosby so intimately from her many years as a director and company stage manager, agreed. Crosby loved Strauss's music, she said, "Because it was very much like his own mind. Very convoluted and complicated. Oom-pah-pah didn't do it for him, and he liked the challenge of the difficulties of the piece." (Once during an orchestral rehearsal for *Salome*, Crosby called Lockwood down from the stage to translate an instruction in the score from the German into English. "Because," he told her loudly enough for the orchestra to hear, "They won't believe me, that I can read it."[50])

Yet Crosby could be uncommunicative about Strauss in odd ways. Noted conductor Kenneth Montgomery, who covered Crosby on three different Strauss productions, recalled, "He never discussed how he liked to approach Strauss. He was quiet in rehearsals. You just knew that he had done his homework."[51] And it was presumed that Montgomery, should he ever be called to the podium, would be expected to emulate the founder exactly.

Throughout his tenure, Crosby held everyone up to his own Straussian standard, even if one had to pick it up through observation rather than from instruction. Any rehearsal pianist with less than complete command of the score was justifiably nervous while working on a Strauss opera. If a mistake occurred, some notes were dropped, or the player was not right on the money, he would be taken off the show for a few days until Crosby had gotten over his pique. Once, in a 1992 *Der Rosenkavalier* rehearsal, Crosby murmured to the pianist to follow his beat better. The long-suffering musician growled, "If I followed you any closer, I'd have to climb up. . . ." Before he could complete the sentence with "into your ass," another pianist quietly eased him off the bench and took over playing.[52]

Crosby had the orchestral sound in his mind at all times. Once, in a piano dress rehearsal of *Die schweigsame Frau*, he turned purple and kept hissing to the répétiteur to play softer—"It's too loud!" The pianist couldn't grasp the problem, as he was playing a solo French horn line, one note at a time.[53] Crosby was evidently hearing the actual horn sounds in his inner ear and matching them to his aural understanding and expectation of the score.

When Crosby had a congenial team for the Strauss operas—directors, designers, and singers he knew and trusted, especially the late Swedish director Göran Järvefelt—he was as artistically content as he could be.[54] All were on the same path and could follow his intensity, even if they could not match it fully. So deep was his commitment, though, that if anything went wrong, or if he felt frustrated in his efforts, he could become annoyed and petulant and everyone would suffer, from the cast to the production crew to his companion of the summer. The tempest could well influence his attitude during the entire season.

In point of fact, the Strauss operas were Crosby's temperature and tolerance indicator. He was all or nothing, with *all* the constantly operative word. If things went well, all was sunny. If not, he went looking for trouble and always found it. "He could get very unhappy over Strauss—a singer, a problem," recalled Hans Fahrmeyer. "And if John was upset, the season was hellacious." Strauss singers were not immune to Crosby's disfavor, especially if Crosby could not express his annoyance directly with an offender for some reason. Triangulating his anger, he would vent it on another person. Tenor Darren Keith Woods, now general director of the Fort Worth Opera, recalled the summer of 1993, when he was singing Monsieur Taupe in *Capriccio*. Singers had come up with a term for being in hot water: being "in the tower." At the first rehearsal, Crosby packed Woods off to prison.

> I was the whipping dog, I could do nothing right. . . . The first read-through, John put down his baton and said, "Well, if you sing it like that, you're just going to ruin the opera." Sheri [Greenawald] took me aside and told me, "Sweetheart, this is your summer in the tower. Just suck it up, sing what you know and go home." It was really bad and really cruel.

Virtually anyone could end up on Crosby's bad side. On one subsequently legendary occasion, an apprentice second cover had to hustle onstage in an emergency to sing the vital role of Marianne in *Der Rosenkavalier*, sans proper costume or notice. Understandably nervous and thrown into the part, she did not do well. Crosby sent a memorandum the next day to the rehearsal department and music staff heads, observing that more than two-thirds of the entrances in the part had been wrong. If he was displeased with the apprentice, he was even more upset with those whose job it was to be sure that every role was properly secure, especially with Strauss performances.[55]

Crosby worked hard on Strauss, perhaps harder than on any other composer. He took great pleasure in solving problems associated with the works. Longtime company percussionist Michael Udow said, "He knew the scores inside and out," and Woods characterized Crosby's skill as "backwards and forwards and upside down—and the scholarly stuff he knew!" Crosby insisted on having all the instruments called for in the score, although even Santa Fe's resources could not extend to the pipe organ called for in many of the operas. If special instruments were needed, such as extra-low chimes, which had to be fabricated for *Die schweigsame Frau*, he would take an eager interest in the process.[56] He would rehearse difficult spots over and over, both for his sake and for the orchestra's. He was specific and detail oriented, guided by his intellect and fueled by his heart. His rehearsal technique was staggeringly thorough.

Plate 1. The picture from Laurence Crosby's family passport, dated 1932. John stands between a seated Laurence and Aileen; James stands behind. Courtesy Caroline Crosby.

Plate 2. Aileen and Laurence Crosby on the lawn of their Bronxville, New York, house, probably circa 1956–1957. Aileen wears one of her usual Liberty of London print dresses; Laurence is natty with a bow tie. Note the cigar in his left hand. Photo by Elizabeth "Betty" Crosby. Courtesy the Crosby family.

Plate 3. Opening night, 1957: the entrance of Cio-Cio San and her retinue from Puccini's *Madame Butterfly*. Aileen Crosby's favorite opera, *Madame Butterfly* opened the season each time a new Santa Fe Opera theater was built. Note the oiled redwood stage surround. Photographer unknown. Courtesy The Santa Fe Opera.

(above) *Plate 4.* Just like Uncle John: Lisa Pasto-Crosby poses by The Santa Fe Opera pool with her uncle in 1959. The land beyond them is today filled with rehearsal studios, halls, a cantina, and landscaping. Photographer unknown. Courtesy the Crosby family.

(top right) *Plate 5.* The Berlin poster for The Santa Fe Opera's performances during the 1961 tour. Photographer unknown. Courtesy The Santa Fe Opera.

(bottom right) *Plate 6.* The red Kohler and Campbell piano that Laurence Crosby bought for James and John Crosby. Photograph by Douglas Pasto-Crosby. Courtesy Lisa Pasto-Crosby.

Plate 7. A volunteer fireman hoses down the smoldering structure after the July 27, 1967 fire. Photo by Alan Stoker. Courtesy The Santa Fe Opera.

Plate 8. The second theater rises proudly from the ashes of the first house in 1968, with the soaring line of the loggia and balcony saluting the sky. Photographer unknown. Courtesy The Santa Fe Opera.

(above) *Plate 9. Madame Butterfly* returns: Maralin Niska in the title role and Helen Vanni as Suzuki head Puccini's opera for the opening of the new house in 1968. Photographer unknown. Courtesy The Santa Fe Opera.

(top right) *Plate 10.* Penderecki's *The Devils of Loudon* in 1969 was one the works that buttressed The Santa Fe Opera's international reputation as a house for the new and startling. Photographer unknown. Courtesy The Santa Fe Opera.

(bottom right) *Plate 11.* Kiri te Kanawa made her U.S. debut in 1971 as the Countess in Mozart's *The Marriage of Figaro.* Here she is shown with Joanna Bruno as Susanna. During this summer, te Kanawa was bitten by a feral cat at her home in Tesuque. John Crosby hired a trapper to secure the feline so it could be tested for rabies. Photographer unknown. Courtesy The Santa Fe Opera.

Plate 12. A premiere to remember: Nancy Shade sang the title role in the 1979 American premiere of the recently completed three-act version of Berg's *Lulu*. She is shown here with Barry Busse as Alwa. Photograph by David Stein. Courtesy The Santa Fe Opera.

Plate 13. Ashley Putnam as Danae has been turned to gold by the kiss of Dennis Bailey's Midas in the 1982 *Die Liebe der Danae*. Photo by David Stein. Courtesy The Santa Fe Opera.

Plate 14. Alan Titus and Elisabeth Söderström in one of Crosby's favorite Richard Strauss productions: the 1984 *Intermezzo*. Photo by Michael Rosenthal. Courtesy The Santa Fe Opera.

Plate 15. The second theater in one of its most famous portrayals, 1980. Photo by David Stein. Courtesy The Santa Fe Opera.

Plate 16. A quiet, introspective Crosby stands in front of his creation, 1987. Photo by Hans Fahrmeyer. Courtesy The Santa Fe Opera.

Plate 17. From left, Mikael Melbye's Eisenstein, Robert Galbraith's Falke, and Gimi Beni's Frank share a confused moment in the 1986 *Die Fledermaus* of Johann Strauss Jr. Despite his generally dour aspect in the orchestra pit, John Crosby loved conducting comic opera and often would be in tears of laughter at the dialogue in *Fledermaus* or similar works, such as Emmerich Kálmán's *Countess Maritza*. Photo by Bayard W. Horton. Courtesy The Santa Fe Opera.

Plate 18. Michael Devlin as the Commander and Alessandra Marc as his wife, Marie, celebrate the end of conflict in Strauss's *Friedenstag*. The 1988 production was paired with another Strauss one-act, *Feursnot.* Photo by Murrae Haynes. Courtesy The Santa Fe Opera.

(below) *Plate 19.* A dramatic moment in Richard Strauss's *Ariadne auf Naxos*: Susan Graham's intense Composer confronts Claude Corbeil's supportive Music Master in the 1990 production, one of Crosby's favorites. Photo by Murrae Haynes. Courtesy The Santa Fe Opera.

Plate 20. Crosby leads a 1991 rehearsal wearing his trademark white shirt and trousers. Though his feet cannot be seen, he is probably wearing espadrilles or possibly running shoes. Photo by Hans Fahrmeyer. Courtesy The Santa Fe Opera.

Plate 21. Eric Halfvarson as Morosus is attended by his not-so-silent "bride" Aminta, Erie Mills, lower left, and other cast members in the 1991 production of Strauss's *Die schweigsame Frau*. Photo by Hans Fahrmeyer. Courtesy The Santa Fe Opera.

Plate 22. The opening scene of the 1992 *Der Rosenkavalier* of Richard Strauss: Ashley Putnam's Marschallin embraces Susanne Mentzer's Octavian. Photo by Hans Fahrmeyer. Courtesy The Santa Fe Opera.

Plate 23. Soprano Sheri Greenawald in the famous blue-and-white, dream-landscape 1993 *Capriccio* of Richard Strauss. Photograph by Hans Fahrmeyer. Courtesy The Santa Fe Opera.

Plate 24. Patricia Racette's Violetta and Raymond Very's Alfredo celebrate their love in the 1997 production of Verdi's *La Traviata*. Racette had made her Santa Fe Opera debut the previous year in the world premiere of Tobias Picker's *Emmeline*. Photograph by Paul Slaughter. Courtesy The Santa Fe Opera.

Plate 25. Nancy Zeckendorf, left, and John Crosby open the new 1998 theater. Photographer unknown. Courtesy The Santa Fe Opera.

(below) *Plate 26.* Puccini's *Madame Butterfly* was the inaugural opera in the company's current house in 1998. Here, soprano Miriam Gauci as Cio-Cio San and mezzo-soprano Judith Christin as Suzuki consult together in act 2. Photo by Paul Slaughter. Courtesy The Santa Fe Opera.

Plate 27. John Crosby's beloved cabin was a refuge in a romantic New Mexico setting. Photographer unknown. Courtesy Thomas B. Catron III and The Santa Fe Opera.

Plate 28. Old friends: Thomas B. Catron III and John Crosby in 1999. They had known each other since 1956. Photographer unknown. Courtesy The Santa Fe Opera.

(above) *Plate 29*. John Crosby, center, with soprano Mary Jane Johnson, center right, and the cast of Richard Strauss's *Elektra* on the production's closing night in 2000. Photographer unknown. Courtesy The Santa Fe Opera.

(top left) *Plate 30*. James Crosby and John Crosby at John Crosby's retirement party in June 2000. Photographer unknown. Courtesy The Santa Fe Opera.

(below left) *Plate 31*. Rolling away: John Crosby, cigarette in evidence, as ever, shows James Crosby his beloved Rolls Royce, June 2000. Photographer unknown. Courtesy The Santa Fe Opera.

Plate 32. Christine Brewer, in the title role of Richard Strauss's *The Egyptian Helen* in 2001. This was the last Strauss opera Crosby ever conducted. Photograph by Ken Howard. Courtesy The Santa Fe Opera.

Plate 33. Charles MacKay, who first joined the company in 1968 and went on to work at the Spoleto Festival and then as general director of Opera Theatre of St. Louis, is the company's third general director. Photograph by Ken Howard. Courtesy The Santa Fe Opera.

Plate 34. Richard Gaddes, John Crosby's chosen successor and the second general director of The Santa Fe Opera, took the company in needed new directions after his predecessor's death while remaining true to Crosby's fiscal and artistic administrative principles. Photograph by Doug Marrion. Courtesy The Santa Fe Opera.

Plate 35. Sailing through time: The Santa Fe Opera as success story—thanks to John Crosby. Photo by Robert Godwin, 2010. Courtesy The Santa Fe Opera.

Plate 36. Painter, baritone, designer, and director Mikael Melbye's affectionate 2002 oil painting of John Crosby. It hangs today in the old Ranch Lounge on the opera grounds. Courtesy The Santa Fe Opera.

Others have observed that although Crosby's intellectual command of Strauss was formidable, he was not emotionally spontaneous with the material in performance. He prepared effects in advance rather than being caught up in a performance moment to initiate a heightened musico-dramatic experience. For a Strauss opera during the heyday of his tenure, Crosby insisted on seven to eight orchestra rehearsals, two orchestral Sitzprobes with the entire cast, a piano dress, and two orchestra dresses leading up to opening night.[57] Perfection was his goal.

Over time, he did become freer and more seductive in his work. Many critics agreed that his final *Elektra* in 2000 and his last Strauss conducted with the company, *The Egyptian Helen* in 2001, were finely paced, warmly effusive, and filled with interesting artistic touches. At those points, Crosby seemed at last to be fully in the moment, able to convey the full arc of the pieces.

Crosby wanted his Strauss to be emotionally vibrant and physically cool. Besides generally emulating Strauss's small beat, he spent his career trying to remain cool enough in performance not to sweat. Over time, he became annoyed that he usually had to change his shirt or waistcoat several times a night during performances. After a 1991 concert *Friedenstag* in Holland, mortified that he had perspired heavily during the performance, he didn't want to go to the celebratory party.[58]

Yet Crosby, who was notorious for his emotional reticence, could be amazingly open in Strauss performances. Harpist Danis Kelly, one of Crosby's closest orchestral friends, said, "John loved every note so much. He just oozed the Strauss music. He was so sentimental about the music—you could see tears coming down his face when conducting. Sometimes he got so teary his nose would start running. Maybe he wasn't even aware of it!" The orchestra would concentrate and play away, trying to ignore the maestro's excessive mucus.

To a tenor: May 26, 1965

I have been looking into the matter of the relief you would like from certain performances with us this summer. At the present time, the only solution that I can consider would be to excuse you from all the performances of Elemer in "Arabella" and schedule (another tenor) for that role. . . . I suppose we can

squeeze (him) into your costume for "Arabella" (which has already
been made), but I might have to ask you to help me pushing him
into it.

During Crosby's tenure, the company staged thirty-eight productions, including revivals, of thirteen Strauss operas.[59] There were nine
of *Salome*; five of *Der Rosenkavalier*; three each of *Arabella, Ariadne,
Capriccio,* and *Daphne*; two each of *The Egyptian Helen, Elektra, Die
schweigsame Frau, Intermezzo,* and *Die Liebe der Danae*; and one
each of *Feuersnot* and *Friedenstag*. Every stage work was represented
except the posthumous *The Donkey's Shadow*; the journeyman, less-
than-stellar *Guntram*; and the immense fairy-tale opera *Die Frau
ohne Schatten*, the ultimate litmus test for any company dedicated to
exploring Strauss.

Strauss aficionados always wondered why Crosby never mounted
Die Frau ohne Schatten. It would have made international news, drawn
a large audience of Strauss lovers who had never been able to see it,
and crowned Santa Fe's Strauss edifice with a large jewel. Granted,
the immense piece might have strained even Santa Fe's resources; it
is more often done in huge houses such as the Metropolitan Opera,
San Francisco, Chicago, Covent Garden, or Berlin, where its complicated stage demands can be imaginatively realized. And yet, Santa
Fe had met many other staging challenges. With an inspired director
and designer joining the creative team, the company might have been
able to use intriguing lighting and minimal stage pieces to produce a
persuasive production.

Some critics felt Crosby thought the opera was beyond his skill level
and that he didn't want to embarrass himself by attempting to conduct
it.[60] However, internationally noted opera consultant Matthew A.
Epstein, who has worked closely with The Santa Fe Opera for more
than three decades, disagrees. Crosby felt able to conduct it, Epstein
said, but Crosby the musician was trumped by Crosby the theatrical
seer. He could not satisfy himself that the house could find a dramatically viable way to do the piece effectively within its capacities.
Discussions became fairly concrete three times, including opening
negotiations with appropriate singers, and three times Crosby veered
away. "Talk about a complex score and a complex mind," scholar

Gilliam said. "I would love to have heard him conduct *Die Frau ohne Schatten*. Certainly his *Egyptian Helen* had those qualities."

All of Crosby's Strauss orchestral scores in the opera archives show signs of heavy use.[61] Their bindings are broken, and the scores lie flat. Many pages are tattered and browned from age. Some scores have been photocopied and bound in wire or plastic, presumably for use in rehearsal as well as in performance. Few personal conducting instructions or alerts are written in the various scores. Every now and then, a correction is noted in a part or parts. Some rare notations about a cue are marked in blue or red pencil. Occasionally a series of slanting lines indicates where 4/4 or 2/4 beats should come in complicated or subdivided measures, or a long line is drawn down through the full score to isolate particular passages where extra care had to be taken or where Crosby wanted to separate sections in his mind. English translations are written in here and there, especially in *Ariadne auf Naxos*, where the English version of the entire prologue is written in Crosby's minute hand. String bowings are rare, for he counted on his concertmaster and section chairs to take care of those indications with the players. The scores are for use, not looks; they are not "ornamented."

Crosby made one notable notation about character development in the score for *Elektra*. On the opening page, he jotted Roman numerals indicating the five female servants whose scene opens the opera, and he gave what seem to be numbers indicating the characters' ages. He also had a few comments on character identification and what the musical-vocal aspects of the parts were. The third maid, for instance, he noted as "tough"—the part as well as the character. Epstein noted how knowledgeably Crosby could speak about the casting of those five servants, and the group of arguing Jews in *Salome*, and the happy skat-playing group in *Intermezzo*—small ensembles with difficult music demanding spot-on, alert singers. "It was so fascinating to me," Epstein noted of conversations he had had with Crosby along these lines, "because one learned so much, because of his tunnel vision on those pieces when he was getting ready to do them."[62]

In the front and back of many of the scores, Crosby indicated what sections were rehearsed on certain dates, sometimes over several productions. He also worked his conducting patterns out in advance and, in at least one instance, notated them on paper. In general in the scores, cuts are notated by pasting over the deleted music with blank paper or by folding back the omitted pages.

After the 1984 *Intermezzo*, which he adored, he noted in a pasted-in memo in the score that the opera was fully staged in just four weeks. He credited soprano Elisabeth Söderström's remarkable musical and dramatic abilities as Christine and Alan Titus's careful preparation of Robert the previous year at Glyndebourne as factors in this speed. But with a new Christine, he commented, the company should allow for five full weeks of rehearsal. That was the same production in which Crosby made sure the piano used looked exactly like Strauss's own instrument—the type of detail that was just as important to him as the broad sweep of the music and characterizations being conveyed both vocally and instrumentally.[63]

For all his dedication to Strauss, Crosby never had an easy time with critics in that repertoire. The main complaint was twofold—that his conducting was weak and that he nonetheless insisted on leading all the Strauss himself. Noted music critic Martin Bernheimer once wrote that the maestro "conducted earnestly, with obvious dedication, but without much flair, tension or finesse. Loud is still his favorite color," although he also praised Crosby's "dauntless fervor" when conducting Strauss.[64]

On the other hand, Allan Kozin of the *New York Times* wrote generously of Crosby's final *Elektra* on August 7, 2000. "His devotion to this music and his deep knowledge of it were clearly a motivating force, and the orchestra responded with the lush string textures, burnished brass sound and, most important, the carefully modulated tension that 'Elektra' requires." It was a fine review to climax forty-five years of dedication.[65]

Critics aside, Crosby's devotion to Strauss was widely acknowledged. In recognition of his services to German music, especially Strauss, he received the Order of Merit from the Federal Republic of Germany in 1992. It was one of the honors he expected least and valued most.

The New and Different

When it came to premiering new works, Crosby was avid.[66] The Santa Fe Opera staged numerous works by American composers in the early

A happy-looking John Crosby shows off his Officer's Cross of the Federal Order of Merit on August 1, 1992, at The Santa Fe Opera. Photographer unknown. Courtesy The Santa Fe Opera.

years, including Levy's *The Tower* in the first season; Carlisle Floyd's *Wuthering Heights* in 1958, which Crosby conducted; Berio's *Opera* in 1970; Eaton's *The Tempest* in 1985; Rochberg's *The Confidence Man* in 1982; and the trio of new works by Lang, Picker, and Lieberson in 1995, 1996, and 1997. Also, fairly early on, The Santa Fe Opera turned to European composers for American premieres. Crosby realized that he could publicize his company and his leadership of it by mining the rich vein of composers from elsewhere—including Berg, Hindemith, Stravinsky, and Shostakovich; Henze and Penderecki (who were, at that time, teaching in America); and Aribert Reimann. Crosby also looked to the past for premieres, with good results. When he mounted Cavalli's 1643 *L'Egisto* in 1974, more than forty critics from different publications attended that season.[67] He followed this up with the same composer's *L'Orione* in 1983 and *La Calisto* in 1989, plus a repeat of *L'Egisto* in 1976.[68] The Santa Fe Opera intended to prove that it could manage early operatic works as well as more standard repertoire.

Crosby could be touchy when critics questioned his motives for producing such pieces. He harrumphed in a 1971 interview, "It wasn't to our credit that we produced these works. It was to the discredit of opera in the United States that they weren't being performed other places."[69]

He knew that American opera companies were not always as adventur-ous as they could be—and as Santa Fe had shown it could be.

In terms of American premieres, *Lulu* made a tremendous mark for The Santa Fe Opera in 1963, 1964, and 1974, when it was performed in the incomplete two-act version. In 1979, the work was presented with the completed act 3. In a 1973 program book interview, Crosby said, "We did it by default—no one else had picked it up. The opera was written in the late thirties and had been presented in Europe before the Second World War. It was played fairly regularly in Europe, cer-tainly by the mid to late fifties."[70] It was left to Santa Fe and Crosby to give the American mounting.

Crosby's adoration for modern German works sometimes bore rich fruit and sometimes Dead Sea apples. Failures, at least from an audi-ence viewpoint, included the Zemlinsky-Korngold double bill from 1984; Siegfried Matthus's *Judith* in 1990; and Hans-Jurgen von Böse's *The Sorrows of Young Werther* in 1992. Wolfgang Rihm's *Oedipus* in 1991 had highs and lows. But although many of the contemporary works were "horrible, absolutely horrible . . . they stirred up inter-est. At least everybody would come and listen to it before they ran screaming into the night."[71]

Greater successes were Britten's *Owen Wingrave* in 1973, Janáček's *The Cunning Little Vixen* in 1975, and Ingvar Lidholm's *A Dream Play* in 1998, an American premiere in the current theater. Shostakovich's *The Nose* proved a popular local favorite in 1965 and 1987. Menotti's *Help! Help! The Globolinks* in 1969 and 1970 had a *succès d'estime*. But Stephen Oliver's 1978 *The Duchess of Malfi*, Reimann's *Melusine* in 1972, Nino Rota's *The Italian Straw Hat* in 1977, Kurt Weill's *The Protagonist* and *The Tsar Has His Photograph Taken* in 1993, and Judith Weir's *A Night at the Chinese Opera* in 1989 and *Blond Eckbert* in 1994 have hardly been seen since Santa Fe mounted them. Penderecki's *The Devils of Loudon* in 1969 was a tour de force of a premiere, but his *The Black Mask* in 1988 fell flat. Arnold Schoenberg had two American premieres—*Die Jakobsleiter* in 1968, repeated in 1980, and *Von Heute auf Morgen* in 1980. Brad Woolbright noted, "The repertoire was heavyweighted to a lot of Germanic composers, a lot of productions we got blasted for. However, they kept Santa Fe in the forefront of the operatic world at the time."[72]

The formal maestro: John Crosby in the pit, 1988. Photo by Hans Fahrmeyer. Courtesy The Santa Fe Opera.

Musicianship and Conducting

John Crosby's conducting, whether of Strauss or of any other composer, caused more dissension and discussion during his life than any other aspect of his legacy. It remains a sensitive topic more than a decade after his death. Although critics uniformly and generously praised his work as a founder and creative genius, many were less kind about his stick technique. A positive analysis of a Crosby-led production often had a caveat in the form of a cutting remark about his ability, or inability, to lead performances effectively. Or his work was damned with faint praise. Critics seemed to compete for who could most effectively gut the founder with one hand and bestow laurels with the other. As critic Bernheimer phrased it once, in an August 2, 2000, remark in the *Financial Times*, Crosby was "A first-rate visionary and a second-rate conductor."[73]

Comments were sharp enough when discussing standard repertoire from Puccini or Verdi tragedies to the musical comedy–like realms of Johann Strauss Jr. or Offenbach, but when the topic turned to Richard Strauss, the knives really came out. Crosby's love of Strauss was no excuse for his constantly misusing the master, some felt. Among critics and pseudo-sophisticated members of the public, it became fashionable to say that the only people who enjoyed a Crosby conducting appearance were those who had never been to an opera before or cognoscenti for whom the chance to hear a *Die Liebe der Danae* or a *Daphne* made up for podium shortcomings.

But positive, if not always effusive, opinions were certainly posted during Crosby's tenure, from provincial and local critics to national and international writers. In the first season, *Opera News* praised his leadership of *Butterfly* with the comment that "Crosby's sensitive conducting transformed the well-worn score into something new and poignantly credible."[74] In contrast, a 2000 *Dallas Morning News* critique of Crosby's farewell *Elektra* noted, "Even in Strauss, the most sumptuous of composers, Mr. Crosby has often seemed a lackluster conductor. His gestures Friday night were no more demonstrative than usual."[75] In 1984, the *Los Angeles Times* commented about the Strauss *Intermezzo* Crosby loved so much, saying it "trampled upon the finesse of the score and, in the lofty finale, made vocal life pretty miserable for [Elisabeth] Söderström."[76] Yet the *Washington Post*, in the maestro's farewell season, noted that although Crosby was sometimes "bedeviled by critics for his sometimes dry conducting," he was "leading a chilling performance of *Elektra* that takes the breath away."[77] The variation in commentary goes from the beginning of the company through the founder's retirement.

No conductor ever gets 100 percent raves, and it is no surprise that Crosby was both buffeted and cosseted in the press. Sadly, the buffeting took on his most cherished desire and determination: to be a truly accomplished conductor. He founded his company because he loved to conduct, then bent all his considerable abilities to mastering the craft. It had to hurt when commentators said that The Santa Fe Opera would have been far greater artistically had he settled for being a brilliant business-side leader rather than a pedestrian podium plodder and that even the superb orchestra he had built as a fail-safe could not compensate for his aimless stick technique.

True, Crosby began his operatic work with little formal or even experiential training. When he led the company's first *Madame Butterfly* in 1957, he had worked at the Columbia opera workshop and led various musical shows at Yale, in the army, and elsewhere. He also had accompanied singers at the Juilliard School. But he had never conducted a full-length opera with orchestra at that point. Everyone starts somewhere, but not every aspiring baton master gets to begin his career as chief conductor in all but name, in a theater built by his own family, and with no one to challenge his supremacy. Being born with a silver spoon in his mouth led Crosby to a career with a silver, or at least nicely plated, baton in his hand. He did feel that those fortunate circumstances sometimes led others to undervalue or even denigrate him, not only in the early years but for decades. The implication was that his way had been paved for him, and he could not be taken seriously because of it. Later, his way was paved by his own efforts, and no one would dare take issue with him. He was there, and he was The Santa Fe Opera incarnate.

Looked at dispassionately, Crosby's technique could range from uninspiring to dependably workmanlike; on occasion, it could even reach glowing heights. He planned his effects carefully, drew them out in rehearsal, and relied on his pliant orchestra and understanding casts to follow his spoken and implied desires. Without a doubt, he did get better with time as he became more seasoned. If one conducts more than 580 times over the course of a career,[78] experience alone dictates growing success. Competence through study and rehearsal was his forte, not in-the-moment magic.

The dichotomy is that desired effects in a piece ideally are devised ahead of time, based in and on the score and the dramatic construction of the work. A performance should not be subject to sudden surprises. It should unfurl before the audience as planned, with an added lift due to the presence of a live audience. Its intrinsic excitement comes from a collective, full-bore effort, with each person using all his or her powers to energize a role or function. But it is entirely possible for performers to respond to the inspiration of the moment—those times when puzzle pieces come together so perfectly that things leap to a new and even more persuasive height. At that point, the person in charge of marshaling all the forces, of keeping things in line yet *en pointe*, is the conductor. That is what Crosby could not do. He could be efficient, full-hearted, and wholly focused on the job at hand, but he could not let things reach a speed or flexibility beyond what had been set. The performance fire would be lit adequately enough, but Crosby would snuff out any attempt to turn up the gas under it. Control, not creative fervor, was the be-all. The result under his baton was solid, but it could be stolid. It was often satisfactory, although seldom soul inspiring, and idiosyncratic but not incisive.

Matthew A. Epstein confirmed that The Santa Fe Opera was founded to give Crosby a podium.

> [For] John, of course, at the start of it, the whole reason for building The Santa Fe Opera was that he wanted to conduct. That's the reason. Let's get real here. The vision of it was complete madness, and yet he knew Glyndebourne had happened, and Bayreuth had happened, and therefore the people—if you do something of quality they would come, and John was cultured enough to know what quality was. . . . It's a miracle what he did, but it all stemmed out of his need to be a conductor. He wouldn't have been a conductor if he hadn't founded this company, I don't think. I don't want to speak badly of him, but I don't think that was his genius. His genius was not music making. His genius was everything but.[79]

While those on the audience side of the footlights were often critical of Crosby's baton technique, a gentler and more understanding assessment comes from many of his orchestra members and singers. None claimed he was a great conductor. He was not in the top ten of conductors, nor in the top two thousand, as one singer put it.[80] Yet there is something to be said for basic professional competence, especially in light of his brilliant work with the company itself.

Miles Davis, longtime orchestra principal bass player, commented, "You kind of had to know the tempos and take some responsibility as principal players" to keep a show moving.[81] Seen from the audience, Crosby's beat was essentially small, but it had occasional broad gestures that, technically speaking, meant nothing. At other times, Crosby's movements looked as though he were sloppily chopping ham. Famed conductor Edo de Waart noted, "He was not, I think, a natural—what shall I say?—inspiring conductor in the sense that he could let go. I think there was much more inside of John than he could ever show, because when he talked about music, it was so thoughtful and so warm."[82]

"In the pit, I always had the feeling he worked very hard at it," recalled Sheri Greenawald, a frequent colleague. "Once he developed what he needed to do for himself, there wasn't a ton of flexibility between the stage and the pit. He was leading the band, and you needed to fit into the band. He would listen to you in early rehearsals, you'd take a breath here and there, and he would listen to all that. But once it was established, you hit those marks or else."[83] One bass-baritone who worked with Crosby often in the early years said, "It was hard to [express] animation onstage because his conducting arm was very spaghetti-like. In *Fledermaus*, his arm would be going like he was conducting 'Ombra mai fu' [of Handel]."[84] A brass player in the early years of the company thought Crosby "a talented amateur" who grew more confident with time.[85]

On the other hand, baritone Richard Stilwell felt that Crosby was "very sympathetic" as a conductor. "I don't think he was dictatorial at all. I thought he knew the score, and was a good collaborator."[86] Pianist and coach David Triestram said, "I thought he got clearer as a conductor as he got older. By the last *Elektra*, I think he had gotten clear. In the beginning, it was wilder. His technique was maybe not the best. The beat wasn't that clear, the patterns weren't consistent. . . . To [John], big beats meant just play louder."[87] But soprano Johanna Meier, who sang under Crosby's baton in a Baltimore Opera *Die Fledermaus*, said, "He seemed to be very much a part of the production. Many conductors, perhaps in the more serious works, are more involved with the orchestra and so forth and there isn't a lot of communication on the stage. I felt he was right there with us and enjoyed the music too."[88] In other words, Crosby, like any conductor, had his ups and downs, his triumphs, his workaday successes, and sometimes his failures.

Reserved as he was, and carefully as he had planned effects in rehearsal, Crosby could sometimes, unexpectedly, become emotionally involved in the story. When he did, it could mean trouble for the cast, as his technique was not solid enough for him to impose a new interpretation neatly and quickly.[89] In Puccini, especially, he could vary his approach from one night to another; he was not always consistent.

Singers might find themselves teetering on the edge of trouble in a fermata, only to have to react to a suddenly speedier tempo as they came off it. Crosby, for all his insistence on maintaining uniform times for an opera's duration over different performances, could also vary significantly within sections of a work. If he was in a bad mood, tempos could suddenly be faster; if he suddenly felt more comfortable and mellow, he would leave singers snatching for breath. When he let his own personal feelings get in the way of a unified production, he felt bewildered and angry if his singers and orchestra did not respond miraculously. He didn't seem to see that his musicians could not follow his fervor when he had nailed their interpretive feet to the floor during rehearsal.

Crosby had few conducting engagements elsewhere during his Santa Fe Opera tenure, for two reasons.[90] Most of his time was given to his own company, and he was not always a satisfactory or sufficiently inspiring colleague. While he was president of the Manhattan School of Music from 1976 to 1986, he led, among other pieces, Rota's *The Italian Straw Hat* and Strauss's *Feuersnot*—both also performed at The Santa Fe Opera—and he took Shostakovich's *The Nose* to Manhattan after doing it in Santa Fe. Over the years, he did Gaetano Donizetti's *Lucia di Lammermoor* and a *La Traviata* with the Edmonton Opera in Canada; *Die Fledermaus* and *Salome* with the Baltimore Opera; *Madame Butterfly* with the New York City Opera; *Elektra* with the Canadian Opera Company; and *Der Rosenkavalier* in Portland, Oregon. He led *Countess Maritza* in Los Angeles. He also conducted with the Miami Opera and led a Netherlands Radio Philharmonic performance of *Friedenstag* in 1991. That's not much in forty-five years, even for someone necessarily wrapped up in his own company. Still, after his 1996 *Elektra*, the Canadian Opera Company orchestra wrote to management asking that Crosby be brought back again. They felt that his organization was good, that rehearsals had gone well, that their parts were superbly marked in advance, and that he had let them do their work, while he did his.

Crosby always was eager for a broader musical outlet for his talents. In a July 12, 1968, letter to agent Ludwig Lustig, he wrote,

Now that the Santa Fe Opera has settled down somewhat, I have

been hoping that there might be a few opportunities for me to get away from paper work in the winter and undertake some conducting, particularly in Europe. This would undoubtedly bring me in more contact with singers, designers, stage directors, which would be beneficial for The Santa Fe Operation.

Crosby would have been happy leading every performance himself, but even he knew that was not possible—although in the early years, he often led up to four operas per season. He therefore acquiesced in the need for colleagues. His closest colleague in the first two decades was Robert Baustian, whom he trusted completely, and who became the house's resident Mozart conductor. Robert Craft conducted not only Stravinsky works but other pieces in modern repertoire regularly throughout the 1950s and 1960s. Conductors with consistent podium appearances in the early 1980s and on included Kenneth Montgomery, Richard Bradshaw, Edo de Waart, and George Manahan, for all of whom Crosby had exceptionally high regard.[91] Other conductors were invited specially at the request of a singer or

A happy conductor: John Crosby lifts his baton with a rare smile, leading Puccini's *Madame Butterfly* at the New York City Opera in 1971. Photographer unknown. Courtesy The Santa Fe Opera.

perhaps director—Lawrence Foster to do Marilyn Horne's final stage *Orfeo ed Euridice* in 1990, for example—but others came relatively seldom or only once, or would come for several years, then vanish. These included Dennis Russell Davies, Michael Tilson Thomas, Mario Bernardi, Raymond Leppard, and Richard Buckley. Not every conductor was made to feel as though the opera could become a long-term home.[92]

Crosby had no patience with tantrums, aside from his own. Once a conductor was having an affair with a principal wind player, and they had an argument. Each wrote to Crosby saying he refused to conduct, or play, if the other person was in the orchestra for the next performance. The founder quietly put a prominent replacement player on hold, prepared different letters for the duo accepting their resignations, and laid plans to conduct the upcoming show if necessary. Nobody resigned, everyone performed, and the day was saved.[93]

"I think there were many instances where his depth of study was very impressive," said percussionist Udow. "I think his meticulousness sometimes was interpreted as being stiff by some people. I found his insistence on wanting to realize the score as precisely as possible . . . inspiring at that level."

Opinions differ on Crosby's ability to learn scores on his own. Some sources stated he learned through listening to recordings or working with a coach.[94] But in general, his musicianship and his general knowledge of any work he led were notable enough. Bass Eric Halfvarson called him "a superb musicologist and a very, very studied conductor." A staff member for many years said, "He loved the music so keenly, but it was hard for him to be vulnerable, or show that through any way except absolute control. I think his reluctance to be open emotionally affected his abilities as a conductor."[95]

He always was thinking of ways to improve the orchestral sound. In a letter of December 11, 1991, he noted that the pit had been enlarged in the winter of 1988–1989 in accordance with specifications from acoustician Jack Purcell. And in 1989–1990, some modifications to the ceiling and rear wall were made in an effort

to reinforce the sound of the string (double) basses. The double basses when positioned in the center of the pit in the newly enlarged area under the stage for ideal musical ensemble were a little weak in sound . . . we also reduced the height of the solid pit railing (separating the first row of the patron seating from the pit) by about 5" and increased the height of the platforms for the first violins which enhanced the presence of the first violins (the "f" holes of the first violins are now about 6" below the top of the pit rail when the instruments are being played upon. . . . We still lack some of the warmth and resonance of tone from the stringed instruments which is so enjoyable in traditional old concert halls.)

Intense Partnerships: From the Board to the Pit

The partnerships John Crosby had with board members, donors, staff, and artistic personnel were marked by deep intensity coupled with his trademark reserve. He relaxed his guard with only a few people he knew and trusted, although when facing a large group—reporters, or board members, or a meeting of the guilds of the opera, or even the general public—he could be amazingly articulate and charming. The contrast between the taciturn and the talkative Crosby was stunning for those experiencing it for the first time.

```
To a music publishing firm: August 17, 1971

If this action represents your regard for us now we should be
well advised to prevent further inconvenience by the simple
means of avoiding dealing with your firm.
```

Crosby's shy, barricaded personality could alienate strangers, people he disliked, and even some he might have been pleasant toward on a previous day. His dismissive attitude toward people outside his circle often embarrassed those close to him or made them uncomfortable, as it did Gilliam when he introduced his friend to the maestro. If Crosby was in a fine mood at a party, his demeanor could sour if someone he did not like approached him. He would either ignore or insult the interloper. Once the husband of a staff member came up to him at a party and held out his hand. Crosby liked the man but did not move. The man put out his hand again. Crosby said drily, "I saw that the first time."[96] He always had someone near him as a buffer—Brad

Woolbright, Richard Gaddes, Carolyn Lockwood, another trusted staff member, or a member of the orchestra whom he liked and could speak with.

Despite his shyness—or more likely, because he built a functional shell around his cryptic personality—Crosby's presence could instantly change the atmosphere in a room. The quality of that presence has been described as "a black hole,"[97] "psychopathic,"[98] and "an immense personality."[99] Everyone who worked for or around him had a huge respect for him—and often a healthy fear of him. Some said they could feel him coming before they saw him, as is the case with certain creatively or mentally or politically powerful personalities. This field of force, as well as his position and experience, made him someone to be treated with both caution and respect, even in cases where he was friendly with a person.

To board chairman: April 16, 1967

Oh how it saddens me to think you feel you can no longer be Chairman of the Opera. Everything seems to be changing so much, and I must grab at straws and try to keep seasons going. Why? There does not seem to be that burning point or reason for Santa Fe anymore. All seems awash in a glut of red, yellow and hugeness—that is all that we notice now. Quantity. What ever happened to quality?

Crosby understood that the basic role of a board of directors in a nonprofit organization was to set policy, raise money, and oversee administration. That did not mean he liked sharing authority. He presented a dichotomy that is typical in nonprofit founders. He realized that the nonprofit model, which offers many benefits to an organization, required an independent oversight board and organization-wide observance of certain rules and protocols. But he disliked having to report to others, even to the nominal extent that he did. When it came to board–general director relationships, he let no one forget that The Santa Fe Opera was John Crosby, although he also knew the value of keeping his determination masked under a layer of collegiality.

Crosby's dislike of board supervision was obvious from the start. Founder-board relations hit several rough spots in the first few years.

The young organization had its growing pains, and the vision Crosby had for its future did not always mesh with that of others. Despite its successes, the company operated precariously during the first decade, administratively speaking. In the company's initial eighteen months, five different people, including Crosby for a brief period, served as president. And before the third season opened, Crosby forced most of the board members to resign when they decided the company should build on its success by turning to musical comedy. This was ridiculous to Crosby, whose own light-music tastes went no further than Gilbert and Sullivan or Viennese operetta. To the proposal, he simply asked where the board planned to present the Broadway offerings. Crosby Development Company owned the theater and grounds and could (and would) block any attempt by the Opera Association of New Mexico to undertake any presenting of its own. When the dust cleared, opera by Crosby's definition was still on the throne, and a new board was being assembled.[100]

Crosby began almost every new board president's tenure by regarding the individual warily. How would the new president get along with him, and what was his or her attitude toward Crosby's working style? With bolder presidents, the relationship could quickly ripen into dislike. With others, it became a strong partnership, especially if the individual shared Crosby's vision and supported his plans. When he found a person intelligent, sympathetic, and straightforward, he could manage the occasional disagreement and be generous with his time—helping a new board president learn about company history and operations[101] or thanking a treasurer in a gracious letter for a fine presentation on company finances and plans.[102]

Despite his dislike for certain people, "John was a great one for observing protocols," one former board president and chairman said.[103] Crosby, he added, had great respect for the office of president, if not always the office's occupier. That held true for the other officers of the board. Their positions demanded diplomacy and support.

While he would listen to others' views and advice, however, Crosby remained firmly in charge and got his way far more often than not. The board really had no alternative but to follow his lead, for he held an unbeatable hand, especially in the later years, when he could wield his decades of experience. Crosby continued to pour all his energy and time into the endeavor; he was contracted to run the company and was not an employee. He was also a generous personal donor, fronted monies for his own opera-related expenses, and permitted the company to use his New York townhouse for an ideally located office. The board had no sword to dangle over his head except the unthinkable: to terminate his contract. Even a fiercely obstreperous board member would be intimidated when Crosby fixed him or her with his straight, stony eyes.

Nancy Zeckendorf, Thomas Catron III, Greig Porter, Edward Gerety, Seth Montgomery, and Gene Rush were among the presidents and chairmen he most respected over his forty-five years. He did not always get along with Catherine "Peach" Mayer, the board president who saw the company through the 1967 fire and the theater rebuilding, but then, Mayer had absolutely no fear of Crosby, and the pair often butted heads. Yet, when she resigned in 1978, Crosby wrote her a conciliatory letter of gratitude on December 5.

Of course, Crosby could be as curmudgeonly to board members as to anyone else. He once showed how much he disliked a new president by, during a meeting, sitting at one of the tables in front of the main executive table rather than near the new president. One of the braver members went up to him and, after a whispered scolding—"John, get your ass in your chair"—got him into his proper place.[104] At other times, a former president recalled, Crosby would grow impatient during committee reports to the board, as he knew the information already. "He would get bored very easily and he would start going 'uh-hhhm, (cough), uhm-hum.'"[105] Both experienced nonprofit volunteers and astute business folk alike recalled their surprise at getting through such meetings without collapse.

Crosby tended to mistrust board members in part because—as many nonprofit administrators can appreciate—a little knowledge may induce enthusiasm, but it can also be dangerous. As he noted in a June 4, 1993, letter,

> It has been my experience that Board members often have good ideas, but that at times they also have ideas which are not practical, or which have been tried by the Opera in years past and proven to be not practical. . . . Quite personally, what is the value and use of

my own experience for some thirty-six years here, and with other institutions at times if I am not to be included in certain decisions concerning policies—at least to the extent of being able to alert persons to possible consequences or inform them of previous experiences.

Crosby did have a proper conscience when it came to his own mortality and what that might mean to the board and the company. An August 11, 1992, letter to the president suggested options in case of an emergency. Crosby conveyed three possibilities with his usual acumen: his sudden death or incapacitation; a three- to nine-months' illness; and a longer period of difficulty, such as a chronic illness, extending beyond a year. His suggested contacts and consultants were Richard Gaddes first and foremost; conductors Montgomery and Manahan; and Epstein, who had been working with the company regularly since the 1970s. The letter was couched in dispassionate, straightforward terms.

Crosby expressed his views of how an executive and a board could work well together in a May 23, 1972, letter to the then president. Some forty-two years later, it remains a reasonable and reasoned statement—although the dollar range of gifts he mentions would now be in the five and six figures.

"The only successful working relationship between a General Director of an opera company and the Board of Directors of such a company is one of absolute mutual confidence and respect," he began, before elaborating,

> The public contributing to the opera company will always hear comments from members of the Board of Directors. If these comments are derogatory to the management of the company, the public will be less inclined to contribute, and in my opinion, wealthy persons who could make gifts of a few thousand dollars may decide to make gifts of only a few hundred dollars as token support of an institution whose product they enjoy, but about whose management they are doubtful. . . .
>
> In my opinion, the Opera Association of New Mexico has an excellent Administrative Staff supporting me in my efforts on

behalf of the Association. That staff does not ask for, nor require, praise from the Directors of the Association, but it does need the same kind of mutual confidence with the Directors that I require. It is only natural to human nature to become discouraged if one knows that one has done everything possible to operate efficiently and economically, and yet one feels that the Directors of the Association do not believe that fact that operations have been so conducted.

John Crosby looks formidable in a 1986 photograph, at the height of his influence and power as head of The Santa Fe Opera. Photographer unknown. Courtesy The Santa Fe Opera.

Opera eats money faster than any other art form. Considerable funds must be raised to close the gap between operating costs and ticket sales and other earned revenue. Despite those needs, Crosby was not always charming and welcoming—what development professionals call "a good schmoozer"—with donors, although he was more so in the earlier years than later. He famously told one director of development, "I'm no good with people. I need you to be out there with the public." His antisocial tendencies did not help. That same director mused that if ten top donors were in a room together, all of them could tell a story of how they had been insulted or ignored by Crosby.[106] It is a tribute to Crosby's intellect and ability to deliver artistically, as well as to his willingness to trust staff members and board members to take on the fundraising aspects of the company's operations, that donated support not only continued but increased so notably over time. This included special gifts for productions and bricks and mortar, as well as operating support and donations to assist the apprentice programs. Of course, nothing succeeds like success, and The Santa Fe Opera in the new millennium has gone forthrightly up the ladder of accomplishment.

With some donors, he was always close and confiding. In the early days, such major givers as the McCunes and Margaret Driscoll, plus Margaret Tobin and her son, Robert L. B. Tobin, were trusted friends and supporters. Later, Crosby's relationships with several supporters were notably confident, including Edgar Daniels, Jane and Arthur Stieren, Nancy and William Zeckendorf, and Susan and William Morris. But in general, with few exceptions, he did not like being personally involved in fundraising, except with the few persons he felt familiar with. Zeckendorf found him open and involved in the fundraising planning for the current house, with a special aptitude where foundations were concerned. When a major grant application was being prepared to request money from a national foundation, Crosby took the first draft prepared by a staff member and then wrote and rewrote it, not only obsessively but to great benefit. He brought board members and other staff members into the process as well. He was not interested in being the sole author of the application, only in producing the best and most competitive application possible. The approach was successful.[107]

The influence and safety net provided by the McCunes and Margaret Driscoll can hardly be underestimated in how they kept the opera afloat from the beginning through the 1980s. Charles MacKay recalled that in his early days with the company, "those two angels" essentially would divide the deficit between them and ante up. "Near the end of the fiscal year, John would arrange to go see them for tea, and we would all be kind of waiting anxiously while he drove off in the big 1962 Cadillac," MacKay explained. "He would return with the checks, then celebrate with a wee dram of Scotch."[108] The McCunes regularly gave $300,000 per year, and sometimes $600,000, gifts that would measure in the millions today. Once Crosby took a paid-off note of high amount to show the McCunes. He was congratulated for the successful repayment, then given yet another check for $300,000. And in 1985, Perrine McCune gave nearly a million dollars to keep the company afloat. The Driscoll and Tobin gifts were equally important then.[109]

When Crosby's emotions were involved, he could be persuasive. He wrote to a major potential donor on May 16, 1996, seeking a gift to recognize Earl Wild. Crosby and the donor, along with others, had tried to have Wild awarded New York's Handel Medallion for contributions to that city's artistic and musical life, to no avail. Seeking another way to honor their common friend and also serve the opera, Crosby suggested a $350,000 endowment to maintain a senior music staff chair or name a space in the new theater for Wild. If the donor would help, Crosby wrote seductively, he would designate $150,000 of his own donation to the opera for the naming opportunity. The donor eventually gave $200,000, which, coupled with Crosby's money, led to the orchestra pit being named for Wild—a fact Crosby kept secret until he could unveil the naming to Wild and his longtime partner, Michael Rolland Davis.

To another donor, on September 28, 1999, he wrote, "The good fairy has whispered in my ear that you like a reminder or a request for your very generous gift to the Opera at this time each year, and the bad fairy has told me I am deputized to be reminderer this time. In spite of the fairies, I hope you will be pleased to know that the Opera is all right, and we have recently learned about two gifts of $1 million each for our Endowment. Most helpful indeed."

For someone eager to find every penny in donations as well as in savings, Crosby could be shortsighted. He never really became accustomed to such events as preview buffets or dinners, even though they introduced potential donors to the charms of the grounds and brought them ever deeper into the opera family. Letting people come onto the company lawns and walk on the grass his parents had planted and nurtured so carefully made him morose. But he also knew that social events were effective parts of any major fundraising campaign. Still, after one of the first such dinners, he was found the next morning picking cigarette butts off the grass while mourning the damage the grass had taken. He demanded that no party detritus be left behind on the next occasion.[110] His keen knowledge of people expressed itself in surprisingly protective gestures. He once advised that any woman seated next to a certain donor at a party would have to be forewarned that she "might be pawed."[111]

When the opera had its own private foundation, Crosby did not always get along with its officers. His rationale was simple: money coming in was for the benefit of the company, and he wanted to have access to it when it was needed. This might mean borrowings, or it might mean using endowment funds that had grown above and beyond their initial value—what fundraisers call quasi-endowment. In board meetings during the foundation's existence, Crosby could often be heard muttering about the quasi-endowment as he sat in his office or strode through the halls.[112] Established in 1976, the foundation was a joint benison and burden to Crosby; it's a shame he didn't live to see the foundation subsumed into the company proper at the end of the 2003 fiscal year.

Crosby's trademark quiet was made to measure for some donors.[113] When the new theater was being built, he showed the model to a potential giver. The woman looked over the model and asked a series of short questions. Crosby answered with equally brief replies. The donor's assistant and the opera's director of development later compared notes. They found that the donor had commented on how charming Crosby was, not difficult at all; and Crosby said the prospect was one of the easiest people he had spoken with. A silent woman had met a silent man, and they had gotten along famously.

Crosby always admired those who could easily ask for money. Speaking about Richard Gaddes once, Epstein said, he expressed amazement at how Gaddes could go to visit a donor, dine with them, discuss topics ranging from interior decoration to history, spend the night, and the next morning, ask his host for a million dollar gift.[114] At least in the latter part of his life, that kind of approach was beyond John Crosby—one of the few things that was.

John Crosby was a brilliant administrator and mentor to scores of people. His organizational and financial abilities strongly suggest that he could have been a success in any profession involving details and numbers, such as banking, investment, or architecture. Many people understood that Crosby's hand needed to lie heavily on his creation. Even as the company grew in size and complexity, and he could no longer supervise everything directly, he made it a point to observe, interrogate, and coach his senior staff members constantly. He would walk the campus quietly, perhaps turning up suddenly in the scene shop or the accounting department, at a chorus rehearsal or the groundskeeper's station. When it came to knowing how things worked, Crosby was unsurpassed, said baritone, director, artist, and Crosby-friend Mikael Melbye, adding,

He was the overpowering reason for the success of the Santa Fe Opera. I have always learned that, you know, good management of anything depends on the top of the pyramid. And John was a very strong and pointed top of the pyramid. That filters down throughout the hierarchy of the company, and everybody felt that the reins were kept very firmly in hand with John. The whole idea of the company was so well defined by him that nobody could doubt it.[115]

Those who knew him intimately knew also that they needed to match his commitment to the company every hour of every day. "The man instilled both genius, admiration and fear in people like me who worked for him," said Brad Woolbright. In fact, Crosby's expectations were sometimes absurdly high. During the paralyzing New York blizzard of 1996, Crosby called Woolbright to ask if he planned to come to work. Woolbright accordingly trudged through snow-packed streets from Greenwich Village to the East 63rd Street brownstone, worked a few hours, was thanked, and went back home through the mess. Crosby frequently informed employees that he had worked eight hours on both Saturday and Sunday, leaving unspoken the expectation that they should have done the same.[116]

To: staff members, July 28, 1993

There has been a general decline in the deportment of audiences at The Santa Fe Opera over the recent years as we have attracted greater attendance. It is not like the "good old days," and it is not the way tradition is maintained at festivals in Europe which we like to compare ourselves to. You may feel these are developments which we have to accept, but, with all respect, I disagree. I wish we could have a better dress code in the Opera Club, and better behaviour on the sold out nights.

One man who worked with Crosby when he was at Opera America as president (1976–1980) found out how different Crosby could be as an employer. "During the five years I worked with him at Opera America he was extremely personable, and warm, and cooperative, and understanding and all of this sort of thing. When I switched and became his employee he became a different person. It was like turning around."[117]

Crosby tended to go through assistants with what seemed like fatal regularity. Assistants would last for a year or two or three, then vanish—not necessarily because they did anything wrong, but because they were expected to live for and with the opera, with personal affairs and lives kept a distant second, and it was too much stress. Other employees also felt the weight of Crosby's expectations. He once became annoyed when a favored staff member had the temerity to get married during an Opera America conference in Santa Fe. From his point of view, the nuptials should have been postponed, and the staffer should have been on duty. She noted in bewilderment, "What was I supposed to do, live in sin?"[118] Another time, he was annoyed rather than sympathetic when an assistant wanted to leave due to a death in his family, in the midst of season preparations.[119]

Although Crosby was a perfectionist, a mistake could be forgiven if accompanied by an explanation, an apology, and a game plan for ensuring the error would not recur.[120] Insolence, insubordination, or defending oneself when in the wrong—and occasionally the right—would prompt a growled reprimand or a furious, full-scale dressing down. As a demonstration of authority, such a reaction was understandable, if deplorable. From a human perspective, especially when Crosby was in the wrong, it was more puzzling. At those times, he would sometimes apologize meekly; at other times, he would demonstrate that he knew he had been in the wrong, even if he could not bring himself to formally admit an error. His attitude toward the injured person would show his regret.[121]

And Crosby could be a caring and thoughtful boss. Once he sent a young staff member to work in a bank for several years to gain financial expertise.[122] Another time, when someone left the company to take another position in town, he was told, "You'll have a better chance of coming back here to the opera if you go somewhere else and get experienced in a leadership position"—and in time, the staff member did return.[123] He repaid loyalty with loyalty, even though the road to the top could be bumpy. He always preferred to promote from within, but he expected loyalty to continue and even increase as advancement occurred.

With Crosby, no news was good news. If you heard nothing, you knew he was satisfied you were doing your job. One simply did not expect lavish praise for doing so. And he enjoyed being a mentor, especially when introducing people to numbers and accurate accounting. "The best way to work with him was to be responsible," one longtime staff member put it. "He was really good at letting people do their jobs. He had clearly defined expectations, he expected the highest level of service and greatest amount of courtesy and the best skills. You lived up to it or you weren't sticking around."[124] Crosby also hated it if people themselves chose not to stick around; he could not imagine why anyone would choose another organization over The Santa Fe Opera or another boss over him. For him to encourage a staff member to leave to gain experience was one thing; for a staff member to leave to further his or her own professional aims was unthinkable.

His courtliness was as legendary as his temper tantrums, but he had definitely a sly side to his personality. Carolyn Lockwood said,[125]

This is another side of John. He would find somebody and you know they would be the best and that was that, that one could do no wrong, and this was great maybe for two years, and then plunk, they just fell out of favor for no reason at all. And he was like that with a lot of people—directors, rarely singers. Conductors, too. Bob Baustian said he was always waiting for the axe to fall. There'd be a conductor that John really liked, and that would go on for a couple of seasons, and then, plunk, they were persona non grata, and I have no idea why. Neither did they.

And he was like that with designers and things. He was particularly fond of Reuben Ter-Artunian . . . and then suddenly, you know, Reuben's gone. It was just so odd. We all thought, we're next. He was like that. In administration, he would have people in that he thought were just great, and two years later, bong, they were gone. For instance Henry Heymann, you know, actually his family gave a lot of money. When his dad took sick, Henry couldn't go to someplace that John wanted him to do or something like that, and suddenly, you know, it was Reuben Ter-Artunian and no Henry from then on.

The odd thing, as close friends as we were, he could scream and holler at me and then just turn around and say, well, come on, I'll take you down, you know, in the car to whatever . . . and it was as if this had never happened. He could swear and scream at us like you could not believe. And yet turn around and with these almost Victorian manners, pull the chair out for you and open the door.

Paul Horpedahl remembers that with Crosby, especially in the theater,

It was old style—here comes the maestro! Stand at attention, be on your guard. If he found a loose screw on the back deck he would pick it up, bring it to you, and draw attention to the fact it should not be left around. If something was wrong, he would tell you right then. If it was not too bad, he would wait till the next day! Usually, if it was critical, he had it typed up in a memo. Or going down to the cantina he would beckon you over, tell you what was on his mind. Sometimes ask you to join him for lunch if it were a bigger topic. His voice was very quiet, and because of the quietness, you felt you needed to pay attention. You got that what he was telling you was very important, and you needed to listen carefully and do what he asked you to.[126]

To a stage director, July 28, 1993

Due to my schedule of activities I have not had the pleasure of attending a rehearsal of the double bill until yesterday. I trust you are very pleased with the development of these productions.
. . . I do have a problem with the pantomime in "The Protagonist" in connection with the scene of the First and Third Player, where the First Player is costumed as a cleric.
   Although a good portion of the pantomime occurs behind a screen, it is evident to the audience that an act of sodomy is being portrayed.
   Given the regulations of the United States Congress and guidelines of the National Endowment of the Arts it could be difficult to prove that this specific portrayal was necessary for realization of the opera, and so I must ask you to modify this action.

In addition the red pom-pom on the biretta of the cleric should be changed to a black pom-pom.

The red pom-pom indicates a rank above that of priest (i.e.: Monsignor, Bishop, etc.). I realize you have been abroad in some of the recent past months, and so it is likely you have not been aware of the very painful experience of the Archdiocese of Santa Fe involving our former Archbishop who resigned his office in April of this year. There was extensive national press coverage of this, and other incidents, and I fear that the red pom-pom could be interpreted by a substantial portion of our audience as an indication that the Santa Fe Opera might be making a reference, albeit oblique, to the misfortune of the recent past Archbishop of Santa Fe.

Crosby was close to the gardeners, groundskeepers, and household staff at the opera, especially those from Tesuque. But he kept an eye on them as well. When the boys took the trash to the dump, he knew exactly how long it should take and would want to know where they'd been if the return varied too much from his own internal clock.[127]

Memo to staff: August 10, 1985

This Saturday morning at 9:30 AM, in anticipation of Sir John Tooley's visit to my office at 10 AM, I undertook the following.

1. Turned off chandelier on west portal.
2. Obtained broom and dust pan and swept up litter (packing chips) from area in front of the switchboard office.
3. Restacked several logs that were strewn about the parking area. . . .
4. Swept up wood chips which have been lying on asphalt driveway. . . .
5. Removed large cardboard carton which was placed by trash bins outside my office about one week ago for removal and noted that trash bins have not been emptied for several days.

Please kindly arrange with the Maintenance Department to attend to affairs such as these in a prompt and orderly manner.

Some staff members saw only his kinder, polite side. A front office employee, whom he always treated with respect, once received word that a family member was gravely ill. Crosby noticed her discomfiture, discovered the reason for her worry, then paid for her airline ticket so she could go home immediately. Another time, he asked if he could use the employee's phone. He used the phone to chastise severely another staff member, then expressed gratitude for use of the phone. Toward the end of his life, his beloved Rolls-Royce was due to be brought back from Palm Springs by truck. When the cargo arrived, it was not his car. Crosby exclaimed, "It's the wrong fucking car!" then clapped a hand on his mouth and said, "Oh, I'm so sorry!"[128]

To a staff member: February 6, 1987

This is for your circular archive. It is from the gentleman who pulled off the best scam on me for free tickets to the Opera by masquerading as the Archbishop of San Francisco.

His sense of humor was sometimes rough, sometimes sly, and he sometimes pulled pranks. When the box office and Crosby were besieged by calls from a mentally disturbed caller one season, the entire staff feared the angry man might show up in person. One night an employee was sitting in the box office when she suddenly heard a voice behind her claiming to be that client and demanding his tickets. She turned to see Crosby smiling mischievously at her from the window.[129] During one evening's intermission of Offenbach's *Orpheus in the Underworld*, a tall and handsome bass wearing blue as the god Zephyr was admiring the view from the back of the stage. Crosby sidled up, cigarette in hand, looked the singer up and down and said, "Darling, that color is *you*."[130]

Staff members knew Crosby would back them up when they had to make decisions in unusual circumstances. One evening, a parking lot attendant found a five-year-old boy wandering around trying to find a bathroom. He had been locked in his grandfather's truck with a package of cookies and a soft drink while the grandfather and his date attended the opera. When Crosby found out, he was livid, and he supported the staff member, who located the miscreant grandfather and packed him off the grounds—and reported the incident to the state police the next day.[131]

Director John Copley, mezzo-soprano Tatiana Troyanos, and Crosby confabulate after a 1987 performance of Handel's Ariodante—still acknowledged as one of the company's most theatrically lush, musically opulent, and artistically successful productions. Photographer unknown. Courtesy The Santa Fe Opera.

John Crosby's relationships with singers and orchestra members echoed his relationships with others. He maintained a distance except with a few people. He could discuss Maalox with a soprano right before a performance, but if he had something on his mind after the show, she would get a memo like everyone else. For example, in a letter after an *Intermezzo* rehearsal on July 14, 1994, one singer was instructed, "Before Number 234, Act I: Exactly three laughs." Yet the same vocalist had the signal honor of being invited to ride in Crosby's golf cart, which carried the secret company sobriquet of the Batmobile, up to the new theater when it was first completed.[132] When a young singer in an audition stopped a song and explained, "You said to sing part of it, and the hard part's coming up," he laughed loud and long.[133]

Singers who saw only his warm side included mezzo-soprano Frederica von Stade, who sang a number of times at Santa Fe, including in *The Marriage of Figaro*, *Yerma*, Handel's *Xerxes*, and Jules Massenet's *Chérubin*; she also sang Melisande in *Pélleas et Mélisande*. Other singers included Elisabeth Söderström, whom Crosby respected as a courtier would his queen, and whom he tried to get to Santa Fe for Pamina in *The Magic Flute* as early as 1967; Evelyn Lear and Thomas Stewart, with whom he had a respectful, if occasionally contentious, relationship; Marilyn Horne, for whom Santa Fe built a prompter's box for her 1990 *Orfeo ed Euridice*; Tatiana Troyanos, the star in *Ariodante*; and Kiri te Kanawa, who sang the Countess in *Figaro* in 1971, in her American debut. When te Kanawa was bitten by a feral cat at her home in Tesuque, Crosby hired an animal tracker to find and catch the feline and then had it tested for rabies at a local veterinarian.

Thinking back on Crosby's influence, von Stade said,

> You'd work extremely hard. We rehearsed harder and longer than many other places [but] there was a great youthful element about it—apprentices, not just singers, they were stage people and build-ing sets. It was all overseen by John and the people he had around him. They were magicians in what they did. For *Pélleas*, they brought aspen trees from the hills! There was a sense of devotion to the cause, everyone pulling in an unusual way. It was fun, silly, goofy, and yet the master had his hand in everything. That never changed in my experience. It makes you feel safe as an artist.[134]

Crosby could sometimes exchange embarrassing confidences with artists he liked and trusted. In 1972, when von Stade was sharing a house with her *Pélleas* costar Richard Stilwell and his wife, a party was thrown. Crosby stayed late, drinking steadily. And von Stade remembered,

> After quite a few vodkas, he said, "I'm not sure I have enough money right now to meet the payroll." Richard and I looked at each other and thought, "Oh, dear. Oh, well. Oh, my." He would scramble and beg; he had to do all of those things you have to do as an impresario. I think for someone like John, it would have been excruciating.[135]

Mikael Melbye was a Crosby intimate. He came to the company as a young singer in 1986 during the thirtieth anniversary and returned frequently for fifteen seasons.

> I enjoyed very much coming there. Even the seasons where I didn't sing, I would very often come over and stay at John's cabin.

We became very good friends. I'm a liberal Dane, and we don't take bullshit from anybody. And so I'm not very easily scared by people. . . . Oh no, I was not afraid of him. We had quarrels, really loud quarrels. It was rare he raised his voice, but we had those as well. I think he really liked that, because so many people were very scared of him. John was quite a timid person and, in combination with power, was often very intimidating to people. They didn't know how to grasp him, somehow. I know there that were very stubborn rumors that we were lovers. That was not the case, though. We were only very good friends.[136]

Soprano Patricia Racette, who made her company debut in the 1996 *Emmeline* world premiere and sang under Crosby's baton in the 1997 *La Traviata*, recalled her experience with him as "A combination of oy and not so bad. Some moments were wonderful. He was a man of few words, but when he did say something, it was like he gave you the Hope Diamond. He loved the way I covered the vowel on 'lui,' in the second act [of *Traviata*], and when he told me, I almost fell off my chair." Mezzo-soprano Beth Clayton agreed, calling Crosby "a man of few words and fewer outfits."[137] Soprano Mary Jane Johnson, who worked many times under Crosby's baton, said, "He was very kind to me, always. But you had to be on top of your game. Oh, yes, I knew when to stay away from him. But I really loved him. The atmosphere was like a family." She recalled singing an *Elektra* in Israel that was a daunting assignment—the conductor never came to rehearsals, there was no prompter, and all in all it was a very uncomfortable experience. "If I can just get home to Santa Fe . . . that's all I kept thinking about," she said.[138]

To *Capriccio* sextet players: July 24, 1993

During the opening sextette of "Capriccio" at the second Dress Rehearsal I had the perception that the sustained accompanying lines were a little loud at times. The inner voices when playing the melodic line are fine, but I think the problem occurs occasionally with the dotted half notes, half notes, and perhaps some of the quarter notes. I also thought the "forte/piano" in the fifth measure after #6 was a little too vigorous, or, in other words, fine if it were an orchestral passage but just a little too strong for a sextette. Thank you for your consideration of these comments.

When it came to the orchestra, the relationship was like that of administrative staff and singers—very much a mix of affection, respect, and healthy fear, with a few players enjoying deep friendships. Although the orchestra members saw his faults, they would play with heartfelt dedication for him despite abuse. "He had the emotional temperament of a 2-year-old," recalled Miles Davis. "His fits! He would be conducting, his face would get red, and he'd curse."[139] His tirades were dreaded—and legendary. On the other hand, on January 17, 1963, he wrote to longtime French hornist Robert Elworthy about Elworthy's wife, Maxine's, due date for delivery of one of the couple's children during the summer.

> Thank you for your interesting letter of January 11th, and the good news about Maxine's plans for the summer. I do hope that Max will be very accurate about her plans which you tell me are for July 12th. This would be quite nice since it is the birthday of Julius Caesar and John Crosby. We could have some interesting parties in the future. . . . I am grateful that Maxine and Jim Burton have discussed ways of taking care of second bassoon activities during her confinement.

Negotiations with Crosby were always an interesting experience, though fraught with tension. The orchestra committee would sit in his office on uncomfortable chairs while he sat behind his dusk enveloped in clouds of cigarette smoke. Proposals would be made, counteroffers stated, and eventually an agreement would be reached, sometimes after lengthy correspondence between meetings. But Crosby appreciated the orchestra, even if he did not always find himself in agreement with the orchestra committee when it came to negotiations. He once told them in the 1980s, "I know you're a $1,000 a week orchestra, but I can't afford to pay you that."[140] When a board member asked if the orchestra cost couldn't be reduced, Crosby compared the players to those in other professions, showing how little they were paid. The orchestra was family to him, and he felt safe in its company. He therefore was careful about what conductors he would permit to come to Santa Fe and work with the ensemble. "Any new conductor that was put on the podium was put under a magnifying glass," Brad Woolbright said. Even without the formal title, Crosby was in essence both music director and chief conductor.[141]

But he also felt that the orchestra owed him plenty. In a letter of July 22, 1980, to the orchestra manager, he pointed out that a softball game injury sustained by the first oboist had both financial and artistic implications. The instrumentalist would have to be replaced by another oboist over the next four days, during which the majority of *Elektra* orchestral rehearsals would take place, and if things went well with the replacement, Crosby was not willing to have to reintegrate the injured player back into the band. "I do not think that The Santa Fe Opera should have to bear expenses which come about as a consequence of sporting injuries," he wrote. "These things are very different from sickness, or unavoidable injuries from, let us say, motor vehicle accidents."

```
To principal trumpet: June 29, 1993

In Boheme Act I, rehearsal #21, can you lift off the second note
in each measure so there is a little separation between the first
and second measures of #21 and also between each pair of eighth
note figures within the second measure, and also going from the
end of the second measure to the third measure. Many thanks.
```

Crosby was always direct, even brutally so, when saying no to any player's continued employment—although he did so with impeccable courtesy, as if that were an ameliorating factor. For a long time, orchestra members would receive a letter in their mailbox after the last intermission of the season's final night, informing them whether or not they would be invited back. Brad Woolbright had the responsibility of delivering that news for years. Danis Kelly remembered, "The last night of the season . . . was scary. Half the orchestra wouldn't be down at the party, because either they or a friend had gotten the letter."[142]

```
Memo for file: August 18, 1976

The charge against (name) is insubordination. The particulars are:

1. Willfully playing wrong bowings (Mozart)
2. Putting in bowings without consulting the principal player
3. Placing hand over entrances when marking parts
4. Turning back a page to mark a part during actual playing
5. Continuing to mark a part during a dress rehearsal when asked
by the principal not to do so
6. Interrupting the principal when conversing with the conductor
on pertinent musical questions
7. Showing hostility to the principal by throwing pencil on the
stand, throwing her purse around, stomping off the stand
8. Continued usurpation of the principal's duties
9. Hostility shown in her playing (unwilling to match pitch,
accenting or jabbing notes, anticipating notes)
```

One annual ritual both pleased and sometimes exasperated the orchestra: dancing for the audience after the opening night, which went on for decades in the second theater. After a busy evening, players would have to schlep their instruments to the balcony, where chairs and stands had been placed. They would put the music on their stands, Crosby would assume a commanding position, and off the group would go with Viennese delights—*Wiener Blut*, *Champagner Polka*, *Tales from the Vienna Woods*, *Auf der Jagd Polka*, *On the Beautiful Blue Danube*. The audience loved the party atmosphere, the orchestra came to accept it as a necessary extra service, and Crosby would conduct the lighthearted repertoire with a forbidding face. Later, when waltzing took place onstage, the orchestra could stay in the pit. But then they had to worry about extravagantly mobile dancers, some with champagne going to their heads, whirling around just above them.

Throughout his life, John Crosby kept most of his energies and time focused on his own company, although he did have two substantial additional professional commitments. From 1976 through 1979, he was president of the national service organization Opera America, then based in Washington, D.C. For a decade beginning that same year, he was president of the Manhattan School of Music in New York. He brought his quietly intense persona and administrative strengths to both organizations. As Marc Scorca, CEO of Opera America, noted, "He was truly an impressive intellect. . . . In every way, The Santa Fe Opera defined the modern American company—a quarter century for sure, almost half a century before the rest of the industry came to that. The Santa Fe Opera was innovative and unique; not imitative but original. I think [Crosby's] imprint on American opera is indelible."[143]

To a correspondent: July 8, 1977

For the past twenty-one years during which I have been directing the Santa Fe Opera I have received a good number of letters from residents of New Mexico complaining about all sorts of things, and often about my work. As a courtesy, I have always tried to respond to these correspondents with candid explanations, but I am at a loss to reply to you, other than to give you the satisfaction of knowing that your letter probably qualifies for first prize in this group. I hope that will be gratifying to you and that it will also please you to know that the Government's postal service did indeed deliver your letter promptly today.

[Note: Unfortunately, no copy of the letter to which Crosby refers could be found. It must have been a doozy for the word-savvy Crosby to resort to a somewhat sarcastic platitude.]

When Crosby became Opera America president, the organization was facing many challenges.[144] With the implementation of the Americans with Disabilities Act, companies had to deal with access issues for the handicapped. There were National Endowment for the Arts issues to consider. An increase in NEA funding was being offset by more competition for grants. There was an increasing push for artistic minority participation in opera, from singers and dancers to directors and designers. (Crosby may well have congratulated himself on The Santa Fe Opera's early hiring of African American singers, including bass Therman Bailey, soprano Reri Grist, and tenor George Shirley[145]—except that he seldom congratulated himself on things he simply knew to be right. If a singer was right for a role, that was the end of the matter.)

The issue of how opera could and should relate to broadcast media and the issue of providing translation grants for companies to render opera librettos into English both needed discussion. There was dialogue about whether Opera America should become a member of Allied Arts, which would lobby Congress and the executive branch on behalf of symphony, opera, theater, dance, and museums. Finally, many small companies were interested in becoming members of Opera America but were not necessarily able to demonstrate the professional capacities the organization required. These included appropriate budget size, a reasonable number of productions per year, and other indicators of professional competency. But those companies, not seeing validity in such a bar, lobbied their senators and representatives for membership. Politics made the mix murky, with the old accusation of opera being elitist coming up now from within the field as well as from outside it.

Crosby was a powerful, if generally understated, president and worked well with the equally powerful personalities of his fellow board members. He dealt effectively with both staff and the board on day-to-day matters as well as on longer-range issues. From the evidence of the minutes from the time of his tenure, the board ran smoothly. Committees were well-structured and well set up to do their work and then present conclusions and recommendations to the board.

Crosby was the first Opera America board member not to come from the East Coast, specifically the Washington, D.C., area, where the organization had its roots. Scorca noted that his selection was "based on credibility, on merit, on authority rather than on geographic proximity" to D.C. Under Crosby, the organization's agenda went from being purely practical to more theoretical and interventionist.[146]

David Gockley, a Santa Fe baritone apprentice from 1965 through 1967, then The Santa Fe Opera box office manager, and later general director of Houston Grand Opera and the San Francisco Opera, recalled Crosby as an excellent president, devoted to parliamentary procedure and capable of running meetings like clockwork.[147] He also had great respect for decorum and process. "He was conservative in his not taking on too much—the organization not taking on too much—[but] being more of an evolutionary leader," Gockley recalled.

John Crosby was president of the Manhattan School of Music from 1976 through June 30, 1986. The school beckoned to him because of his interest in education and also because it offered a challenge. He certainly did not need the trouble of running another major institution while he was dealing with The Santa Fe Opera. The fact that the school offered an additional salary doubtless appealed to him, though. He generally went to the school on Mondays, Wednesdays, and Fridays in the afternoon.[148] He did not have an office of his own, preferring to work in the boardroom.[149] And his generous heart, as in Santa Fe, showed in quiet ways. For example, he would pass a check along to a staff member so that a promising student could buy a proper suit or a nice dress for auditions, always with the proviso that the gift remain anonymous.[150]

According to his assistant Peggy Tueller, a longtime personality in the arts administration world, he was "ninety-nine percent more involved than most full-time persons. He was always available, no matter when you needed him.[151]

"John had his quirks and his weaknesses," Tueller also recalled. "But he was a financial genius. He knew where every penny went." His personality in day-to-day dealings tended to be moody, and she, like Santa Fe Opera personnel, learned when to avoid him and how to approach him when avoidance was impossible. And she could hold her own. Once when he upbraided her for a situation not of her devising, she picked up a chair, slammed it down, said, "Don't yell at me for something I didn't do!" and left the room and went to her own desk. Within a few minutes he was there, apologizing for the outburst.

Tueller realized early on, like so many Santa Fe Opera employees, that in a job demanding social graces, Crosby was lacking. On the practical side, he was brilliant and capable. On the relationship side, he was socially inept. The comparison to his Santa Fe behavior is obvious. "At small social functions," where he knew those with whom he was interacting, "he was amusing and lots of fun," Tueller confirmed. "But when it came to business social gatherings, he became difficult." Still, she stressed, "He was so good at actually running the place. . . . No subsequent president could match him. I adored John, I really did."[152]

Harpsichordist and music administrator Paul Wolfe, who was first director of admissions and then dean at the Manhattan school during Crosby's tenure, subsequently knew him very well in Santa Fe. "He was easy to communicate with on school matters. He was interested in music education, in the whole process of schools. He was old fashioned and very formal at the school. But his real interest was Santa Fe."[153]

On one memorable occasion, Wolfe went to the Baldwin piano company studios to meet Crosby for a reception for Liberace. When he arrived, he found many Crosby friends and cronies there, including Earl Wild. But Crosby was huddled in a corner, not speaking to anyone. He grabbed Wolfe's arm and whispered, "I'm so glad you're here," clearly considering his colleague to be a vital crutch and helper. Then the red carpet was literally rolled out for Liberace, who arrived wearing a plain business suit rather than any of his wild concert outfits. Despite his trademark shyness, Crosby said to Wolfe, "We have to get some money," and went right up to Liberace. In a relatively short conversation, he convinced him to give an endowed scholarship to Manhattan School.[154]

Two musical giants: John Crosby shakes hands with Liberace at a reception at the Baldwin studios in New York in the early 1980s. This is presumably the occasion when Crosby charmed the pianist into giving an endowed scholarship to the Manhattan School of Music. Photograph by Henry Grossman. Used by permission.

A Personal Life in the Opera House

Even in the closeted 1950s and 1960s, it was no secret that John Crosby was homosexual. Close friends at Yale knew of it early on from his relationship with Frank Magee. The arts world knew of it from the beginnings of The Santa Fe Opera, if not before. In time, everyone in the music business was cognizant of Crosby's sexual orientation. For some, his gayness was a topic for prurient gossip and inspired a legend that a gay Don Juan himself could not have managed without a nervous breakdown. For others, it was just a part of who Crosby was, on a par with his mental acuity, his chain-smoking, and his preference for having the costume shop make his pajamas. Given the times he grew up in and his emotional reserve, it was definitely a private matter for him. He was not an activist; he was essentially self-closeted, living as a gay man without ever coming out publicly.

From all evidence, it seems clear that he never confronted his parents about his sexual orientation, and he kept his amours restrained and low-key during his parents' lives out of respect for them and their Roman Catholic faith. (Afterward, although he never tried to hide a relationship as such, he did not advertise or discuss it.) His parents might have suspected or even known: Aileen's machinations at removing Frank Magee from the opera and from John's immediate presence strongly suggests this possibility.

Of course, the world of the arts has always welcomed talented people of every sexual stripe. One is judged by ability and creativity rather than sexual preference. Crosby's artistic and management genius made him respected; that he had boyfriends was beside the point to most people. If the occasional male auditioning for an apprentice spot felt that the tightness of his pants was more important than the arias he had planned to sing, such was life.

Even in the accepting climate of today, some people shy away from the topic of Crosby's homosexuality. Concern for his legacy and the view that one's private life should stay private are the reasons most often given. But it was a major facet of his character and thus essential to discussion. Crosby's gayness was, after all, an integral part of his personality, although he subsumed it, as he did so much else that was part of him, in his professional life. His company was wife, child, and lover to him, and everything was focused on its health and success.

As such, his personal life never interfered in any way with the running of the company, nor did he date full-time opera staff members after Magee. He was scrupulous about maintaining a professional distance, sexually speaking, with regular employees. Inside the company, he was a professional, not a pasha. There was no perching on knees, either literally or figuratively.[155] He did have a succession of companions over the years, as Brad Woolbright recalled.

> There were friends of John from summer to summer. Anyone who had one brain cell knew who that person was. . . . John was very careful about all that. He was very realistic in terms of the friends he had. It never affected the day to day operations of the company. We all have personal lives . . . but his first and foremost love was The Santa Fe Opera.[156]

A great tragedy of Crosby's personal life was that, after Magee, he never again established an emotional relationship of such intensity. He had many friends and companions over the years, some of whom later became regular parts of his life. He had briefer encounters for a season or two, often enough with a male apprentice artist or perhaps a member of the opera's music staff, or relationships of shorter duration with young men he met at bars in New York during the winter.[157] One man who worked as Crosby's assistant for four years in the 1970s, when the maestro was in his fifties, recalled, "He occasionally had young people in on an individual basis. Young friends, very polished usually." They would come in at the end of the workday to the 63rd Street office and be sent upstairs to Crosby's private quarters. "One was a circus performer. I didn't ask what his act was."[158] Most of John Crosby's boyfriends were young, slender, blond, and boyish-looking men, sometimes swishy, the kind unkindly called "twinks." A Texas matron and patron once commented about Crosby's current favorite, in a broad accent, "I declare, if John Crosby wanted a girl, why didn't he just get one?"[159]

Old friends together: John Crosby and acclaimed pianist-composer Earl Wild, a Santa Fe Opera conductor in 1963 and decades-long Crosby friend, celebrate during the 1996 season. Note Crosby's standard-issue white zip shirt under his blazer. Photographer unknown. Courtesy The Santa Fe Opera.

Despite, or perhaps because of, his short-term sexual encounters, Crosby could be jealous of people in established relationships. He once ranted at director Bliss Hebert and designer Allen Charles Klein at a dinner at his home that he hated them because they had each other and were not alone.[160] He showed *Schadenfreude* when his friends' relationships broke up and was jealous of Earl Wild's long and deep relationship with lover Michael Rolland Davis.[161]

In the late 1960s and into the 1970s, many of Crosby's boyfriends came from Germany.[162] He would travel there between seasons on company business. Friends, several from the early opera days who had relocated to Germany, would introduce him to various young men who fit his type and were of equable temperament. (Crosby could fall on occasion for a gold digger, but he did expect good manners and couth.) Occasionally his boyfriends were singers or otherwise involved in the field. He would bring these German men back to the United States with him, then engage them as personal assistants or find other jobs for them, usually in some capacity at the opera. (When he was smitten with attractive American boys, whether or not he established a relationship with them, he similarly found jobs for them at the opera, often in the box office.) They would stay with him some months, perhaps a season or two, then move on. Crosby was an erratic, shy, and moody person, not easy to be with. He expected his young friends to fit into his idea of a relationship, which was definitely not an equal partnership. This included falling in with all his plans and likes, with little attention to the other's wishes. He might take his friends on trips, give them expensive gifts, and often be moony in the early stages of a relationship, but the difficulty of keeping up with Crosby and coping with his moods would finally become too much for each of his partners. Eventually the encounter would end, and to Crosby's credit, often with the young men remaining friends. As he aged, and his interest in young men remained constant, the possibility for a long-term relationship became even more unlikely.

"They had to fit into his schedule is the problem," recalled Michael Rolland Davis. "He had a lot of people for a while, really nice guys. Sometimes he took kids to the Bahamas. But they had to conform to what John wanted to do or where [he wanted] to go. It would last for as long as somebody could put up with John. And then as soon as they had maybe their own ideas or [thought of] moving on, it just fizzled, and John moved on to somebody else. Nobody really wanted to take on his life, I guess."[163]

To the Executive Director: July 1, 1994

I noted five or six teenagers left the Theater at the beginning of Act II (of the youth opera) and when I drove home about

30 minutes later these same teenagers were walking up the road
from the lower parking lot to the main paved parking lot. The
lower lot was not illuminated since there was no need for the
Opera to park vehicles there. I assume these teenagers occupied
themselves with non-musical diversions for which the Opera
cannot bear any responsibility. However, perhaps there may be
a question about that on the part of some parents; the situation
calls for some review on our part.

Crosby, with his decorous upbringing, kept his personal life as private as possible except on a few occasions. Once, in the late 1960s, he took to riding horses with one of his young German friends around Santa Fe, even down to the Plaza. It became so obvious that the relationship involved more than riding horses that a tough board president demanded he stop. The aftermath was pure Crosby. He sent the young man back to Germany but then regularly sent him money to attend school. Several years later, Crosby looked the lad up when he was in Europe, only to find that he had saved all the money Crosby had sent and bought himself a business—a bar—rather than attending school. Crosby, to his credit, found the young man's business acumen amusing.[164]

Two of the men closest to John, first as companions and later as friends, were the German-born Fahrmeyer and Timo Myllys, from Finland. Fahrmeyer became intimate with Crosby in the early 1980s and then became an important component of the opera staff as a photographer and recording engineer; he began the company's archives of performance recordings. The first mention of Myllys comes in a June 7, 1990, letter Crosby wrote to a travel agent, asking that tickets be arranged for Myllys to visit. He was with Crosby when he died in Palm Springs twelve years later.

Fahrmeyer believes that he and Myllys were perhaps the closest companions John Crosby had. Fahrmeyer recalls Crosby as

Extremely insecure, very lonely, not good in communication. I feel sad for him. Basically he had it all, but I've never seen anybody so unhappy in my life. He was always complaining about how people put him down. It's not his fault alone. I think it had to do with his parents, who were extremely straight. He was brought up very strictly. You could not tell from his facial expression if he ever enjoyed anything. . . . I could be his boyfriend but not live with him.[165]

Crosby treated Fahrmeyer from the beginning as someone who worked for the opera, not just as a summer companion. He was someone whom Crosby was helping to find a voice. Crosby treated many of his special friends that way, with generosity and a recognition of their abilities.[166] Still, there was always the problem of his persona. One music staff member who dated Crosby in the early 1970s recalled,

He was often fun to be with; at other times he would be very silent. I never quite knew how to get through that. But I think part of it was that I was so much younger than he was—22 versus 45. I didn't ask John out because at that age I was way too naïve about a lot of things. I didn't have a lot of experience, in any sort of romantic way. So John was the one who had to ask me out. . . . It was a quiet evening kind of thing—I think we just had dinner. John was very restrained, but I definitely think he was kind. He would help people if they needed it, but [he was] restrained probably due to his upbringing.[167]

Crosby's regular Sunday pool parties were legendary gossip fodder. Popular legend had them assuming an orgiastic reputation of Tiberian proportions, with the founder ravaging his way through apprentices like a hot knife through butter. No interview supports this viewpoint; food, drink, and perhaps some skinny-dipping and horsing around were involved, but not much else. One once-company member said, "I heard that in 1962 there was a [wild] party . . . and everybody who was there talked about it in legend. I think it was a little like a unicorn— who's seen one? I think all of those other pool parties were overstated. I went to a lot of them and I never saw anything I couldn't write home to my mother about. Admittedly, I left at a certain time."[168]

In earlier years, from the very beginning of the company, people would gather at Crosby's pool at the ranch for an early afternoon cookout. Hot dogs were the main item on the menu. Families attended, as did single company members whom Crosby considered friends. Longtime concertmaster Michael Ma would grill the wieners, and his wife would prepare side dishes. The pool would be filled with playing children. It was like a Fourth of July or Memorial Day picnic—camaraderie, fun, relaxation, and story after story about notable moments in the company's history.

After Crosby built his cabin home in 1981–1982, the parties had two phases.[169] The lunch party was inevitably family oriented and wholesome, with guests of both sexes gathered for drinks, swimming, grilling the inevitable hot dogs, and conversation, as they had at the ranch pool in earlier years. Ladies and gentlemen would change in different rooms. Then the wholesome fun would begin. But at a certain point in the afternoon, almost as if they were seated at a formal dining table, the ladies would "gather eyes," rise, and depart. So would families. Only men would be left—some handsome gay and straight male apprentices, some staff members, perhaps some artists—for more swimming and sunbathing and, eventually, a simple dinner. But Crosby wasn't a potentate eyeing a harem. He had his friend of the moment, and that was enough; he simply liked to be surrounded by like-minded, attractive people. And his personal rectitude ensured that he would never descend to something as notorious as chasing young men around the pool, even if he would invite those in attendance to shuck off their swimsuits if they wished.[170]

Still, the pool party invitations could be problematic. Some invited staffers would decline, mainly because they practically lived at the opera during the season, and their one day off was precious.[171] But not everyone had the temerity to turn down a Crosby invitation. To his credit, he did not retaliate if someone preferred not to attend his parties, but the person would be moved from the A list to the B or C list.

Besides companions, Crosby had regular home assistants, young men who combined the duties of housemen and valets. The relationships were platonic and the work and pay reasonable, although the hours were long.[172] Ideally, Crosby wanted someone who could and would work both in Santa Fe and New York. In Santa Fe, duties would include all purchasing of food, drink, toilet necessities, and other items for Crosby's personal use; making lunch and dinner; helping out at postperformance receptions at Crosby's home or at cocktail parties;

caring for clothing; and assisting at the Sunday pool brunches.[173] Given Crosby's smoking habit, emptying ashtrays was specifically mentioned as a duty, although housekeeping staff were around for heavy work. Duties would be similar in New York, although not at the level of intensity found in Santa Fe. An ideal valet would have been able to cut hair as well, as Crosby wistfully described in a March 21, 1969, letter. In Santa Fe in the earlier years, the valet had a private room and bath at the ranch; later, when the ranch was converted into an office, housing would be found for him. In New York, he would have the fifth floor bedroom, bath, and sitting room as a rent-free accommodation. Sometimes the valets were young musicians. One letter confirming a summer job states that the valet would be afforded at least one voice lesson a week and would attend apprentice master classes and similar events as his schedule permitted.

Not all of the housemen worked out, and in any event, Crosby seldom kept one longer than a season or two. He never found the kind of male servant who would work for him for decades at a stretch. One hapless lad from England was trying to cook the maestro's breakfast one morning using an electric skillet but did not know it had to be plugged in. Someone trying to be kind, but also mischievous, told him the problem was the altitude, after which he put the skillet on the floor, presuming that would solve the problem.[174]

Crosby expected his shopping lists to be followed exactly. If he called for three small white boiling potatoes, that was what he expected to be served. In one instance, he reported, aghast, to a staff member that the helper had served mashed potatoes instead.[175] The insistence on exactness is both amusing and endearing.

CHAPTER FIVE

The Fall of the Curtain

Retirement: Transition and Tension

"Founder syndrome" is the intransigence of persons who have set up and guided an organization for a significant time and cannot see that they must step down for the entity's good, if not for their own. Few founders escape the infection, whether the organization is an altar society or a bridge club, an international business or an artistic endeavor. It often brings trouble with its bow wave and in its wake. Board relations get prickly, and parties talk around a point or mutter subversively to test the waters, because the founder often holds so much institutional memory and prestige that his leaving is fearfully perceived by those around him as potentially shattering, even if desirable.

In defiance of the norm, John Crosby handled his transition from four-plus decades as general director of The Santa Fe Opera to an emeritus éminence grise with outward dignity and the same meticulous attention to artistic planning and administrative detail that he was known for. He embraced the idea of departure calmly enough when it was first proposed to him, too, although with some initial surprise. Matters only became turgid after his departure, when he continued to be involved in the company as a conductor. At that point, he seemed to realize how much he missed artistic control; whether he admitted it to himself or not, he resented giving it up.

It was then–board president Greig Porter who first spoke frankly about the situation.[1] Porter recalled that when he was on the phone with the founder one day in 1997, "We were talking, and John just complained and complained and complained. He complained about everybody. He complained about the board. He complained about me. He complained about everything. It just wasn't going the way he thought it should."

Porter pondered his response. The next morning, he called Crosby at the New York office. "I said, 'John, quite frankly, if I felt about my job like you do, I would quit.' And there was a pause. And he said, 'Well, perhaps that's something I should think about.'"

Crosby took several days for reflection. When Porter called him back for further discussion, "He said, 'Well, I haven't changed my mind.'" When asked what that meant, he quietly replied, "'I'm going to retire,'" Porter recalled. "And I said, 'Do you think you might want to think about that another couple of days? It's a big step.' And he said, 'No, I don't think so.'" After a few more days, the board's executive committee was informed of Crosby's decision; Porter had previously only told a few inner-circle board members that their founder was considering leaving.

Of course the possibility of—and the need for—Crosby's eventual retirement had been anticipated for a long time. Well before his decision, some board members were already murmuring that the inflexible founder should be eased (or, if necessary, pried) out. Crosby's health was not good; his temper was shorter, and he was more irritable than in years past; and people were impatient with his years of dictatorial behavior. Porter worked well with him, as had Nancy Zeckendorf and other presidents, but the undercurrent of decided feeling was that forty-five years was plenty of time for one person to control an artistic enterprise.[2]

Crosby had referred to his retirement as early as June 19, 1991, when he wrote to Nancy Zeckendorf and Gene Rush, then president and chairman of the board, respectively:

The Officers and Directors of the Opera have always been most supportive of my efforts, and have, I feel, placed great trust in me. I am sure that from time to time some Officers and Directors may have wondered why I took certain actions in artistic or business matters, but they have always supported me. At this time I believe the Officers and Directors may feel they might want to take a special look at our operations in depth. . . . If the Board

should come to the conclusion that The Santa
Fe Opera needs a different kind of management I shall certainly understand, and will step
aside gracefully. Indeed, perhaps we do need a
younger and more vigorous General Director,
or some combination of a chief for Business
Management and someone to look after artistic
matters.

The Opera has grown and should continue
to do so. . . . above all I would like to see the
institution which I was so involved in starting
have every opportunity to flourish.

Of course, there was no need to replace Crosby
on the spot, once he had decided to retire. Such
overnight changes are rare, and The Santa Fe Opera
situation did not call for such extreme actions. Crosby also wanted to
see his company through the final season he had in planning, 2000.
This offered plenty of time to decide on the kind of person desired
for a replacement, set up a search committee, and seek out candidates.

Richard Gaddes and
John Crosby in May
1998, shortly after
the announcement
that Gaddes would
succeed Crosby as
general director at the
beginning of the 2001
fiscal year.

Yet it was soon clear that such a search was superfluous. An obvious candidate was on staff—Richard Gaddes. After leaving Opera
Theatre of St. Louis in 1985, Gaddes had become chief executive for
St. Louis Grand Center, an organization working to revitalize the
city's downtown cultural and theatrical district. After leaving that
position and then doing occasional consulting for The Santa Fe Opera
in the late 1980s, he had come back to the company in 1993 as a valued
adviser to the apprentice artists program.[3] As we have seen, Crosby
had named him, in a 1992 letter, as the person to whom the board
should turn if something "precipitous" happened to him. Now, the
board felt that hiring a new general director from outside, possibly
from Europe, might cause Crosby to be forced out immediately, cut
off in an untimely fashion from the enterprise he had created. That
was a possibility they could not or would not consider.[4]

By 1995, then, Gaddes was already acknowledged in the program
book as associate general director.[5] In effect, he was where he had
been in 1969 as a trusted Crosby coworker, with the added benefit of

decades of operatic experience—clearly the heir apparent. The anger Crosby had felt when Gaddes left Santa Fe for St. Louis had evaporated, and he was relieved to have his former lieutenant back at his side. Here was someone he could count on for loyalty, he felt, but also for the frank opinions that few others would dare voice.

Gaddes was an obvious choice in other ways. He knew finances, board relations, the opera business, and singers. And he was a successful fundraiser and friend-raiser, something Crosby didn't do well. True, Gaddes was not a conductor. He did not have the kind of first-hand orchestral experience Crosby did after decades on the podium. But he had ample experience working with conductors and orchestras, including experience in matching conductors with singers, directors, designers, and production teams. As a marketer and community-outreach specialist, he had no rivals and few peers—certainly not Crosby, who regarded the opera as something of a castle on a hill and the greater Santa Fe community as the proletariat squatting in the village below. This feeling of entitled isolation grew with Crosby over the years, as success followed on success: in the early years, he had been more involved in and receptive to the community at large and, as we have seen, always friendly in a business sense with vendors.[6]

In considering Gaddes, Crosby certainly recalled his past experiences of trying to find a masterful executive who could work comfortably with him while deftly managing The Santa Fe Opera's administrative side.[7] The company's first executive director, the gifted Anthony Riolo, was a great success in his job and was completely accepted by the community and by his chief. The opera programs list him as executive director from 1985 through 1988, when he died of AIDS. Three other executives followed in dizzying succession, as the program book listings testify. Philip Semark was acknowledged in 1989 and 1990, Barbara Zarlengo in 1991, no one in 1992, and Nigel Redden in 1993 and 1994. The next year, Gaddes was in place, promoted from his consultancy to the associate general director position. Having him step into the top position would save the company valuable time, energy, and money. The executive committee of the board quickly agreed, and Crosby's retirement and Gaddes's forthcoming control of the company were confirmed.

With retirement pending, many details needed to be discussed, including money. Personally, Crosby was hardly in want. He had his own substantial personal investment portfolio and a 401(k) retirement account to which he had contributed regularly throughout the years. He still owned a great deal of prime land near the opera, as well as his beloved cabin. When the New York brownstone was sold to the company in December 1999, Crosby was paid $1.45 million and guaranteed a life income of $75,000 per year against the balance of the property's $2.9 million assessed value. In return for this, he agreed to relinquish his retirement pension of $75,000 per year; he had simply exchanged one payment instrument for another.[8]

Although Crosby outwardly embraced the idea of retirement, his reaction became more testy and cautious when he actually began descending the slippery slope. He and Gaddes began to clash. Gaddes was younger and more energetic than his former patron, ready to take on the challenge of Santa Fe. Although grateful to Crosby, he was eager to make his mark. Crosby was stubborn and tired, but he clung to his creation; he could not change his essential character.[9] As a family member observed after his death, "If John had worked for John, they'd have butted heads."[10] And as an astute observer noted, "not all the divas were onstage" during this period at the company.[11]

Crosby had another challenge, one he shared with many who reach retirement age after a lifetime dedicated to one end: inchoate, ill-defined expectations. He had devoted his whole life to one company; even with substantial means and free time, he would not be able to find any endeavor that compared to it. His child was grown up and could function without him. Admitting these things was as unthinkable as conceding that he could make a mathematical mistake in a financial projection or miscalculate a well's pumping capacity.[12]

Yet Crosby's health was reason enough for him to retire. Decades of living up to the opera's and his own expectations had taken a toll. So had years of overwork, drinking and smoking, and frequent emotional explosions. As he grew older, more corpulent, and slower, his ability to find pleasure in exercise diminished. He no longer could swim vigorously, ride horses, water-ski, or ice-skate; he could loll in his own pool, but he couldn't use it as energetically as he once had. The excesses caught up with him, as when he had to use oxygen while conducting the 1999 *Ariadne auf Naxos*—amazing the singers, who had not previously been warned—but nothing would stop him from leading a work by Richard Strauss, then or later.[13]

What is sad is that Crosby had to work hard to reach this parlous state. He came from sturdy stock, with both parents living well into their eighties. And aside from an occasional accident—including having a briefcase fall on his head before a plane flight[14] and once shutting his thumb in the East 63rd Street door, for which he refused medical attention[15]—his ills seem to have been limited to the occasional cold, flu, or bronchitis, or, more seriously, occasional bouts of exhaustion that demanded a few days of hospital stay.

The ill effects of his tobacco and alcohol use had become magnified over time. His childhood respiratory problems had returned, exacerbated by chronic obstructive pulmonary disease.[16] He had survived urinary cancer;[17] he had cataracts;[18] and he had long been on a blood thinner, as well as on cardiac medications.[19] He suffered from heart arrhythmia and had to have electric shock treatment every few years to regulate his heartbeat.[20] As early as 1967, he had reported internal spasms that might be due to an esophageal problem or cardiac stress. He had suffered from a slipped disc at different times, and from 1995 on, he wore custom orthotics to cushion his feet. An end had to be inevitable, as no one could imagine Crosby negotiating the opera grounds in a motorized wheelchair.

Crosby nonetheless felt he could look forward to a number of pleasant, if not operatically productive, years, but he had to decide where to live. Santa Fe in winter did not seem attractive, given that he would not have an opera company to run every day. In 1999, he began looking for a possible retirement site. On September 15, 1999, he wrote to a friend that his Santa Fe doctor had given him permission to fly to Phoenix and Palm Springs to look for lodgings for the coming January; he eventually settled on Palm Springs.

He wrote in the winter of 2000 to Hans Werner Henze of his health and his hopes for future involvement with his company. Given his blood-thinning pills and hypertension medication, he wrote, air travel was a terrible strain. But he exulted that Gaddes had invited him back in 2001 and 2002 to conduct *The Egyptian Helen* and *Die Liebe der Danae*. He expressed positive feelings about moving to Palm Springs' low altitude and dry, warm, and sunny climate.

And yet, said Charles MacKay, "I think he was very ambivalent about it. This was the organization that he created; it was his baby. To be able to let go of it, when it was his whole life. . . . I'm not sure he could really face that. One of the things John used to say to me, over and over again, was, 'Charles, when you're so immersed in a job like this, it occupies virtually all of your waking hours.'"[21] (In a letter of June 17, 1993, he deprecated the naming of two roads in Casas de San Juan after operas, noting that when one worked with music all the time, not having to see anything about it going home was ideal.) "John hated retiring," Brad Woolbright confirmed, "much as he realized it was inevitable given his age and that he was slowing down."[22]

Crosby's actual departure from the opera was both dramatic and workaday. Shortly after his final fiscal year end on September 30, 2000, he packed his Rolls-Royce and rolled off into the sunset toward what he had come to believe would be a great reward and a wonderful time. Then reality shouldered imagination aside.[23]

Maestro without Portfolio

To many, Palm Springs seemed an odd choice for a new home for Crosby. True, it offered a change of climate and pace from Santa Fe. It offered luxury, privilege, and, given its demographics, excellent medical care. Crosby eventually acquired a big house with a pool, tennis courts, and even an elevator, the acme of indulgent comfort.[24]

Yet Crosby knew few people there, and his few friends there he quickly alienated just by being himself, only more so. He was still so interlocked emotionally with The Santa Fe Opera that he could not establish an identity for John Crosby the retiree versus John Crosby the founder and guide. It was no surprise that he soon built a new Santa Fe house on one of the highest points in Casas de San Juan—an aerie to which he planned to return every summer. It was complete with comfortable pool, a file room where he planned to store his personal and professional materials and write his memoir, great comfort, and a magnificent view.[25] This could not have pleased Gaddes, who was trying to put his imprint on what was now his company and yet wished to be kind to the man who had given him the chance to make a name and reputation for himself.

Crosby felt the company was now serving strange gods, and he did not like it one bit. And he simply did not have enough to do. The energy he had expended day in and day out for four decades had nowhere to go except in obsession. That quickly became apparent in Palm Springs. He soon alienated Earl Wild and Michael Rolland Davis, who had helped him decide where to live in retirement and even inspected potential houses for him, sending him information and pictures and opinions. The relationship that had begun even before Wild conducted in Santa Fe in 1960 had grown into something approaching the back-and-forth of an old married couple. "They would bitch at each other and grouse here and there," Davis said. "It just went on like that. Sometimes Earl would snap, 'John, stop it!'"—and Crosby would draw up short.[26] During the two years before Crosby's death, Wild and Davis visited him frequently. Wild had a grand piano placed in Crosby's house for afternoon and evening gatherings as well as for practice. Wild and Davis had spent a lot of time in Palm Springs, so they knew plenty of people and tried to introduce John into the city's social circles. They also recommended doctors and dentists. He appeared happy at first and was grateful to the couple for being friends and attentive hosts. They even found restaurants where he could sit outdoors and smoke—which, Davis said, meant a great deal to him, as might be expected.

That changed on Thanksgiving 2001 at Crosby's house. Many other guests had been coming and going, and Crosby had been drinking heavily, which made him even more morose and touchy than usual. The particular outburst that fractured the friendship came during the holiday dinner. Crosby had prepared a turkey cooked with three liqueurs, including cognac and rum—a heavily heightened version of coq au vin. He was nodding off at one end of the table when Wild asked what wine was being served. Crosby snapped to attention and snarled, "Well, if he doesn't like it, let him buy his own!" This was the end for Wild, who was deeply hurt both by Crosby's tone and the implication that he was a freeloader. After an uncomfortable period during which the two men did not speak to each other and Wild avoided being in the same room with Crosby, the two old friends parted. They never met or spoke again before Crosby's death.

Crosby did change in positive ways as well as negative ones in retirement. When he came back to Santa Fe to conduct Gilbert and Sullivan's *HMS Pinafore* in winter 2001 in the newly renovated Lensic Performing Arts Center—which he admired—he seemed softer and more yielding, more mellow but also more frail.[27] He spoke of his love for conducting and his affection for the orchestra. It must have been comforting to go back to his musical roots with something as familiar as a Gilbert and Sullivan operetta.

Crosby was disappointed in 2001, when the planned 2002 production of *Die Liebe der Danae* had to be canceled. The day after the September 11, 2001, attacks, Gaddes decided the uncertain state of the world and the new cultural and political reality made the expense of a complex new *Danae* production unwise and called his mentor to let him know.[28] Disappointed, but ostensibly understanding the reasons behind Gaddes's decision, Crosby acquiesced and agreed to lead a revival of Verdi's *La Traviata*—an opera he knew quite well but that could hardly be called his favorite.[29]

(Canceling *Danae* may have saved money and trouble, but other big projects remained on the slate, including new productions of Tchaikovsky's *Eugene Onegin*, Rossini's *The Italian Girl in Algiers*, and Kaija Saariaho's immense *L'amour de loin*. In retrospect, it begs the question: If the company could manage all those new productions, why not a *Danae*?)

In any event, Crosby began to feel he was becoming persona non grata at the company he had founded and nurtured for so long. Bryan Gilliam recalls that Crosby was smoking even more than usual and seemed bitter in those days. "I don't think he felt fully appreciated, to put it bluntly," Gilliam said. "I remember he called me up one time— that was the last time I talked to him—it was in 2002 shortly before he died. He read some interview out loud to me, which suggested he didn't feel fully appreciated in this interview. The idea [was] that 'This is our company now and we're not going to do Strauss every year.' It just didn't go over well."[30]

The *La Traviata* experience turned out badly. The soprano assigned to the role left early in the run, leaving a replacement to take on the difficult title part. During rehearsals, Crosby was alert for even a perceived slight; with so much time on his hands, he could take offense even more quickly than before. When he found out that his production

Three ladies and a gentlemen: John Crosby with his three mares, circa 1970. In a letter to a supporter, he likened them to the three ladies in Mozart's *The Magic Flute*. Photographer unknown. Courtesy The Santa Fe Opera.

was assigned fewer rehearsal pianists than the show opposite him, he insisted on an additional pianist being assigned. His reasoning was that when rehearsing outdoors in the wind, three pianists were needed, one on each side of the regular coach, to hold back the score's pages if it was windy. In addition, he needed another one sitting beside him to take notes for the orchestra or singers. The fifth coach was needed to help out in any other way the conductor might think of. He also at one point discussed with a music staff member that he was considering conducting a certain second-act, off-the-beat passage *on* the beat, in order to make sure the orchestral passage was perfectly coordinated. That could be seen as an interesting example of a musician's constant consideration of how to make a performance more effective, or a perfect example of someone with too much time on his hands.[31]

By the last few weeks of the season, he and Gaddes were communicating only by letter. Matthew A. Epstein intervened with both men, as did Ragnar Ulfung. As a result, Crosby and Gaddes had lunch the Tuesday after the season ended. Both wrote Epstein that they had made up their differences and parted cordially. It was the last time the mentor and the new general director met.[32]

Crosby knew he had not been at his best during this podium outing, and he was sensitive to the suspicion that new orchestra members, who did not know him by experience, found his conducting a subject for badinage. Veteran orchestra members found the experience painful. At the closing party, where he had his own "deposed king" table, Crosby asked two players he trusted to come speak with him. He asked them directly if they thought he was "losing it as a conductor." Their frank reply was that surely Crosby knew the *La Traviata* had not been good. "Well, maybe I should just pack it in," he said. But the players encouraged him in another option. Let his swan song be a Strauss opera, the *Intermezzo* planned for the next season. Crosby definitely perked up at that idea and became, if not more cheerful, at least less morose.[33]

Death and Transfiguration

John Crosby's final illness began a few days after Thanksgiving 2002 in Palm Springs.[34] Timo Myllys was staying with him. Crosby began to experience abdominal pain and bloating. Rather than calling the doctor that had been recommended earlier by Wild and Davis, Crosby picked one out of the telephone book. Diverticulitis was initially diagnosed and treated with pain pills and a restricted diet, but time bought no improvement. Crosby even began experiencing pain when being driven about, especially when the car went over a bump in the road. All indications pointed to something that demanded immediate care. But Crosby had always been a stoic about illness and accidents, and he refused to seek a second opinion until the pain forced him to consult another physician. X-rays revealed a hugely inflamed appendix. Because of the blood thinners Crosby had taken for years, surgery was postponed. Before the operation could take place, the appendix burst, filling his peritoneal cavity with infectious fluids. During surgery on December 7, Crosby's abdomen was drained. Despite initial positive progress, his system began to fail within the week. The illness and surgery were too much for what had been a basically healthy constitution weakened by years of neglect. Crosby died at 1:17 p.m. Pacific Time on December 15, 2002, of "cardiopulmonary arrest, septic shock, peritonitis, [and] appendicitis with perforation."[35] He was seventy-six years old—six years beyond the psalmist's three score and ten, but young, given his family's longevity. One reason he had chosen Palm Springs as a main residence was because he was concerned about the level of medical care available in Santa Fe. Now he had died there due to a tragedy of errors.

Before Crosby died, as he lay unconscious, Myllys put headphones on him and played a recording of Crosby's own conducting of Strauss—the 1984 *Intermezzo* that had meant so much to the maestro. He was looking forward to reprising the work in 2003. He died with the sound of his oldest musical friend in his ears.[36]

As far as is known, Crosby did not receive the final Roman Catholic sacrament, Anointing of the Sick; he had not been a practicing Catholic for decades. Nor is it known if his earlier wish to be an organ donor on his death was fulfilled. His body was embalmed and shipped from Palm Springs back to a Santa Fe funeral home. As one critic noted sadly, "It should have been sent in a golden chariot, to the music of the march from *Aida*."[37]

Acknowledging his World War II service, a private gathering and interment took place on December 20, 2002, at the Santa Fe National Cemetery. Few people attended—his brother James Crosby and James's three children; a Crosby cousin and her daughter, who had been close to the maestro; and three friends: Thomas Catron III, Miranda Levy, and Benjamin Saiz. There was no music, not even a Johann Strauss waltz or a Richard Strauss aria. And religious aspects were absent at the burial. The gathering simply sat with the body at the funeral home, then went to the cemetery in a simple and short cortege.[38]

Some workers at the opera had hoped the funeral procession might pass through the grounds, so the company could pay final respects to the founder and Crosby could symbolically return to his creation one last time. But James Crosby felt the company had turned against his brother, and he decided that the small procession would go straight from the funeral home to the cemetery. A few words were spoken, a salute was fired, "Taps" was played, and the flag that had covered the coffin was given to the family. With a private lunch after the burial, the societal part of Crosby's passing was completed. A few days after the burial, a small bottle of vodka and a pack of cigarettes were found resting on the gravesite, placed there by orchestra members.[39]

Crosby received countless tributes in national and international publications, including the *New York Times*, the *Dallas Morning News*, *Opera News*, *Opera*, the *Denver Post*, and of course the *Albuquerque Journal* and the *Santa Fe New Mexican*. Hundreds of other newspapers picked up the Associated Press story on his death. All spoke of his vision, his business acumen, his brave programming, his creation of the American apprentice program concept, his insistence on quality, and his supposed shortcomings as a conductor versus his dedication to the operatic canon, especially Richard Strauss. Some noted his five honorary doctorates—the University of New Mexico in 1967, the College of Santa Fe in 1968, Cleveland Institute of Music in 1974, the University of Denver in 1977, and Yale University in 1991—as well as his receipt of a National Medal of Arts in 1991 and the 1992 Verdienstkreuz.[40] But sardonic humor had its place in the memorials. One critic observed that John Crosby's death was the nicest Christmas present Richard Gaddes could ever have received.[41]

Seven months after his death, on what would have been his seventy-seventh birthday—Saturday, July 12, 2003—a memorial was held in the theater.[42] Attendees included members of his close and extended family, board members, donors, artists, and company friends. It was a solemn, somewhat sad, yet triumphant occasion.

The first speaker was board president Susan F. Morris, whose father had been Crosby's pediatrician decades ago and thus instrumental in his seeking health in the New Mexico mountains. She announced that henceforth the soaring building would be known as the Crosby Theatre—a generalized name that honored Aileen and Laurence Crosby and their son. It was a neatly conceived way to commemorate Crosby's name and accomplishments on the portico of his own house while not formally doing so, for he had often stated his reluctance—in fact, his refusal—to have a building, even the theater, named after him. In a July 9, 1996, letter to a donor, he wrote, "There was talk about it amongst some of our Board members, and involving my name, but I made it very clear, absolutely not!"

After touching tributes from friends and colleagues—including Catron, Rickless, Davis, Zeckendorf, Johnson, and Gaddes—soprano Christine Brewer and the company orchestra under the baton of Kenneth Montgomery gave a refulgent reading of Strauss's *Four Last Songs*. The final song, "In Abendrot," seemed especially poignant in the moment, with its final words, "Can this, perhaps, be death?" A moment of silence followed, and the theater then emptied quietly. Some who attended, though, wondered if the founder had not been present in some fashion. Even though no clouds were visible in the sky, a sound of thunder had permeated the afternoon. At least Crosby's spirit would have been delighted that, after the memorial, the theater was set for the opening night performance of Strauss's *Intermezzo*, the work he had been slated to conduct.[43]

CHAPTER SIX

Encore

The Santa Fe Opera after John Crosby

A friend in the orchestra once asked John Crosby what would happen to his company after he died. His reply was simple. "Well, if it doesn't go on like it always has, then I haven't done my job."[1] But he had, and it did, and it does.[2]

In the thirteen years since the founder's death, under both Richard Gaddes and Charles MacKay, the organization has seen tremendous growth in administration and facilities. It has continued to present a mix of repertoire from the comfortably familiar to the startlingly audacious, with plenty of world and American premieres. Its education and community programs, which include the landmark Pueblo Opera Program implemented in 1973, are nationally noted models for intelligent and viable outreach. It is in the midst of traversing a new master plan with success, and the annual budget is now a balanced $20 million. Crosby might not agree with every decision the company has made or every step that it has taken—he would not be either an operatic impresario or himself, if he did—but he would surely nod in approval at its success and solidity and agree that there is nothing stolid about it.

Administratively, much has taken place that Crosby would smile on. An apartment complex in Santa Fe has been acquired to house the hardworking apprentice technicians. Water remains a company attention and concern: up to 600,000 gallons of water is harvested annually from the theater roof. The fabled water storage treatment facility treats 40,000 gallons of recycled gray water for the grounds planting. And a recent facilities renovation, although it did change the interior of the old ranch complex, has maintained its footprint. The theater remains the king building at the company's campus, with major renovation and construction of the backstage and support areas slated through the 2017 season.

From even before 2001 through 2008, the tall, lean, distinguished, and sometimes waspish Gaddes pushed the company in new artistic directions with notable success. He mounted a welcomed community production of Britten's *Noye's Fludde* while he was still the associate general director; put in place special ticket offers and purchase discounts for first-time New Mexico ticket buyers; and encouraged regular postseason rental of the theater by community groups, arts presenters, and even for-profit entrepreneurs. This was something Crosby himself had grudgingly permitted occasionally, although he himself would not attend such events. He once growled that when he left the theater at the end of the season, he would not enter it again until the following May.

Even more importantly, Gaddes offered a sincere and friendly, if calculated, hand to the community at large. Crosby had generally ignored if not alienated politicians, patrons, and many movers and shakers in Santa Fe. Gaddes, although he kept The Santa Fe Opera at the forefront of his efforts, was not averse to discussing the possibility of partnerships and joint lobbying and seeing them through. He also was bold in putting the opera out into the community during the off-season. His programming was generally safe in terms of choices but well-suited to the new audiences he hoped to reach, and he did strike off in bold, audacious repertoire directions.

The company's Santa Fe–oriented off-season presentations included an intimate production of John Gay's *The Beggar's Opera* in 2000 at El Museo Cultural de Santa Fe, complete with a Santa Fe Southern train ostensibly delivering the cast to the theater. Gilbert and Sullivan were represented by *HMS Pinafore* in 2001 (conducted by Crosby) and *The Pirates of Penzance* in 2002, both in the Lensic Performing Arts Center. One-act operas presented later on were Bizet's *Dr. Miracle* in 2006 and Donizetti's *The Night Bell* in 2007.

The main stage saw its share of interest, too, in terms both of personnel and productions. Kaija Saariaho's *L'amour de loin* received its American premiere in 2002; her *Adriana Mater* was similarly honored in 2008. Other notable productions included, in 2002, a return of

Eugene Onegin for the third time, the company premiere of Rossini's *The Italian Girl in Algiers*, and the *La Traviata* that marked Crosby's final bow. In 2003, superstar soprano Natalie Dessay made her American concert debut; she returned to The Santa Fe Opera in 2004 for the title role of Bellini's *La sonnambula* (which was simulcast to Fort Marcy Park's ball field in a company first). Additional landmarks during Gaddes's years were Janáček's *Kátya Kabanová* in 2003, the first opera by the Czech master that The Santa Fe Opera had mounted since 1975's *The Cunning Little Vixen*; Verdi's towering *Simon Boccanegra* and Handel's deliciously malicious *Agrippina* in 2004; and in 2005, the company premiere of Puccini's massive *Turandot* and its first production of Britten's emotionally towering *Peter Grimes*.

The company's fiftieth anniversary in 2006 was the occasion for a year-long celebration and some major leading singers. Repertoire looked back and forward, with *Carmen* (with Ann Sofie von Otter in the title role), *The Magic Flute* (with Dessay as Pamina), Massenet's *Cinderella* (with former apprentice artist and now world star Joyce DiDonato), *Salome* (with Janice Watson), and the American premiere of Thomas Adès's *The Tempest* (with American baritone Rod Gilfrey as Prospero and Cynthia Sieden as Ariel). That opera mandated one of the company's most intriguing set ventures: building a desert island surrounded by water on the stage. A gala fiftieth anniversary concert was held that, for assembled Santa Fe Opera star power, could compare and overtake any previous season. Other works of note during the Gaddes years were a *Daphne* in 2007, the first since 1996, and the same year, the American premiere of Tan Dun's sonically intricate theater piece *Tea: a Mirror of Soul* and Santa Fe's first take on French Baroque opera, Rameau's wry comedy *Platée*. Britten's probing *Billy Budd* received a stunning production in 2008, with Teddy Tahu Rhodes as the able seaman of the title and William Burden as Captain Vere.

With the advent of the quietly passionate and brilliantly astute Charles MacKay, beginning in the 2009 fiscal year and season, the artistic explorations continued. The world premiere of *The Letter* by Paul Moravec starred Patricia Racette, who had bowed with the company in the 1996 *Emmeline*. Dessay returned in *La Traviata*. Donizetti's *The Elixir of Love* was mounted for the first time since 1968, and the company premiere of Gluck's *Alceste* also took place. Then, 2010 saw *Madame Butterfly*, *The Magic Flute*, *The Tales of Hoffman*, the world premiere of Lewis Spratlan's Pulitzer Prize–winning *Life Is a Dream*, and Britten's *Albert Herring* in a charming production with a stellar cast. In 2011 came *Faust*—rather late in the day, at that, in its company premiere; *La Bohème*; Santa Fe's first venture into Vivaldi with *Griselda*; a revival of the disturbing yet masterful 2001 production of *Wozzeck*; and a MacKay gamble that paid off splendidly: Menotti's comic yet philosophically tart *The Last Savage*. That year it was also announced that the Building for a Sound Future Campaign, started in 2007 under Gaddes, had exceeded its goal of $30 million by $4.6 million. The total provided important monies for endowment, production, the apprentice program, and education initiatives. Crosby would have nodded with great satisfaction at such success.

The next year, 2012, saw a return of *Tosca* for the first time since 1994; the company premiere of Bizet's *The Pearl Fishers*; yet another Rossini, the rarely heard *Maometto II*; Strauss's *Arabella*, for the first time since 1997; and the company premiere of Szymanowski's *King Roger*. The mix of repertoire was critically successful, although audiences were a bit slow at first to respond to the number of more-or-less rarities.

The 2013 season confirmed that Crosby's audacious project remained alive and well in Santa Fe under MacKay's hands. A comedy opened the season—*The Grand Duchess of Gerolstein*—and it starred a singer who had begun her career with the company in 1989, singing Flora in *La Traviata*: superstar mezzo-soprano Susan Graham. *The Marriage of Figaro* returned for the seventeenth time, with a sterling cast in a sparkling production revived from 2008. A Rossini rarity, *La Donna del Lago*, continued the company's recent attention to the Italian composer, for *La Donna* was the fifth Rossini opera mounted since 2000, with DiDonato the eponymous heroine. *La Traviata* was back in a revival of the 2009 production that had starred Dessay. World premiere territory came with *Oscar* by Theodore Morrison, a co-commission and coproduction with Opera Philadelphia. Starring American countertenor David Daniels, who had previously been heard at Santa Fe in three Baroque roles, it persuasively told the story of poet, playwright, and wit Oscar Wilde

A 1967 discussion: John Crosby and baritone John Reardon in a lighthearted moment in the company's New York headquarters. Reardon was one of Crosby's favorite singers until he took another engagement one summer at Wolf Trap. It took a long time for the breach to be healed. Photo by James Clois Smith Jr. Courtesy James Clois Smith Jr. and Sunstone Press.

during the darkest period of his life. It was accompanied by a large-scale community seminar series that included films—a cooperative concept established since Crosby's departure. In the pit, there were familiar faces and one debutant—Leo Hussain for *La Traviata*. Returning maestros were Emmanuel Villaume, John Nelson, Stephen Lord, and Evan Rogister for the Offenbach, Mozart, Rossini, and Morrison, respectively.

Notably, Harry Bicket was named as chief conductor effective October 1, 2013. His podium duties in Santa Fe during the Gaddes years had comprised Handel's *Agrippina* and *Radamisto* in 2004 and 2008, respectively, and Rameau's *Platée* in 2007. His appointment continued Santa Fe's seemingly fruitless attempt to find a permanent podium occupant, be the title music director or chief conductor, to replace the founder. Alan Gilbert, now music director of the New York Philharmonic—and a former violinist in the company orchestra—was music director in 2004, 2005, and 2006. Trusted Crosby associate Kenneth Montgomery, who first conducted in Santa Fe in 1982 with *Mignon*, was acting music director in 2007. (Montgomery returned in 2013 as conductor laureate. He was in residence the entire summer and served as an adviser in orchestra matters.) Edo de Waart, who likewise has a long company association, beginning with *The Flying Dutchman* in 1971, was chief conductor in 2008 and 2009. Frédéric Chaslin took over that position in 2010, 2011, and 2012. Between Chaslin's sudden departure at the end of the 2012 season and Bicket's appointment, the company considered many potential chiefs before choosing the British maestro.

In other 2013 administrative news that would have pleased John Crosby, there were 123 new parking spaces and a new picnic area to serve the incoming crowds. Those may sound like small fry, but such amenities contribute greatly to a positive audience experience—and happy audience members are more likely to buy more tickets, as well as to potentially become donors to the organization. Another upcoming major project will be improving the mezzanine and balcony air flow system, something that had long been on Crosby's mind. Another project is to resurface the parking lot, which in some places has been untouched for decades. In what is sure to be a thumbs-up from everyone, the number of restrooms will soon be increased yet again. Crosby would be delighted at that change, although surely he would caution everyone to keep a weather eye on water. Backstage, as there has been no major renovation of facilities since the 1968 theater was built, technical and mechanical equipment will be upgraded to modern-day specifications.

To technical director: August 21, 1997

Just to confirm our conversation yesterday evening, the problem with the Sysco double roll toilet paper holders in the Opera Club new ladies' lounge is not the location, but the difficulty of pulling paper out.

The paper tears off frequently, one sheet at a time.

It is difficult to pull paper from the roll in the forward position (nearest the lavatory door.)

There is a white button which may need to be pushed to switch from one roll to another, but it is confusing.

Carolyn Lockwood and I checked each dispenser in each stall. It was very frustrating to try and use these dispensers.

I urgently recommend the simplest possible dispensers (double roll probably a good idea) for the new lavatories and a change-out of any of the impractical dispensers.

With all due respect for our patrons we have to remember many of them are elderly, frail, and do not necessarily see well. We also must bear in mind that patrons arrive having just had a full meal with wine and spirits. They have digestive problems and fainting spells.

Finally, the company possesses 166 acres, with twenty-five buildings scattered over them, from the theater and Stieren Orchestra Hall to offices, rehearsal studios and pavilions, the cantina, and maintenance facilities—one of the few companies in the world with such a large-scale, wholly owned campus.

Artistically, the 2014 season broke new ground as well as restoring a few staples. Stravinsky's *Le Rossignol* returned in its fifth company production, slated on a double bill with Mozart's *The Impresario* in its Santa Fe Opera debut. *Carmen* was back for the seventh time, and Donizetti's *Don Pasquale* returned for the first time since its house debut in 1983. The company mounted Ludwig van Beethoven's *Fidelio* for the first time. Continuing the tradition of American and world premieres, Huang Ruo's *Dr. Sun Yat-sen* received its American premiere. Conductor Carolyn Kuan, leading it, was the first woman to step onto the company podium for a full-length production since Margaret Hillis led Marc Blitzstein's *Regina* in 1959. The mix was deliciously Crosbyean

John Crosby appears slightly bemused between two chorus girls—Rockettes, perhaps—at an event in the early 1980s, presumably for the Manhattan School of Music. Photograph by Henry Grossman. Used by permission.

in its approach, and its combination of offerings had, if not something for everyone, then something certainly for any sincere opera-goer.

The 2015 season, announced in May 2014, presents a carefully balanced seesaw of choices, all new productions. Donizetti's *The Daughter of the Regiment* will be presented in its company debut, followed by an unfamiliar Mozart comedy, *La Finta Giardiniera*. Strauss's *Salome* is due back on the stage after nine years—something Crosby surely would have approved—and Verdi's classic *Rigoletto* is slated to return after fifteen years. The world premiere, greeted at its announcement with much acclaim, is *Cold Mountain*, by composer Jennifer Higdon and librettist Gene Scheer, based on the 2003 novel by Anthony Minghella.

To a board member about a new Opera Club manager: November 29, 1966

He has worked with young people as a Scout Master, and, of course, (his) delicate and gentlemanly assistance to inebriated members of the (Metropolitan) Opera Club of all ages has been a remarkable accomplishment for many years. He would be just perfect for us, with respect to our directors, subscribers, distinguished guests, general public, and the parking lot boys.

In addition to the artistic slate, MacKay announced that the company was undertaking a major three-year reconstruction and revitalization project, as previously referenced. As of this writing, $24.3 million has been raised of a $35 million total campaign. As with all previous Santa Fe Opera renovations and building, the work was slated to take place during three off-seasons so that the artistic preparation and audience experience would remain unhampered. The first year is devoted to work on the front of house, to make the patron experience easier and more pleasant. The second year will involve major renovation and enlarging of the backstage and production areas as well as of the Opera Club—no updates in those areas have been

John Crosby conducts a group of Apprentice Artists in a 1985 rehearsal of Offenbach's *Orpheus in the Underworld*. Although his stern presence might suggest otherwise, Crosby loved conducting operetta as well as the works of Richard Strauss. Photographer unknown. Courtesy The Santa Fe Opera.

made since 1968, even when the new house was built in 1997–1998. Finally will come the renovation and repair of the patron parking lot and construction of onsite storage facilities for productions, replacing the semitrucks that currently dot the property.

To President, Opera Association of New Mexico: June 6, 1980

We shall be taking in bar stock soon for all the theatre bars. We plan to charge $2.00 for drinks (hard liquor), and last year we had some complaint about our bar Scotch ("Dawsons").

For about $2.00 more per case we can pour Haig & Haig 5-star. On a 1-1/2 oz. basis we estimate twenty drinks per bottle—or 240 per case. (Our distributors) can supply Haig & Haig, and we like to do business with them because of fast delivery and good pricing on their part.

Please let me know if the above is not agreeable.

How would you feel about our pouring Haig & Haig 5-star at the Club. Last year I believe we offered J & B.

So even with John Crosby gone, his organization continues to sail forward in time, navigating financial, social, and artistic waters with the confidence he instilled in so many people and following the course and directions he set out during that first 1957 season. The small flat headstone in the Santa Fe National Cemetery marks where his body lies, but his living memorial soars into the sky three miles north, amid sound and wonder. The old ranch kitchen and its refrigerator, once packed with Crosby's cigarettes, has vanished in a recent renovation, and the white petunias he loved are gone from the theater entrance. But for as long as there is a Santa Fe Opera, the vision of voices flourishes, and John Crosby abides.

Acknowledgments

Material for this study came from original and secondary printed sources, from some online proprietary and free sources, and through scores of interviews with persons who knew, worked with, or were friends of John Crosby. One and all, their memories were sharp with the distinctness that comes from deeply etched experiences.

Nancy Zeckendorf's warm affection for Crosby is equaled only by her knowledge of him attained through years of interactions as a Santa Fe Opera board president, chairman, and champion fundraiser—and as Nancy King, a dancer with the company in early seasons. Her help has been vital to this work.

I heartily thank James O. Crosby, John Crosby's elder brother, for his participation. His loving memories of his sibling have brought accuracy and warmth to the story of their early days and proven John Crosby's sincere, if quietly understated, affection for his family. I also acknowledge a deep debt of gratitude to John Crosby's nieces and nephew for sharing generously their remembrances, family pictures, and anecdotes of him: Elizabeth Anne (Lisa) Pasto-Crosby, Laurence Alden Crosby (named for his grandfather, James and John Crosby's father), and Caroline Leland Crosby. They provided an interesting second-generation appraisal of their famous uncle.

Santa Fe Opera General Director Charles MacKay graciously allowed me access to the company's files, including John Crosby's surviving company correspondence, plus years of clippings, images, photographs, scores, program books, and reviews. He also allowed me access to transcriptions of John Crosby's oral history, taken at the opera in May 1997, and to the short autobiographical sketch John

Crosby was writing at the time of his death. I am grateful both for this access and for his generously sharing his own close memories of John Crosby with me.

Many current Santa Fe Opera staff members were more than helpful, including those who worked closely with Crosby and, as of this writing, remain pillars of the company. Brad Woolbright, who worked with Crosby day in and day out in various positions for decades and is now Director of Artistic Administration, offered telling insights. So did Benjamin Saiz, currently Controller and now the longest-serving staff member still with The Santa Fe Opera—he has been with the company more than forty years. Tom Morris, Director of Administration and Operations, brought keen insight to the book concerning what it was like to work with John Crosby for more than twenty years. Paul Horpedahl, Production and Facilities Director and a former technical apprentice, offered fascinating anecdotes about Crosby's attention to production matters. Joyce Idema, Director of Press and Public Relations, and Brian Dailey, Senior Major Gifts Officer, were equally generous with their recollections. Together, their input covered the company's entire life. Many thanks to all.

Thomas B. Catron III was John Crosby's friend and attorney for forty-five years. His sharp memories of the ongoing years of the company and his personal experiences with Crosby shone light into dark corners and clarified uncertain matters. He also kindly provided access to files of Crosby's correspondence with Paul Hindemith and Hans Werner Henze.

Designer Henry Heymann provided interesting information about the early years of the company and John Crosby's relationship with Frank Magee Jr. His carefully considered stories of The Santa Fe Opera's working structure in the first six seasons have proven invaluable, as have his memories of specific personalities.

James Clois Smith Jr. was a superb source of information about his experiences with John Crosby during the period when baritone John Reardon was a frequent performer at The Santa Fe Opera and after. He also kindly supplied important photographs, as well as permission to use information from Sunstone Press's 1976 landmark *The First Twenty Years of The Santa Fe Opera*, by Eleanor Scott. All quotations and information gleaned from that book appear courtesy of Sunstone

Press. I am exceptionally grateful for this permission, which made researching the company's early years a pleasure.

Many other people willingly and fully assisted me in various ways through consultations and interviews and smoothed the way for me in research both at The Santa Fe Opera and elsewhere. They include administrative staff members, technical personnel, board members, and orchestra members; singers; and donors, critics, and community members. As well as those noted elsewhere, especially this study's funders, they include Peter Ader, Tracy Armagost, David Ater, Richard Balthazar, Jefferson Baum, Robert Baustian, Martin Bernheimer, Richard Best, Andrea J. Bishofberger, Jeanne Chieffo Boyles, Thomas Cirillo, Beth Clayton, Carl Condit, E. H. Corrigan, Michael Rolland Davis and the late Earl Wild, Miles Davis, Edo de Waart, Bruce Donnell, Carole Ely, Matthew A. Epstein, Hans W. Fahrmeyer, Mary Lou Falcone, Bryan Gilliam, Robert Glick, David Gockley, Sheri Greenawald, Reri Grist, Eric Halfvarson, Bliss Hebert, David Holloway, Paula Hunter, Paul G. Hutton, Mary Jane Johnson, Danis Kelly, Allen Charles Klein, Winnie Klotz, Gene Kuntz, Jane Stieren Lacy, Cynthia Layman, Sue La Liberté, Steven Landrum, Carolyn Lockwood, Susan MacKay, Patricia A. McFate, Johanna Meier, Mikael Melbye, Gordon Micunis, Erie Mills, Kenneth Montgomery, Dominique Moralez, John Moriarty, Jerome Nelson, Kirt Pavitt, MacGregor Wilson Peck, Tobias Picker, James Polshek, Patricia Racette, Theodora Raven, Dan Rice, JoAnn Rice, Molly Rose, Dale Scargall, Marc Scorca, Linda R. Shockley, Dale R. Smith, Nadine Stafford, Richard Stilwell, Lore Thorpe, David Triestram, Michael Trujillo, Peggy Tueller, Robert Tweten, Michael Udow, Jan Van Dooren, James A. Van Sant, Helen and Mario Vanni, Frederica von Stade, Andrea Fellows Walters, Gary Thor Wedow, Julie Wheeler, Paul Wolfe, and Darren K. Woods. My thanks to all.

I am grateful to Robin McKinney Martin, owner of the *Santa Fe New Mexican*. She provided a work space for me in the company's offices during the course of my researching and writing this study. It was tremendously helpful to have a central source for work in the midst of a creatively busy newsroom. Former publisher Ginny Sohn and many staff members have also been supportive about the progress of the book, including former editor Rob Dean, current editor Ray Rivera, and especially *Pasatiempo* editor Kristina Melcher.

I acknowledge additionally the sympathetic encouragement of biographer and choreographer Judith Chazin-Bennahum, kind assistance from Peter Rawson of the Hotchkiss School and the staff of the Yale University Library, and all those who provided illustration and textual quotation permissions. John Byram of the University of New Mexico Press has been generous with time and counsel throughout the course of this project. Sandra Nelson's professionalism and insight as a consulting editor are deeply appreciated. Debra Ayers, Joseph Illick, Robert Nott, Devon Jackson, and Nancy Zeckendorf read the manuscript and made valuable suggestions. Bill and Alicia Miller kindly permitted me to tour John Crosby's beloved cabin home, which they purchased in March 2000, and which they have cared for in a way that would greatly please its original builder. Virginia Browning, Joseph Illick, and Carolyn Vantress provided attentive support during the writing of this book and throughout our long and valued friendships.

I have received much deeply appreciated support from many people, but no person has dictated the conclusions or opinions stated in this biography. Those, and any errors of fact, are my own.

Appendix

The Santa Fe Opera Repertory, 1957–2015

Thomas Adès
  The Tempest, 2006 (American premiere)
Ludwig van Beethoven
  Fidelio, 2014 (Santa Fe Opera premiere)
Vincenzo Bellini
  La Sonnambula, 2004
Alban Berg
  Lulu, acts 1 and 2, 1963 (American premiere), 1964, 1974
  Lulu, with act 3, 1979 (American premiere)
  Wozzeck, 1966, 2001, 2011
Luciano Berio
  Opera, 1970 (world premiere)
Hector Berlioz
  Beatrice and Benedict, 1998, 2004
Georges Bizet
  Carmen, 1961, 1964, 1967, 1975, 1999, 2006, 2014
  The Pearl Fishers, 2012
Marc Blitzstein
  Regina, 1959
Hans-Jürgen von Böse
  The Sorrows of Young Werther, 1992 (American premiere)
Benjamin Britten
  Albert Herring, 2010
  Billy Budd, 2008
  Noah's Flood, 1996, 1999, 2013

Owen Wingrave, 1973 (American premiere)
Peter Grimes, 2005
The Turn of the Screw, 1983
Pier Francesco Cavalli
La Calisto, 1989
L'Egisto, 1974 (American premiere), 1976
L'Orione, 1983 (American premiere)
Domenico Cimarosa
The Secret Marriage, 1984
Claude Debussy
Pelléas et Mélisande, 1972, 1977
Gaetano Donizetti
Anna Bolena, 1959, 1970
The Daughter of the Regiment, 2015
Don Pasquale, 1983, 2014
The Elixir of Love, 1968, 2009
Lucia di Lammermoor, 1965, 1979, 2001
John Eaton
The Tempest, 1985 (world premiere)
Manuel de Falla
La Vida Breve, 1975
Carlisle Floyd
Wuthering Heights, 1958 (world premiere)
John Gay
The Beggar's Opera, 1992, 2000 (showcase production*)
Umberto Giordano
Fedora, 1977
Christoph Willibald Gluck
Alceste, 2009
Orfeo ed Euridice, 1990
Osvaldo Golijov
Ainadmar, 2005
Charles Gounod
Faust, 2011

*A showcase production is an off-season production mounted off the main stage.

George Frideric Handel
  Agrippina, 2004
  Ariodante, 1987
  Radamisto, 2008
  Semele, 1997
  Xerxes, 1993
Hans Werner Henze
  The Bassarids, 1968 (American premiere)
  Boulevard Solitude, 1967 (American premiere)
  The English Cat, 1985 (American premiere)
  The Stag King, 1965 (American premiere)
  Venus and Adonis, 2000 (American premiere)
  We Come to the River, 1984 (American premiere)
Jennifer Higdon
  Cold Mountain, 2015 (world premiere)
Paul Hindemith
  Cardillac, 1967 (American premiere)
  News of the Day, 1961 (American premiere), 1981
Arthur Honneger
  Joan of Arc at the Stake, 1962, 1963
Leoš Janáček
  The Cunning Little Vixen, 1975 (American premiere)
  Kátya Kabanová, 2003
Emmerich Kálmán
  Countess Maritza, 1995, 1999
Erich Wolfgang Korngold
  Violanta, 1984
David Lang
  Modern Painters, 1995 (world premiere)
Franz Lehár
  The Merry Widow, 1973
Marvin David Levy
  The Tower, 1957 (world premiere)
Ingvar Lidholm
  A Dream Play, 1998 (American premiere)
Peter Lieberson
  Ashoka's Dream, 1997 (world premiere)

Jules Massenet
  Chérubin, 1989
  Cinderella, 2006
Siegfried Matthus
  Judith, 1990 (American premiere)
Gian Carlo Menotti
  Help! Help! The Globolinks, 1969 (American premiere), 1970
  The Last Savage, 2011
Claudio Monteverdi
  L'Incoronazione di Poppea, 1986
Douglas Moore
  The Ballad of Baby Doe, 1961
Paul Moravec
  The Letter, 2009 (world premiere)
Theodore Morrison
  Oscar, 2013 (world premiere)
Wolfgang Amadeus Mozart
  The Abduction from the Seraglio, 1959, 1994
  La clemenza di Tito, 2002
  Così fan tutte, 1957, 1958, 1962, 1969, 1975, 1977, 1988, 1990,
    1997, 2003, 2007
  Don Giovanni, 1963, 1966, 1972, 1992, 1996, 2004, 2009
  La Finta Giardiniera, 2015
  Idomeneo, 1999
  The Impresario, 2014
  Lucio Silla, 2005
  The Magic Flute, 1968, 1969, 1971, 1974, 1979, 1980, 1984, 1986,
    1993, 1998, 2006, 2010
  The Marriage of Figaro, 1960, 1961, 1964, 1965, 1967, 1970, 1971,
    1973, 1976, 1982, 1985, 1987, 1991, 1995, 2000, 2008, 2013
  Mitridate, 2001
Jacques Offenbach
  La Belle Hélène, 2003
  The Grand Duchess of Gérolstein, 1971, 1972, 1974, 1979, 2013
  Orpheus in the Underworld, 1983, 1985
  The Tales of Hoffmann, 2010

Stephen Oliver
   The Duchess of Malfi, 1978 (American premiere)
Stephen Paulus
   Shoes for the Santo Niño, 2012 (showcase production)
Krzysztof Penderecki
   The Black Mask, 1988 (American premiere)
   The Devils of Loudun, 1969 (American premiere)
Giovanni Battista Pergolesi
   La Serva Padrona, 1957
Tobias Picker
   Emmeline, 1996 (world premiere)
Francis Poulenc
   Dialogues of the Carmelites, 1966, 1999
Giacomo Puccini
   La Bohème, 1958, 1961, 1964, 1967, 1973, 1974, 1981, 1990, 1993,
      2007, 2011
   La Fanciulla del West, 1991, 1995
   Gianni Schicchi, 1960, 1964
   Madame Butterfly, 1957, 1959, 1963, 1965, 1968, 1972, 1987, 1996,
      1998, 2010
   Tosca, 1960, 1962, 1966, 1969, 1978, 1994, 2012
   Turandot, 2005
Jean-Phillippe Rameau
   Platée, 2007
Maurice Ravel
   L'Enfant et les Sortilèges, 1963, 1964, 1973, 1975
Aribert Reimann
   Melusine, 1972 (American premiere)
Wolfgang Rihm
   Oedipus, 1991 (American premiere)
George Rochberg
   The Confidence Man, 1982 (world premiere)
Gioachino Rossini
   The Barber of Seville, 1957, 1959, 1965, 1967, 1981, 1994, 2005
   Cinderella, 1958, 1960, 1966
   Count Ory, 1978

La Donna del Lago, 2013

Ermione, 2000

The Italian Girl in Algiers, 2002

Maometto II, 2012

Nino Rota

The Italian Straw Hat, 1977 (American premiere)

Huang Ruo

Dr. Sun Yat-sen, 2014

Kaija Saariaho

Adriana Mater, 2008 (American premiere)

L'Amour de loin, 2002 (American premiere)

Aulis Sallinen

The King Goes Forth to France, 1986 (American premiere)

Arnold Schoenberg

Erwartung, 1980

Die Jakobsleiter, 1968 (American premiere), 1980

Von Heute auf Morgen, 1980 (American premiere)

Bright Sheng

Madame Mao, 2003 (world premiere)

Dmitri Shostakovich

The Nose, 1965 (American premiere), 1987

Lewis Spratlan

Life Is a Dream, 2010 (world premiere)

Johann Strauss Jr.

Die Fledermaus, 1959, 1963, 1982, 1986,1988, 1992

Richard Strauss

Arabella, 1965, 1983, 1997, 2012

Ariadne auf Naxos, 1957, 1990, 1999

Capriccio, 1958 (American premiere), 1966, 1993

Daphne, 1964 (American premiere), 1981, 1996, 2007

The Egyptian Helen, 1986 (American premiere/Vienna version), 2001

Elektra, 1980, 2000

Feuersnot, 1988

Friedenstag, 1988 (American premiere)

Intermezzo, 1984 (American premiere), 1994, 2003

Die Liebe der Danae, 1982 (American premiere), 1985

Der Rosenkavalier, 1961, 1963, 1968, 1989, 1992

Salome, 1962, 1967, 1969, 1972, 1976, 1978, 1979, 1995, 1998, 2006, 2015

Die schweigsame Frau, 1987, 1991

Igor Stravinsky

Mavra, 1962

Oedipus Rex, 1960, 1961, 1962

Perséphone, 1961 (American premiere), 1962, 1968

The Rake's Progress, 1957, 1960, 1962, 1966, 1970, 1981, 1996

Renard, 1962

Le Rossignol, 1962, 1963, 1969, 1970, 1973, 2014

Arthur Sullivan

The Gondoliers, 1960

H.M.S. Pinafore, 2001 (showcase production)

The Pirates of Penzance, 2002 (showcase production)

Karol Szymanowski

King Roger, 2012

Tan Dun

Tea: A Mirror of Soul, 2007 (American premiere)

Peter Ilyitch Tchaikovsky

Eugene Onegin, 1978, 1980, 2002

Ambroise Thomas

Mignon, 1982

Virgil Thomson

The Mother of Us All, 1976

Giuseppe Verdi

Don Carlos, 1971

Falstaff, 1958, 1975, 1977, 2001, 2008

Rigoletto, 1964, 1966, 2000, 2015

Simon Boccanegra, 2004

La Traviata, 1960, 1962, 1965, 1968, 1970, 1976, 1980, 1989, 1991, 1997, 2002, 2009, 2013

Heitor Villa-Lobos

Yerma, 1971 (world premiere)

Antonio Vivaldi

Griselda, 2011

Richard Wagner

The Flying Dutchman, 1971, 1973, 1988

Kurt Weill

   The Protagonist, 1993 (American premiere)

   The Tsar Has His Photograph Taken, 1993 (American premiere)

Judith Weir

   Blond Eckbert, 1994 (American premiere)

   A Night at the Chinese Opera, 1989 (American premiere)

Alexander von Zemlinsky

   A Florentine Tragedy, 1984 (American premiere)

Notes

Preface

I wrote this preface before realizing that Phillip Huscher had followed much the same approach in his 2006 *The Santa Fe Opera: An American Pioneer*. I have let the duplication stand, much in the manner of Ralph Vaughan Williams's point that a composer (and by extension, a writer) should feel no compunction in using the mot juste, even if it has been used previously by someone else.

1. Several persons of undoubted unflappability have reported receiving definite impressions of John Crosby's presence at the opera in the years following his death. These experiences have included hearing his voice addressing them with a "Good evening" or "Good morning," smelling powerful cigarette smoke suddenly when no person anywhere around was smoking, and having the feeling of being watched with the same kind of intensity that a living John Crosby could produce. These impressions have been experienced singly and in small groups. However, no widespread manifestation to a large group has been reported.

2. This information comes from http://gravelocator.cem.va.gov/index.html and a personal visit to the gravesite.

3. For example, Brad Woolbright and Nancy Zeckendorf believed this. Two physicians and two clinical psychologists whom I consulted declined to attempt to diagnose John Crosby at the distance of more than a decade and without access to medical records. (All declined to go on the record by name.) However, standard sources offer an interesting list of behavioral symptoms that accord with an Asperger's diagnosis, including the definition and list of symptoms in the Diseases and Conditions section of the Mayo Clinic site, http://www.mayoclinic.com/health/aspergers-syndrome/DS00551 (accessed July 24, 2014).

4. This writer often saw Crosby walking the aisles of the DeVargas Center Albertsons grocery store in north Santa Fe on Sundays in the summer, his shopping basket filled with hot dogs, buns, and condiments. He would stand peering at an item, then push his glasses back onto his nose in a characteristic gesture. Even in such an informal setting, he radiated a sense of defined personal space. It kept people from approaching him, even when whispers from other shoppers indicated they were discussing his presence.

Chapter One

1. Weather conditions noted here and elsewhere were confirmed via interviews with persons present on the various occasions, including Thomas B. Catron III, Miranda Levy, and Regina Sarfaty Rickless, as well as from various references in Eleanor Scott, *The First Twenty Years of The Santa Fe Opera* (Santa Fe, NM: Sunstone Press, 1976). Online weather records, such as those in the Historical Weather section of the Weather Underground website, http://www.wunderground.com/history (accessed 25 July 2014), also were consulted.

2. Over the years, Crosby himself sometimes spoke of the theater as having just 450 seats, but numerous references in his letter files and in Scott, not to mention company records, confirm the 480 count.

3. Crosby maintained a 9:00 p.m. performance start time for decades despite more or less constant requests from audience members—including members of the board of directors—to advance the clock. He maintained that conditions would not be right for an outdoor theater to present a dramatically viable performance until that time. Today, roughly half of the performances begin at 8:30 p.m. and half at 8:00 p.m. However, see the schedule listings in the *Santa Fean Magazine* for May 1981, which states that starting time in the first season was 8:30 p.m.

4. Different versions are extant of how Sachse came to speak to Aileen and Laurence Crosby and whether he approached one of them first or both together. What is certain is that his intervention helped weight the Crosbys' decision toward funding their son's undertaking. Sachse had impressive port and presence, as well as being a powerful figure in the musical world of New York at the time.

5. Recollections from persons active in the company's early days, including Henry Heymann, Regina Sarfaty Rickless, Gordon Micunis, Theodora Raven, and MacGregor Wilson Peck, all speak to the astonishingly general youth of the participants.

6. Scott, *First Twenty Years*, 115.

7. From a photostat of the 1957 program book. Only the productions

are listed: the number of performances and the dates are not given, and specific information could not be located in the files.

8. Local newspapers the *Santa Fe New Mexican* and the *Albuquerque Journal* provided the bulk of the coverage the first season. But the *New York Times* and *Time* also sent representatives, as well as *Opera News*. The acceptance of the repertoire by the season's audience bore out John Crosby's belief that when operagoers knew little, classic and modern musico-theatrical works would be equally accepted.

9. Some early participants' recollections are that *The Rake's Progress* was the second opera to take the company stage. What is certain, per Scott, *First Twenty Years*, 11, is the rainout.

10. "His regular singers, directors, and designers see him as a desperately shy man who can, as a consequence, appear taciturn and difficult. His detractors—and there are many in the opera world and even on the streets of Santa Fe—find him dictatorial, overbearing, sullen, prickly, and fickle." Thor Eckert Jr., "High on Opera," *Connoisseur*, June 1988, 94–98.

11. Crosby's capacity for alcohol and tobacco was legendary. See The Man and the Myth section in chapter 4.

12. John Crosby, notes for an autobiography, 4–5, supplemented by checking historical records, including the files of the *Santa Fe New Mexican*.

13. Crosby's conducting was the most controversial aspect of his career. See the Musicianship and Conducting section in chapter 4.

14. See "Top 10 Destinations for Opera Lovers," *Opera News*, April 23, 2009, accessed July 25, 2014, http://www.frommers.com/articles/5996.html. In 2013, Santa Fe was also ranked second in *Condé Nast Traveler*'s Readers' Choice Awards; see "Top 10 Cities in the United States," November 2013, accessed July 25, 2014, http://www.cntraveler.com/readers-choice-awards/united-states/best-cities-america_slideshow_2-Santa-Fe_9.

15. This information is from Ancestry.com.

16. "Family Record of James Crosby: 1790–19," *Buried Treasures* 11, no. 3 (July 1979): 5–8, published by the Central Florida Genealogical and Historical Society, Orlando; interviews with Lisa Pasto-Crosby, Laurence Crosby, and Caroline Crosby.

17. From family trees provided by Lisa Pasto-Crosby and Laurence Crosby.

18. Information on this accident and its subsequent impact on the family comes from interviews with Lisa Pasto-Crosby, Laurence Crosby, and Caroline Crosby.

19. Biographical information in this and ensuing paragraphs is drawn from the MarquisWho'sWho.com online biography of Laurence Crosby,

accessed July 25, 2014, https://cgi.marquiswhoswho.com/OnDemand/Default.aspx?last_name=crosby&first_name=laurence.

20. FreeBMD Birth Index, 1837–1915, England & Wales, Ancestry.com, accessed August 11, 2014, http://search.ancestry.com/cgi-bin/sse.dll?rank=1&new=1&MSAV=0&gss=angs-c&gsfn=aileen+Mary&gsln=O%27Hea&gsln_x=NS_NP_NN&msbdy=1885&msbpn__ftp=London%2c+London%2c+England&msbpn=85535&msbpn_PInfo=8-%7c0%7c0%7c3257%7c3251%7c0%7c0%7c0%7c5274%7c85535%7c0%7c&uidh=6v5&msbdd=23&msbdm=10&_83004003-n_xcl=m&pcat=34&h=25304113&recoff=7+8+9&db=FreeBMDBirth&indiv=1&ml_rpos=3.

21. Interview with Caroline Crosby.

22. Information about Crosby family history here and throughout this chapter comes variously from interviews with James O. Crosby, Lisa Pasto-Crosby, Laurence Crosby, and Caroline Crosby.

23. From interviews with James O. Crosby, Lisa Pasto-Crosby, Laurence Crosby, and Caroline Crosby and from the John Crosby transcribed interview/oral history, May 29, 1997, 4.

24. Find My Past, accessed August 10, 2014, http://search.findmypast.co.uk/record?id=gbc%2f1911%2frg14%2f03313%2f0533%2f1&highlights=%22%22.

25. Laurence Alden Crosby, Passenger Search, The Statue of Liberty–Ellis Island Foundation, Inc., accessed July 26, 2014, http://ellisisland.org.

26. Biography of Laurence Crosby, MarquisWho'sWho.com.

27. Ancestry.com, accessed August 11, 2014, http://trees.ancestry.com/tree/52537130/family.

28. This quotation and succeeding quotations from James Crosby are drawn from interviews with and information supplied by him.

29. From conversations with the late Miranda Levy, 2003.

30. Foreign Claim Settlement Commission of the United States Cuban Claims Program: Certified Claimant List, United States Department of Justice, April 22, 2009, accessed July 28, 2014, http://www.justice.gov/fcsc/readingroom/ccp-listofclaims.pdf.

31. Interview with Lisa Pasto-Crosby.

32. Information in this and ensuing paragraphs about the Crosby family home in Bronxville is drawn from John Crosby's oral history, interviews with family members as identified in earlier notes in this chapter, and a "Housing History of John O. Crosby," provided courtesy of Thomas B. Catron III. Crosby drew up this extensive document when attempting to convince the New York State taxation and revenue department that he was a resident of New Mexico, not New York. It is an excellent example of

Crosby's obsessive record keeping and lists every place he lived, either as a family member, owner, or renter, from his birth through 1991.

33. Interview with Lisa Pasto-Crosby.

34. Interviews with Lisa Pasto-Crosby and Laurence Crosby.

35. Interview with Lisa Pasto-Crosby.

36. Crosby was famous for wearing a casual shirt until it became thread-bare, even though he had at least a score of identical outfits in his closet. Male staff members attending pool parties, at which the women changed into their bathing suits in one room and the men in Crosby's bedroom, couldn't resist looking in his closet on one occasion, only to find the same outfit, over and over, neatly hung up (per Robert Tweten).

37. Interview with Lisa Pasto-Crosby.

38. Interview with Laurence Crosby.

39. Interview with Winnie Klotz and Paul Hutton.

40. Information from John Crosby, oral history, 1, 4, and interviews with James Crosby.

41. Information here and in ensuing paragraphs about John Crosby's musical education and private study comes from his oral history.

42. Interview with Lisa Pasto-Crosby, who currently owns the instrument.

43. The Allagash River trip was especially pivotal for both James and John because, given Laurence's busy business and travel schedule, they generally saw their mother more often than they did their father. The chance to spend time with Laurence and a favorite uncle was life-changing.

44. From interviews with James Crosby.

45. There are numerous web references to be found relating to James Crosby's notable career as a Spanish scholar, and many of his books can be located today on Amazon.com or Abe.com.

46. John Crosby, oral history, 4.

47. Confirmed by Santa Fe Opera staff members, including Brad Woolbright and former apprentice artist Darren Keith Woods.

48. This and preceding information in this paragraph is taken from John Crosby, oral history, 6.

49. Ibid., 7, 8.

50. Ibid., 8.

51. Ibid., 9.

52. "History of the Los Alamos Ranch School," Los Alamos Historical Society, accessed July 26, 2014, http://losalamoshistory.org/ranch_school.htm.

53. John Crosby, oral history, 12.

54. Conversations with Miranda Levy, 2002. In his oral history,

however, Crosby states he did not meet Mirandi until 1948 and that she first began helping publicize The Santa Fe Opera project in 1956 (20).

55. John Crosby to Lesley Poling-Kempes, letter, October 21, 1991.

56. Interviews with Brad Woolbright.

57. Information from the 1944 yearbook *The Mischianza* (published by the graduating class of the Hotchkiss School), 44, 97, 111, 124.

58. *The Mischianza*, 101.

59. John Crosby, oral history, 20-21.

60. James Crosby interviews.

61. Information from John Crosby's file in the offices of Catron, Catron, Pottow & Glassman, attorneys at law, Santa Fe, NM, courtesy of Thomas B. Catron III.

62. General information on Crosby's military activity, from here to the end of this section, is drawn from John Crosby, oral history, 22–34.

63. Ibid., 23-24.

64. Ibid., 25; Crosby files in the Catron et al. offices.

65. John Crosby, oral history, 28

66. Crosby files in the Catron et al. offices.

67. John Crosby, oral history, 31.

68. Crosby files in the Catron et al. offices.

69. Ibid.

70. Ibid.

71. Interview with Lisa Pasto-Crosby.

72. Information from a copy of the show's program book, courtesy Henry Heymann.

73. John Crosby, oral history, 35.

74. Ibid., 36.

75. Ibid., 38.

76. Ibid., 38

77. Interview with Caroline Crosby.

78. Information on Crosby's relationship with Magee supplied by Henry Heymann, an active and brilliant stage designer in the early years of The Santa Fe Opera and also a Yale attendee during this period; he was close both to Crosby and to Magee. Magee was still living as of this writing but was unavailable for interviews. He died on January 1, 2015.

79. Per Magee's undated résumé in the Crosby letter files at The Santa Fe Opera.

80. Per Santa Fe Opera program books, 1958–1963.

81. Yale University digital scan of John Crosby's listing in the 1950 Yale yearbook; see photo on page 29.

82. Columbia information in this paragraph from a letter and résumé of

April 8, 1954, sent to a Miss Charlotte Griggs, indicating Crosby's interest in the position of conductor of the Tri-City Symphony, based in Davenport, Iowa.

83. John Crosby, housing history.

84. Interview with Edgar Foster Daniels.

85. Crosby's views on the Metropolitan Opera and its role in re-creating operatic viability in the United States come from his oral history, 43–47. Many other commentators have discussed this artistic revival, including the special effect the Metropolitan Opera's landmark *Così fan tutte* had on opera production around the country.

86. Ibid., 43–44.

87. John Crosby to rodeo manager, letter, July 15, 1964, commenting on Bing's short stay at the rodeo.

88. John Crosby, notes for an autobiography, 6.

89. This and subsequent information on Crosby's early relationship with Sachse is in ibid., 7.

90. Ibid., 6; but see 5, where he states that he had decided in 1954 on Santa Fe as the best site for a theater. "I had not progressed any further than to settle on Santa Fe as the most desirable location for a summertime festival of opera."

91. This and subsequent information from John Crosby, notes for an autobiography, 7–8.

92. Interview with James A. Van Sant.

93. John Crosby to Leopold Sachse, letter, July 21, 1956.

94. John Crosby to Mrs. Pierre Monteux, telegram, July 1, 1964.

95. John Crosby to Benjamin Saiz, letter, August 19, 1994.

Chapter Two

1. In his oral history John Crosby speaks only of one summer at Bishop's Lodge, 1943. Lore Thorpe, whose late husband was one of the past owners of the lodge, was certain that the young men were there in the summer of 1947 and 1948. Crosby told Thorpe later that her mother-in-law, the senior Mrs. Thorpe, taught him how to be frugal by means of the breakfasts served to the help: they could have cereal or eggs in the morning, but not both foods. See also John Crosby to Edward Purrington, letter, February 22, 1968, wherein Crosby says that he knew the manager of Bishop's Lodge well "in 1946–47 and 48."

2. John Crosby, housing history.

3. Interviews with James O. Crosby.

4. Interview with Laurence Crosby.

5. Interviews with James O. Crosby.

6. Interview with Laurence Crosby.

7. Interview with Realtor Dale Scargall, who sold the property for James and John in July 1973.

8. John Crosby, housing history.

9. Interview with Jeanne Chieffo Boyles.

10. Interview with Susan MacKay.

11. Interview with Regina Sarfaty Rickless.

12. Conversations with Miranda Levy, 2006.

13. Interview with Carolyn Lockwood.

14. Interview with Theodora Raven.

15. Interview with Carolyn Lockwood.

16. Interviews with Charles MacKay.

17. Interview with Caroline Crosby.

18. Information in this paragraph comes from interviews with Benjamin Saiz.

19. Interview with Lisa Pasto-Crosby.

20. Interview with Laurence Crosby.

21. Interview with Sue La Liberté.

22. John Crosby to Joseph D'Addesio, letter, December 12, 1971.

23. John Crosby to Joseph Regan Jr., letter, October 25, 1971.

24. Crosby, Aileen O'Hea, Nationwide Gravesite Locator, National Cemetery Administration, last updated April 30, 2014, accessed July 29, 2014, http://gravelocator.cem.va.gov/index.html.

25. John Crosby to Bernard Zielinski, letter retaining Zielinski as a nurse and companion for Laurence Alden Crosby, November 23, 1974.

26. Interviews with Charles MacKay.

27. John Crosby to Elizabeth "Betty" Crosby, letter, March 25, 1975.

28. Crosby, Laurence Alden, Nationwide Gravesite Locator, National Cemetery Administration, last updated April 30, 2014, accessed July 29, 2014, http://gravelocator.cem.va.gov/index.html.

29. Crosby, Laurence Alden, Nationwide Gravesite Locator, National Cemetery Administration, last updated April 30, 2014, accessed July 29, 2014, http://gravelocator.cem.va.gov/index.html.

30. John Crosby to Lisa Pasto-Crosby and Caroline Crosby, letters, September 18, 1984.

31. Interview with Laurence Crosby.

32. John Crosby to James Crosby, letter, May 20, 1993.

33. Information in this paragraph comes from an interview with Laurence Crosby.

34. Information in this paragraph comes from an interview with Lisa Pasto-Crosby.

35. Information in this paragraph comes from an interview with Caroline Crosby.

36. Information in this paragraph comes from an interview with Lisa Pasto-Crosby.

37. This story was charmingly recounted by both Caroline Crosby and Lisa Pasto-Crosby.

38. John Crosby, notes for an autobiography, 4.

39. Ibid., 5.

40. Scott, *First Twenty Years*, 8.

41. John Crosby, notes for an autobiography, 4.

42. Ibid.

43. Ibid.

44. Information and quotations in this paragraph are from ibid., 5.

45. Ibid., 5–6.

46. Ibid., 6.

47. Information drawn from Miranda Levy obituary in the *Santa Fe New Mexican*, "Spark Plug Helped Breathe Life into Santa Fe Opera," June 9, 2011. Also see the special supplement to the *Santa Fe New Mexican*, "The Santa Fe Opera 50th Anniversary," June 28, 2006. A somewhat different version of the story is in John Pen LaFarge, *Turn Left at the Sleeping Dog: Scripting the Santa Fe Legend, 1920–1955* (Albuquerque: University of New Mexico Press, 2001). Levy, though acute well into her nineties, did not always recount a story the same way twice.

48. John Crosby, notes for an autobiography, 6.

49. Ibid., 8.

50. Ibid., 7.

51. Ibid., 8.

52. Ibid., 8–9.

53. Information in this paragraph is from ibid., 12–13.

54. Variously in Scott, *First Twenty Years*, and John Crosby, notes for an autobiography, 11.

55. Information from conversations with Miranda Levy, 2006, and interviews with Thomas B. Catron III.

56. Marian F. Love, "From Beans to Grand Opera," *Santa Fean Magazine* 9, no. 4 (May 1981): 20–21.

57. John Crosby, notes for an autobiography, 9.

58. Information in this paragraph is from a memo of March 4, 1967, unsigned but presumably written by John Crosby. It sets out the details of the lease-purchase agreements and provides details of other theater and company history.

59. John Crosby, notes for an autobiography, 10.

60. Ibid., 13.

61. Ibid.

62. Ibid.,14.

63. John Crosby's relationship with the American Guild of Musical Artists (AGMA) over the years ranged from cordial to testy, but he respected the organization's mission and reach, if not always its proposals, according to Brad Woolbright.

64. Information in this paragraph is from John Crosby, notes for an autobiography, 14–15.

65. Copy of original Articles of Incorporation provided by Thomas B. Catron III.

66. Information in this paragraph is from the John Crosby housing history.

67. John Crosby to Greig Porter, letter, November 9, 1999, discussing the sale of the brownstone to the opera company and proposing that half of the value of the building go to the opera as a gift annuity and half as an outright sale.

68. This information comes from Scott, *First Twenty Years*, 11.

69. John Crosby, notes for an autobiography, 11.

70. Ibid.

71. Crosby often spoke of his reliance on and affection for Purcell.

72. Crosby referred at various times to the theater costing $50,000 rather than $115,000. The higher figure is correct as per comparison against the cost of the initial land purchase in 1957: 76.46 acres for $77,000.

73. Scott, *First Twenty Years*, 9; John Crosby to Leopold Sachse, letter, January 6, 1957.

74. This information is from the 1957 program book.

75. Interview with Susan MacKay.

76. John Crosby, notes for an autobiography, 2.

77. Unsigned memo of March 4, 1967.

78. Levy maintained over and over that she met the Stravinskys on August 4, 1949, but the fiftieth anniversary history of the Aspen Music Festival makes it clear that Maestro Stravinsky appeared there only in 1950. There is no record of his participating in the 1949 Goethe Bicentennial Convocation and Music Festival that was the precursor of the Festival proper. Vronsky and Babin, however, took part in the 1949 concerts. See LaFarge, *Turn Left*, 332–33. In addition, Paul Horgan, in *Encounters With Stravinsky: A Personal Record* (New York: Farrar, Straus and Giroux, 1972), makes it clear that 1950 is the correct year. The Aspen Festival history by Bruce Berger, *A Tent in the Meadow: 1949–1999* (Aspen, CO: Sojourner Publications, 1999), clinches the fact.

79. The information that follows on the Stravinskys' first experiences of northern New Mexico is from an interview with Miranda Levy, published in the 2006 "The Santa Fe Opera 50th Anniversary," a special supplement to the *Santa Fe New Mexican.*

80. John Crosby, notes for an autobiography, 16–17.

81. This story exists in multiple versions, from both Miranda Levy and John Crosby, in oral lore as well as in written form. Scott gives another version in *First Twenty Years,* 11. Paul Horgan discussed the encounter in yet other terms in *Encounters with Stravinsky.* What is certain is that Stravinsky did become intrigued by the possibility of The Santa Fe Opera and seeing a production of *The Rake's Progress* performed by a young and dashing company. He only asked that Crosby let Robert Craft conduct and that the opera hire three young singers who had previously done the work in Boston in 1954: Loren Driscoll, Robert Rue, and Marguerite Willauer. Crosby gladly agreed. See John Crosby, notes for an autobiography, 17.

Chapter Three

1. This may have been the night, as recounted by Theodora Raven, when a bonsai-like tree at the rear of the stage began to topple at one point during a performance of *Madame Butterfly.* A doughty volunteer working the show crawled up behind it to prop it up and avoid a possibly risible moment.

2. Miranda Levy in the 2006 "The Santa Fe Opera 50th Anniversary" supplement to the *Santa Fe New Mexican.*

3. Crosby referred to this cleansing operation years later in a letter to Polshek and Partners, January 18, 1996.

4. See Frank Magee Jr., "Opera and the Royal City: A Double Anniversary," *New Mexico Magazine,* June 1960, 11, for confirmation of both white petunias and yellow snapdragons in the flower beds. Aileen Crosby has always been given credit for choosing those flowers, and their regular reappearance was important to John Crosby. The petunias by the theater entrance recently were replaced by xeriscaping.

5. Miranda Levy in the 2006 "The Santa Fe Opera 50th Anniversary" supplement to the *Santa Fe New Mexican.*

6. Scott, *First Twenty Years,* 10.

7. Santa Fe Opera program book, 1957.

8. Santa Fe Opera Program books and the repertoire list in Phillip Huscher, *The Santa Fe Opera: An American Pioneer* (Santa Fe, NM: Santa Fe Opera, 2006), 188–92.

9. Interview with Matthew A. Epstein.

10. Interview with Regina Sarfaty Rickless.

11. Derived from Huscher, *Santa Fe Opera*, 188–92.

12. Santa Fe Opera program book, 1980.

13. But see the May 1981 *Santa Fean*, as noted in chapter 3, note 3.

14. Anecdote related in conversation with Joseph Illick, December 2013. Illick, a former member of the opera's music staff, is now artistic director of Performance Santa Fe and music director of Fort Worth Opera.

15. Information in this paragraph comes from a survey of Santa Fe Opera program books, 1975–2014.

16. Santa Fe Opera program book, 1987.

17. Santa Fe Opera program book, 2000.

18. Huscher, *Santa Fe Opera*, 188–92.

19. Ibid.

20. Santa Fe Opera box office records.

21. Interview with Tom Morris.

22. Santa Fe Opera program book, 1985, and personal observation of the season.

23. Scott, *First Twenty Years*, 73, 79.

24. Interview with Regina Sarfaty Rickless.

25. Scott, *First Twenty Years*, 13.

26. This saying was common currency when the author was a young singer on the audition circuit.

27. Baritone John Reardon felt Crosby's wrath one year, when, kept on the string for months, Reardon took a position at Wolf Trap. He never sang at The Santa Fe Opera again, although the pair remained somewhat friendly in an aloof way. James Clois Smith Jr., interview.

28. Scott, *First Twenty Years*, 28.

29. Information in this paragraph comes from a report to the company by Lillian Libmann on fundraising, July 2, 1959.

30. There have been differing accounts of the years Stravinsky came to The Santa Fe Opera during the company's early years. This list is drawn from Scott, *First Twenty Years*.

31. These anecdotes from the interview with Susan MacKay.

32. Scott, *First Twenty Years*, 11.

33. From Huscher, *Santa Fe Opera*, 64–65, and the plaque in the St. Francis Auditorium in the New Mexico Museum of Art that commemorates the premiere of *The Flood*. See also Scott, *First Twenty Years*, 50.

34. Interview with Regina Sarfaty Rickless.

35. Santa Fe Opera program book, 1971, 26.

36. Robert Craft to John Crosby, letter, April 28, 1971.

37. Santa Fe Opera program book, 1957, and interview with Susan MacKay.

38. John Crosby to Hans Busch, letter, December 30, 1974.

39. Scott, *First Twenty Years*, 10

40. Interview with Mary Lou Falcone. Falcone, who worked with Crosby for some years, recounted how she would advise reporters that the best way to get Crosby to open up was to ask him about his passion for opera and his company. "Any time I brought in a reporter thereafter . . . I would always open it, you know, with 'John, talk about your passion.' And immediately the reporter would see the opening [up] of John Crosby. And this was consistent. It was quite amazing."

41. John Crosby to Mr. and Mrs. William Butler, letter, January 13, 1964.

42. Interview with Daniel Rice.

43. Interview with Gary Thor Wedow.

44. Interview with Daniel Rice.

45. Apprentice Programs, Santa Fe Opera, accessed August 1, 2014, http://www.santafeopera.org/apprenticeprograms/index.aspx.

46. John Crosby, notes for an autobiography, 14.

47. Interview with Benjamin Saiz.

48. John Crosby to Ellyie Schwaartz, letter, March 2, 1970.

49. Interview with David Holloway.

50. Ibid.

51. From Santa Fe Opera press information and a review of company casting.

52. Program & Application Information, Technicians, Apprentice Programs, Santa Fe Opera, accessed August 1, 2014, http://www.santafe opera.org/apprenticeprograms/technicians/programrequirements.aspx.

53. Interview with Paul Horpedahl.

54. Several of these programs were grant driven, and they perished when funding was not renewed.

55. Interviews with David Holloway, Robert Tweten, and Paul Horpedahl.

56. Apprentice Singers, Apprentice Programs, Santa Fe Opera, accessed August 1, 2014, http://www.santafeopera.org/apprenticeprograms, and per confirmation from David Holloway.

57. Interviews with David Holloway and Paul Horpedahl.

58. Santa Fe Opera program book, 2014; interview with Paul Horpedahl.

59. Interview with David Gockley.

60. Scott, *First Twenty Years*, 9, 15.

61. Santa Fe Opera company records.

62. Scott, *First Twenty Years*, 9, 65.

63. Santa Fe Opera company records.

64. Scott, *First Twenty Years*, 65, 77.

65. Unsigned memo, March 4, 1967.

66. Scott, *First Twenty Years*, 32.

67. Ibid.

68. Information in this paragraph is from ibid., 35.

69. Information about the tour is taken from ibid., 38–43.

70. Interview with Carolyn Lockwood.

71. Scott, *First Twenty Years*, 45.

72. Ibid., 47, 53.

73. General information in this section is heavily drawn from ibid., 79–88.

74. From an extract from John Crosby, notes for an autobiography, provided by James Crosby.

75. Interview with Bruce Donnell.

76. Scott, *First Twenty Years*, 80.

77. Ibid.

78. Interviews with Benjamin Saiz.

79. Even two decades after the fire, in 1988, the author heard ongoing cackle about Crosby's possible role in it. Today, time—and the fact of a third theater—has made the topic less general.

80. Scott, *First Twenty Years*, 83.

81. Memo of July 28, 1967, "Western Union Telegrams Received by Santa Fe Opera." Those expressing support included Stravinsky and representatives of the National Council on the Arts, the Metropolitan Opera, the Metropolitan Opera Guild, Lyric Opera of Chicago, and the American Opera Society.

82. Scott, *First Twenty Years*, 81, 83, 84–85.

83. Ibid., 88; interviews with Thomas B. Catron III and Benjamin Saiz.

84. Scott, *First Twenty Years*, 85.

85. Ibid., 90–91.

86. In its materials and records documents, The Santa Fe Opera consistently speaks of the $2 million figure. However, see Scott, *First Twenty Years*, 95, where a total of $1.8 million is given, including $1.45 million for construction, $116,000 in design and professional fees, and seating at $41,000, among other costs.

87. Scott, *First Twenty Years*, 95.

88. See ibid., 90–95, for information in this and ensuing paragraphs.

89. Ibid., 91, 93.

90. Ibid., 95.

91. Santa Fe Opera program book, 1968.

92. Scott, *First Twenty Years*, 95–97.

93. Interviews with Benjamin Saiz; and see Scott, *First Twenty Years*, 122.

94. Interviews with Charles MacKay; and see *Pasatiempo*, the arts magazine of the *Santa Fe New Mexican*, July 3, 2009.

95. This information per Richard Gaddes résumé in The Santa Fe Opera files, dated September 1971.

96. Interviews with Charles MacKay; and see John Crosby to Richard Gaddes, letter, June 2, 1976, discussing Opera Theatre of St. Louis using part of the office space of Crosby's brownstone for a New York office.

97. Interviews with Charles MacKay.

98. From repertory list, Santa Fe Opera program book, 2013, 146–49.

99. The facilities plan study was underwritten by longtime Santa Fe Opera donors Jane and Arthur Stieren. Their generosity is acknowledged in the naming of Stieren Orchestra Hall.

100. Interview with Nancy Zeckendorf.

101. Quoted by Nancy Zeckendorf, with details from Tom Morris, at the John Crosby memorial gathering at The Santa Fe Opera, July 12, 2003.

102. Information on Crosby's attention to restroom details permeated a number of the interviews held for this book. Information on the current expansion plans comes from the 2013 program book.

103. Interview with James Polshek.

104. Ibid.

105. Ibid.

106. Ibid.

107. Interview with Nancy Zeckendorf.

108. Interview with James Polshek.

109. Ibid.

110. Interview with Nancy Zeckendorf.

111. Information about the technical updates is from The Santa Fe Opera program book, 1998.

112. Interview with Regina Sarfaty Rickless.

113. See Hollis Walker, "Saving Water's an Old Habit at Santa Fe Opera—Founder Takes Pride in Wetlands," *Santa Fe New Mexican*, June 6, 1996. The opera suffered a famous power outage on August 5, 2002, at a performance of *Eugene Onegin*, when a snake incinerated itself in an electrical box. The opera's first act was performed in concert without sets; by the second act, the safety generators had been brought fully on line and the production proceeded.

114. John Crosby to William Sullivan, letter, September 7, 1983.

115. John Crosby to William Paty, letter, October 10, 1972.

116. Interviews with Benjamin Saiz.

117. Interview with Paul Horpedahl.

118. Ibid.

119. Interview with Susan MacKay; interview with Robert Glick.

120. Interview with Robert Glick

121. Interview with Dale Scargall.

122. John Crosby to Ike Kalangis, letter, February 24, 1982.

123. Interview with Dale Scargall.

124. Land issues that might affect the opera's operations, even if not on opera property, were as germane to Crosby as the company's own issues.

125. John Crosby to accountant, letter, March 29, 1993.

126. At no time in his life could John Crosby have conceivably been called poor.

127. Like his father, Crosby had a keen eye for a good real estate deal and could see the value of holding property over the long term for the best eventual return.

128. Interview with Dale Scargall.

129. Scott, *The First Twenty Years*, 59.

130. John Crosby to William Hunker, letter, December 7, 1963, insisting on use of the word "estimate" rather than "budget."

131. John Crosby to Nigel Redden, letter, April 15, 1994.

132. Managing this sort of detail may sound impossible, but not for a savant like Crosby. Stories such as this abound on the opera campus, with enough examples to confirm that they are not just apocrypha. Interviews with Brad Woolbright, Tom Morris, Robert Glick, Benjamin Saiz, and others confirm the fact.

133. Interview with Nancy Zeckendorf.

134. Interview with Daniel Rice.

135. Interview with Brad Woolbright.

136. Interview with Charles MacKay.

137. Information in this paragraph comes from an interview with Nancy Zeckendorf, plus perusal of her 1961 company contract as Nancy King.

138. John Crosby to Blake Middleton, letter, January 10, 1992.

Chapter Four

1. General information on John Crosby's physical characteristics comes from comments by staff and family members, photographs, and personal observation of Crosby by the writer from 1983 through 2000.

2. Interview with Theodora Raven.

3. Interview with Winnie Klotz and Paul Hutton.

4. This information comes from an interview with James Crosby, the Hotchkiss School yearbook, and various references to riding, skating, and

swimming in the John Crosby letter files.

5. Interviews with Brad Woolbright and Michael Rolland Davis.

6. John Crosby to Perrine and Marshall McCune, letter, April 26, 1969.

7. See chapter 1.

8. Interviews with Benjamin Saiz.

9. John Crosby to Mrs. Edgar Tobin, letter, June 24, 1970.

10. Interview with Matthew A. Epstein.

11. Interview with Theodora Raven.

12. Personal observation by the author at the home of a person who had been given the shot glass by Crosby.

13. Interview with Danis Kelly.

14. Interview with Thomas Cirillo.

15. Interview with Carolyn Lockwood.

16. In an interview, Robert Tweten, head of the music staff at The Santa Fe Opera, recalled a member of the staff saying that Crosby conducted the opening of *La Bohème* as "(quick inhale) da-da-da-dum."

17. Information in this paragraph comes from interviews with Benjamin Saiz, Peter Ader, and Matthew A. Epstein.

18. Numerous interviewees discussed Crosby's speech patterns, including Paul Horpedahl, Charles MacKay, Tom Morris, Andrea Fellows Walters, Julie Wheeler, Carole Ely, Allen Charles Klein, and Brad Woolbright.

19. Interview with Sheri Greenawald.

20. Interview with Andrea Fellows Walters.

21. Interviews with Brad Woolbright and Paul Horpedahl.

22. Interview with Paul Horpedahl.

23. Interview with John Moriarty.

24. Ibid.

25. From interviews with Allen Charles Klein and Bliss Hebert.

26. Interviews with Charles MacKay.

27. Interviews with Michael Rolland Davis, Bliss Hebert, and Brad Woolbright.

28. Interviews with Charles MacKay.

29. Interviews with Brad Woolbright.

30. Information in this paragraph comes from ibid.

31. Interview with Hans Fahrmeyer.

32. Interview with Paul Wolfe.

33. John Crosby to Cynthia Robbins, letter, February 11, 1980.

34. Crosby's reluctance to use the word *vomit* is interesting.

35. Interview with Martin Bernheimer.

36. Interview with Linda Shockley.

37. Anecdote related by Joyce Idema, July 2013.

38. Interview with Paul Wolfe.

39. Interview with Susan MacKay.

40. In conversation with Michael Trujillo, summer 2013.

41. Information in this and ensuing paragraphs comes from interviews with Brad Woolbright.

42. John Crosby to William Sullivan, letter, March 31, 1984.

43. Author inspection of John Crosby literary works and music score possessions in Santa Fe Opera archives.

44. Stories of Crosby's listening to his own recordings at the cabin—often while relaxing in the swimming pool—are ubiquitous among The Santa Fe Opera staff, both past and current.

45. A long-time and astute observer of The Santa Fe Opera, Van Sant also was deeply involved in the beginnings of Opera Theatre of St. Louis as a businessman, planner, and donor.

46. Crosby, notes for an autobiography, 7.

47. Repertoire list, Santa Fe Opera program book, 2013.

48. All quotations by Bryan Gilliam in this section are from the interview with Bryan Gilliam.

49. Molly Rose to Nancy Zeckendorf, letter, January 8, 2013. Molly Rose was a longtime dancer at The Santa Fe Opera.

50. Interview with Carolyn Lockwood.

51. Interview with Kenneth Montgomery.

52. Anecdote related by a former member of the music staff who requested anonymity.

53. Interview with Robert Tweten.

54. Interviews with Brad Woolbright and Hans Fahrmeyer.

55. Interview with Robert Tweten.

56. Interview with Michael Udow.

57. Interview with Peter Ader.

58. Interview with Gary Thor Wedow.

59. Repertoire list, Santa Fe Opera program book, 2013.

60. Interview with James A. Van Sant.

61. Personal inspection by the author of Crosby's orchestral scores in The Santa Fe Opera archives.

62. Interview with Matthew A. Epstein.

63. Interview with Brad Woolbright.

64. Martin Bernheimer, "Strauss' Unhappy 'Helena' and Other Exotica in Santa Fe," *Los Angeles Times*, August 3, 1986.

65. From Santa Fe Opera press clippings files.

66. All information on operas, composers, and years of production in

this section comes from Santa Fe Opera program books for respective years and from the repertoire list in the 2013 program book.

67. Scott, *First Twenty Years*, 138–39.

68. Repertoire list, Santa Fe Opera program book, 2013.

69. Scott, *First Twenty Years*, 138.

70. Interview with John Crosby, by Margaret Carson, Santa Fe Opera program book, 1972.

71. Interview with Daniel Rice.

72. Interviews with Brad Woolbright.

73. Other critics often hinted at the same opinion, but without being quite as bold as Bernheimer.

74. Constance Mellen, "A Passion in the Desert," *Opera News*, October 1967.

75. Scott Cantrell, "'Elektra' captures essence," *Dallas Morning News*, August 6, 2000.

76. Martin Bernheimer, "Novelty for Novelty's Sake in Santa Fe," *Los Angeles Times*, August 1984.

77. Philip Kennicott, "In Santa Fe, An Operatic Oasis Looks to the Future," *Washington Post*, August 14, 2000.

78. This figure comes from a combination of the approximately 567 times Crosby conducted at his company from 1957 through 2000, per Santa Fe Opera figures in 2000, plus performances of *The Egyptian Helen* in 2001 and *La Traviata* in 2002.

79. Interview with Matthew A. Epstein.

80. Conversation with Regina Sarfaty Rickless.

81. Interview with Miles Davis.

82. Interview with Edo de Waart.

83. Interview with Sheri Greenawald.

84. Interview with Richard Best.

85. Interview with Gene Kuntz.

86. Interview with Richard Stilwell.

87. Interview with David Triestram.

88. Interview with Johanna Meier.

89. Information in this paragraph comes from the interview with Daniel Rice.

90. Information on Crosby's conducting for companies or in venues other than The Santa Fe Opera comes from examination of Santa Fe Opera program books, Crosby biographical listings, and various letters in the company files.

91. Santa Fe Opera program books.

92. Interview with Matthew A. Epstein.

93. Interview with Gary Thor Wedow.

94. Interview with James A. Van Sant.

95. Interview with Gary Thor Wedow.

96. Interview with Jeanne Chieffo Boyles.

97. Interview with Allen Charles Klein.

98. The opera staff member who used this term would only permit it to be used on guarantee of anonymity.

99. Term used by this writer after first meeting Crosby during a 1984 interview at The Santa Fe Opera.

100. Interview with Thomas B. Catron III.

101. Interview with Carole Ely.

102. Interview with Patricia A. McFate

103. Interview with Greig Porter.

104. Ibid.

105. Interview with Carole Ely.

106. Interview with Robert Glick.

107. Interview with Nancy Zeckendorf.

108. Interviews with Charles MacKay.

109. From various letters in The Santa Fe Opera files, including John Crosby to Mrs. Walter Mayer, March 19, 1976, and to Perrine McCune, September 10, 1986.

110. Interview with Carole Ely.

111. John Crosby to Nancy Zeckendorf, letter, November 25, 1996.

112. Interview with Robert Glick.

113. The source of this anecdote, a former staff member, requested anonymity.

114. Interview with Matthew A. Epstein.

115. Interview with Mikael Melbye.

116. Interviews with Brad Woolbright.

117. Interview with Richard Balthazar.

118. Interview with Jeanne Chieffo Boyles.

119. The former staff member who recounted this story requested anonymity.

120. Interview with Julie Wheeler.

121. Interviews with Charles MacKay, Tom Morris, Brad Woolbright, and Benjamin Saiz.

122. Interview with Charles MacKay.

123. Interview with Brian Dailey.

124. Interview with Julie Wheeler.

125. Interview with Carolyn Lockwood.

126. Interview with Paul Horpedahl.

127. Information in this paragraph from interview with Sue La Liberté.

128. Interview with Sue La Liberté.

129. Interview with Julie Wheeler.

130. Interview with Darren Keith Woods.

131. Interview with Julie Wheeler.

132. Interview with Sheri Greenawald.

133. Interview with Darren Keith Woods.

134. Interview with Frederica von Stade.

135. Ibid.

136. Interview with Mikael Melbye.

137. Interviews with Patricia Racette and Beth Clayton.

138. Interview with Mary Jane Johnson.

139. Interview with Miles Davis.

140. Interview with an orchestra member who preferred to remain anonymous.

141. Interviews with Brad Woolbright.

142. Interview with Danis Kelly.

143. Interview with Marc Scorca.

144. Opera America board minutes for the period of Crosby's tenure were graciously supplied by Opera America.

145. Santa Fe Opera program books, 1957–1976.

146. Interview with Marc Scorca.

147. Information in this paragraph comes from the interview with David Gockley.

148. Interviews with Brad Woolbright.

149. Interviews with Peggy Tueller and Paul Wolfe.

150. Interview with Paul Wolfe.

151. This and ensuing information come from the interview with Peggy Tueller.

152. Interview with Peggy Tueller.

153. Interview with Paul Wolfe.

154. Ibid.

155. This point was made independently by at least ten interviewees. It seems unlikely that a cabal existed to assure a conspiracy of silence on this point.

156. Interview with Brad Woolbright.

157. Interview with Hans Fahrmeyer.

158. Interview with Richard Balthazar.

159. Interview with Paul Wolfe.

160. Interviews with Allen Charles Klein and Bliss Hebert.

161. Interview with Hans Fahrmeyer.

162.   Information in this paragraph comes from interviews with Allen Charles Klein and Bliss Hebert.

163.   Interview with Michael Rolland Davis.

164.   Interviews with Allen Charles Klein and Bliss Hebert.

165.   Interview with Hans Fahrmeyer.

166.   Ibid.

167.   Interview with David Triestram.

168.   Interview with Gary Thor Wedow. A number of persons interviewed expressed the same viewpoint.

169.   According to Darren Keith Woods.

170.   After his conducting, Crosby's penchant for private pool parties was the most gossiped-about aspect of his life.

171.   Interviews with Brad Woolbright, Thomas Cirillo, Richard Balthazar, and others.

172.   Crosby's valets and house help comprise another gossip central of his life. One constant story, with no proof presented, is that one year he had twin eighteen-year-old blond houseboys whose skills encompassed more than cooking, laundry, and cleaning. This story, and similar ones, always seemed to come to the writer via a friend of a friend.

173.   For examples of job duties, see John Crosby's letters to various recipients from February 8, 1966; May 11, 1972; and May 11, 1979.

174.   Interview with Jeanne Chieffo Boyles.

175.   Ibid.

Chapter Five

1.   Information here and in ensuing paragraphs is from the interview with Greig Porter.

2.   Members of the board also were concerned about Crosby's health and about the possibility that he might suddenly die and leave the company in a bereft and difficult position.

3.   John Crosby to Richard Gaddes, letter, February 24, 1993.

4.   Interview with Greig Porter.

5.   Santa Fe Opera program book, 1995 season.

6.   Gaddes's abilities, including his expertise in working with other arts organizations and executives, was common currency in the opera world from his long and successful tenure in St. Louis.

7.   In this paragraph, the dates and responsibilities as listed for the various executives are from the noted Santa Fe Opera season program books.

8.   John Crosby to Greig Porter, letter, November 9, 1999.

9. Many persons interviewed discussed this situation with candor as well as respect for the difficulties Crosby went through as the transfer of power began—and the difficulties Gaddes faced as a result. Brad Woolbright was especially forthright: "Richard tried to make John as comfortable as possible when he was back at opera, but he could not be seen as John Crosby, Part II."

10. Lisa Pasto-Crosby, as quoted by Laurence Crosby.

11. Interview with Greig Porter.

12. October 1, 2000, the day Richard Gaddes formally assumed the general directorship of the company, Crosby drove down to the office in the morning and parked in the general director's parking place—possibly deliberately, and certainly setting up an awkward situation. This was a foreshadowing of more troubles to come. The person who stated this fact requested anonymity.

13. Interview with Brad Woolbright.

14. John Crosby to John Sweeney, letter, March 18, 1985.

15. Interviews with Brad Woolbright.

16. John Crosby to Luther Brady, MD, letter, September 9, 1999.

17. John Crosby to Edo de Waart, letter, April 24, 1990.

18. Interview with Jeanne Chieffo Boyles.

19. John Crosby to various recipients, letters, December 31, 1998; July 22, 1996; August 18, 1999; and September 9, 1999.

20. Interviews with Mikael Melbye and Nancy Zeckendorf.

21. Interviews with Charles MacKay.

22. Interviews with Brad Woolbright.

23. Ibid.

24. Interview with Michael Rolland Davis.

25. Interview with Mikael Melbye; personal visit by the author to Crosby's home, now owned by The Santa Fe Opera, courtesy of Charles MacKay.

26. Information here and in the following paragraphs comes from the interview with Michael Rolland Davis.

27. Interviews with Peter Ader and Robert Tweten.

28. Interviews with Brad Woolbright.

29. According to Robert Tweten, Crosby considered *La Traviata* to be "hurdy-gurdy music."

30. Interview with Bryan Gilliam.

31. Information in this paragraph comes from the interview with Robert Tweten.

32. Interview with Matthew A. Epstein.

33. Interviews with Miles Davis and Jeanne Chieffo Boyles.

34. Information about Crosby's final illness and death has been assembled from interviews with Thomas B. Catron III, Benjamin Saiz, Brad Woolbright, and Michael Rolland Davis.

35. From Crosby's death certificate, courtesy of Thomas B. Catron III.

36. Myllys did not respond to repeated requests for an interview. However, the story of Crosby's dying with Strauss playing in his ears has been confirmed as accurate by interviewees, including Thomas B. Catron III and Brad Woolbright.

37. The critic in question was this writer.

38. The service, and the fact that so few persons associated with John Crosby locally were present, were decisions made by James Crosby, according to Laurence Crosby.

39. Interviews with Thomas B. Catron III.

40. John O'Hea Crosby, biography, MarquisWho'sWho.com, accessed August 17, 2014, https://cgi.marquiswhoswho.com/OnDemand/Default.aspx?last_name=crosby&first_name=john.

41. Understandably, the person who made this crack requested anonymity.

42. Information drawn from Santa Fe Opera program for this memorial service.

43. Information from Santa Fe Opera program book, 2003.

Chapter Six

1. Interview with Danis Kelly.

2. The following information about programs, singers, operas, and company activities has been drawn from Santa Fe Opera program books for 2003–2014.

Sources

The Santa Fe Opera Archives

Crosby, John. Correspondence and memos. Fifteen boxes dating from January 1, 1963, through December 31, 1999. One box with miscellaneous material from 1956 through 1962.

———. Notes for an autobiography. Version of July 26, 2002. Seventeen pages.

———. Transcribed interview/oral history. May 29, 1997. Sixty-four pages.

Music holdings of John Crosby: music scores (full scores and piano-vocal scores of operas, piano music, chamber music, and other sheet music) and books on music (scholarly studies, biographies, and general musical culture).

Santa Fe Opera program books, press information, clippings of previews and reviews, and image files (photographs, negatives, slides, transparencies). 1956–.

Sarfaty (Rickless), Regina. Transcribed oral history. July 2, 1996. Forty-six pages.

Interviews

Ader, Peter. September 9 and October 5, 2012.

Ater, David. January 5, 2013.

Balthazar, Richard. August 31, 2012.

Baustian, Robert. July 25, 2012.

Bernheimer, Martin. December 17, 2012.

Best, Richard. January 21, 2013.

Boyles, Jeanne Chieffo. December 12, 2013.

Catron, Thomas B., III. January 22, 2013.
Cirillo, Thomas. March 28, 2013.
Clayton, Beth. January 18, 2013.
Corrigan, E. H. January 10, 2013.
Crosby, Caroline. September 18, 2013.
Crosby, James O. March 26, April 1, and April 17, 2013.
Crosby, Laurence. December 27, 2012.

Dailey, Brian. October 10, 2012.
Daniels, Edgar Foster. August 2, 2012.
Davis, Michael Rolland. January 10, 2013.
Davis, Miles. July 3, 2013.
De Waart, Edo. January 5, 2013.
Donnell, Bruce B. July 19, 2012.

Ely, Carole. December 28, 2012.
Epstein, Matthew A. July 21, 2013.

Fahrmeyer, Hans. January 14, 2013.
Falcone, Mary Lou. January 9, 2013.

Gilliam, Bryan. January 4, 2013.
Glick, Robert. July 30, 2012.
Gockley, David. February 14, 2013.
Greenawald, Sheri. July 10, 2012.
Grist, Reri. August 4, 2012.

Halfvarson, Eric. January 28, 2013.
Hebert, Bliss. January 25, 2013.
Heymann, Henry. July 10 and 24, 2012.
Holloway, David. August 27, 2012.
Horpedahl, Paul. October 30, 2012.
Hutton, Paul. January 17, 2013.

Idema, Joyce. July 2013.

Johnson, Mary Jane. January 19, 2013.

Kelly, Danis. August 15, 2012.
Klein, Allen Charles. February 4, 2013.

Klotz, Winnie. January 17, 2013.
Kuntz, Gene. January 27, 2012.

Lacy, Jane Stieren. January 24, 2013.
La Liberté, Sue. December 10, 2012.
Landrum, Steven. August 29, 2012.
Levy, Miranda. 2002, 2003, 2006.
Lockwood, Carolyn. August 3, 2012.

MacKay, Charles. January 18 and February 1, 2013.
MacKay, Susan. February 7, 2013.
Micunis, Gordon. July 12, 2012.
McFate, Patricia A. December 5, 2012.
Meier, Johanna. July 30, 2013.
Melbye, Mikael. December 10, 2012.
Mills, Erie. August 4, 2012.
Montgomery, Kenneth. October 9, 2012.
Moriarty, John. January 28 and 30, 2013.
Morris, Tom. October 22, 2012.

Pasto-Crosby, Lisa. January 3, 2013.
Pavitt, Kirt. January 23, 2013.
Peck, MacGregor Wilson. August 20, 2012.
Picker, Tobias. August 25, 2012.
Polshek, James. December 18, 2012.
Porter, Greig. August 7, 2012.

Racette, Patricia. January 18, 2013.
Raven, Theodora. July 31, 2012.
Rice, Daniel. December 20, 2012.
Rickless, Regina Sarfaty. June 26, 2012.
Rose, Molly. January 8, 2013.

Saiz, Benjamin. December 10, 2012, and January 25, 2013.
Scargall, Dale. January 23, 2013.
Scorca, Marc. February 7, 2013.
Shockley, Linda. July 7, 2013.
Smith, James Clois, Jr. July 6, 2012.
Stilwell, Richard. January 11, 2013.

Thorpe, Lore. July 6, 2012.
Triestram, David. November 14, 2012.
Trujillo, Michael. July and August 2012, and July and August 2013.
Tueller, Peggy. January 25, 2013.
Tweten, Robert. December 31, 2012.

Udow, Michael. January 7, 2013.

Van Dooren, Jan. October 9, 2012.
Vanni, Helen, and Mario Vanni. June 1, 2012.
Van Sant, James A. September 26, 2012.
von Stade, Frederica. January 8, 2013.

Walters, Andrea Fellows. December 10, 2012.
Wedow, Gary Thor. September 1, 2012.
Wheeler, Julie. November 6, 2012.
Wolfe, Paul. May 31, 2012.
Woods, Darren Keith. January 4, 2013.
Woolbright, Brad. November 15, November 16, and December 31, 2012.

Zeckendorf, Nancy. September 27, 2012.

Newspapers and Magazines
Albuquerque Journal
Chicago Sun-Times
Chicago Tribune
Connoisseur
Dallas Morning News
Denver Post
Financial Times
Los Angeles Times
Musical America
Newsweek
New Yorker
New York Times
Opera
Opera News
Santa Fean Magazine
Santa Fe New Mexican
Santa Fe Reporter
Time

Books and Articles (Partial List)

Berger, Bruce. *A Tent in the Meadow: 1949–1999.* Aspen, CO: Sojourner Publications, 1999.

Butcher, Harold. "Stravinsky Conducts His Work at Fourth Santa Fe Festival." *Musical Courier,* August 1960, 4.

Central Florida Genealogical and Historical Society. "Family Record of James Crosby: 1790–19." *Buried Treasures* 11, no. 3 (July 1979): 5–8.

Church, Fermor S., and Peggy Pond Church. *When Los Alamos Was a Ranch School.* Los Alamos, NM: Los Alamos Historical Society, 1974.

Craft, Robert. *A Stravinsky Scrapbook: 1940–1971.* New York: Thames and Hudson, 1983.

Dizikes, John. *Opera in America: A Cultural History.* New Haven, CT: Yale University Press, 1993.

Eckert, Thor, Jr. "High on Opera." *Connoisseur,* June 1988, 94–98.

Farrington, William. "The Santa Fe Opera." *Sunstone Review,* summer 1975, 13–15, 44.

Gilliam, Bryan, ed. *Richard Strauss and His World.* Princeton, NJ: Princeton University Press, 1992.

Gilliam, Bryan, ed. *Richard Strauss: New Perspectives on the Composer and His Work.* Durham, NC: Duke University Press, 1992.

The Graduating Class of The Hotchkiss School 1944. *The 1944 Mischianza.* Lakeville, CT: Hotchkiss School, 1944.

Henze, Hans Werner. *Bohemian Fifths: An Autobiography.* Translated by Stewart Spencer. Princeton, NJ: Princeton University Press, 1999.

Horgan, Paul. *Encounters with Stravinsky: a Personal Record.* New York: Farrar Straus and Giroux, 1972.

Hürlimann, Martin, Gertrud Hindemith. *Paul Hindemith: Die letzten Jahre; Ein Zeugnis in Bildern.* Mainz, Germany: B. Schott's Söhne, 1965.

Huscher, Phillip. *The Santa Fe Opera: An American Pioneer.* Santa Fe, NM: The Santa Fe Opera, 2006.

Kolodin, Irving. "Santa Fe's Operatic Oasis." *Saturday Review,* August 30, 1969, 39–42.

La Farge, John Pen. *Turn Left at the Sleeping Dog: Scripting the Santa Fe Legend, 1920–1955.* Albuquerque: University of New Mexico Press, 2001.

Lisagor, Nancy, and Frank Lipsius. *A Law Unto Itself: The Untold Story of the Law Firm of Sullivan & Cromwell.* New York: Morrow, 1988.

Love, Marian F. "From Beans to Grand Opera." *Santa Fean Magazine* 9, no. 4 (May 1981): 20–21.

Magee, Frank, Jr. "Opera and the Royal City." *New Mexico Land of Enchantment*, June 1960, 8–11, 37–38.

Osborne, Charles. *The Complete Operas of Richard Strauss*. North Pomfret, VT: Trafalgar Square Books, 1988.

Reardon, John. "The First Time." *Sunstone Review*, summer 1975, 5–7.

Santa Fean Magazine. "Celebrating the 25th Season." 9, no. 4 (May 1981).

Santa Fe New Mexican. The Santa Fe Opera 50th Anniversary. Special supplement. June 28, 2006.

Santa Fe Opera. *Bravo, John Crosby*! Commemorative videotape, 2000.

Santa Fe Opera Guild, ed. *Cooking with The Santa Fe Opera: Thirtieth Anniversary Edition*. Santa Fe, NM: Sunstone Press, 1986.

———. ed. *On Stage: A Cook Book*. Santa Fe, NM: Vergara Printing Co., 1963.

Scott, Eleanor. *The First Twenty Years of The Santa Fe Opera*. Santa Fe, NM: Sunstone Press, 1976.

Stravinsky, Igor, and Robert Craft. *Memories and Commentaries*. Garden City, NY: Doubleday, 1960.

Walker, Hollis. "Saving Water's an Old Habit at Santa Fe Opera—Founder Takes Pride in Wetlands." *Santa Fe New Mexican*, June 6, 1996.

Wild, Earl. *A Walk on the Wild Side: A Memoir*. Palm Springs, CA: Ivory Classics Foundation, 2011.

Wirth, John D., and Linda K. Aldrich. *Los Alamos: The Ranch School Years, 1917–1943*. Albuquerque: University of New Mexico Press, 2003.

Index